STEP BY STEP:
A PROGRAM FOR CHILDREN AND FAMILIES

CREATING
INCLUSIVE
CLASSROOMS

ELLEN R. DANIELS AND KAY STAFFORD
INTRODUCTION BY PAMELA A. COUGHLIN

CHILDREN'S RESOURCES INTERNATIONAL, INC.
WASHINGTON, DC

Library of Congress Catalog Card Number: 99-72258

The Soros Foundations/Open Society Institute is a network of foundations, programs, and institutions established and supported by philanthropist George Soros to foster the development of Open Societies around the world, particularly in the former communist countries of Central and Eastern Europe and the former Soviet Union. To this end the Soros Foundation cooperates with Children's Resources International to develop and implement the project called Step by Step: A Program for Children and Families.

CRI, a nonprofit organization located in Washington, D.C., promotes the implementation of sound educational practices developed in the United States while maintaining the cultural traditions of the participating countries.

Open Society Institute, New York
400 West 59th St.
New York, New York 10019
212.547.6918 *phone*
212.548.0660 *fax*
E-Mail: osnews@sorosny.org

Children's Resources International, Inc.
5039 Connecticut Ave, NW, Suite 1
Washington, DC 20008
202.363.9002 *phone*
202.363.9550 *fax*
E-Mail: criinc@aol.com

TABLE OF CONTENTS

PART III: Facilitating Learning in Inclusive Classrooms

Acknowledgments

The Step by Step program began in 1994 as an experiment linking sound early childhood educational practice with the concepts of democracy. In Step by Step classrooms children practice choice, take responsibility for their decisions, express their ideas with creativity, embrace differences, develop critical thinking skills, and practice independent thinking. Parents actively participate in the education of their children. Research has demonstrated that the Step by Step methods have achieved these goals of democracy. This publication extends the concepts of democracy to include children with disabilities in classrooms with typically developing children.

We thank George Soros who has identified inclusion as a major initiative of the Open Society Institute. He is a hero to us and to countless children and families who experience the exuberance of freedom for the first time. There is no adequate way to express our gratitude to our partners in this endeavor— Liz Lorant, Director of Regional Programs, and Sarah Klaus, our project director. Their flexibility, support, and insight have been without peer. We laugh and cry with them, argue over the best way to do the job, and then work hard to accomplish what some might think the impossible.

It is an unparalleled privilege to work with the international Step by Step teams. They recognize that including children with disabilities in classrooms with typically developing children is a necessary expression of democracy. They understand that the principles of choice, individualization, parental involvement, and personal freedoms are only fully practiced when children with disabilities and their families experience the same benefits.

There have been many collaborators who have participated in the production of *Creating Inclusive Classrooms*. We thank our authors, who willingly wrote and rewrote the book. Jean Iker, whose whimsical art enlivens all of the CRI publications. Our reviewers, Julie Empson, Sharon Scholem, and Carol Norrish, who contributed their suggestions to make this both a reference as well as a practical book for classroom teachers. The editors, Judy Cusick and Shelly Nicoll, who lived with the rewriting process until we got it right. We thank Callie Crosby of the Crosby Group, who designed the covers of all CRI publications with such professionalism and good humor. And finally, thanks to Cassie Marshall, who has produced this attractive and easy to read document and who makes everything run smoothly.

The staff of CRI

INTRODUCTION

The Purpose of This Manual

This manual is intended to help educators design and implement programs in which young children (ages three to six years) with special needs learn alongside their typically developing peers. It provides hands-on information for how to help children with disabilities function in schools and child care centers.

For administrators, teachers, and parents interested in developing inclusive schools, the task of including children with disabilities may seem overwhelming. In truth, the process of creating inclusive, child-centered classrooms is a matter of creating complex school change. It requires a comprehensive commitment from the entire school community, from the principal to the custodian, and especially from the parents and families.

This manual explores many of the practices that have resulted in successful inclusive experiences for all children, with or without disabilities. It provides both theoretical and practical information on how to build inclusive classrooms. It is important to keep in mind that inclusion is not a fixed methodology or a set of procedures and techniques. Fundamentally, inclusion is the belief that learning should be tailored to each child's individual needs and that each family is entitled to have their child educated in regular schools.

Advocates for inclusion strive to ensure that every child has the opportunity to reach his or her full potential. That is no small task. Yet, teachers with experience in sound early childhood practice—knowledge of child development, observation and assessment skills, setting individual educational goals and objectives, working as a team, communicating with families, respecting the individual differences in children—have the requisite skills to teach children with disabilities in their classrooms.

Philosophy of the Step by Step Program

The Step by Step Program is based on the belief that children grow best when they are intrinsically involved in their own learning. A carefully planned environment encourages children to explore, to initiate, and to create. The teaching team, in partnership with other school staff, use their knowledge of child development to create the learning environment and provide the materials for learning.

The team's role is to set appropriate goals for individual children and for the group as a whole, to respond to the interests of the children, to respect the individual strengths and needs of each child, to keep alive the natural curiosity of the young child, and to foster cooperative learning. The involvement of families in the education of their children extends classroom learning from school to home and from home to school.

The Step by Step Program, which embodies the early childhood practices discussed above, promotes democracy in fundamental ways. These practices give very young children and their families opportunities to practice choice, respect diverse strengths and needs, and develop appreciation for individuality.

It is in this environment that inclusive practices are most likely to be successful—that is, in child-centered education programs, where individual children's needs and interests are respected. Such caring classrooms are effective for children with a wide range of abilities, learning styles, and needs.

Principles of the Step by Step Program
The Step by Step Program promotes practices for teachers and administrators that incorporate exemplary early childhood principles including:

- developmentally appropriate practice
- child-centered learning
- family participation
- democratic practice.

Developmentally Appropriate Practice
The National Association for the Education of Young Children, the major professional early childhood organization in the United States, ascribes two dimensions to the term *developmentally appropriate*: age appropriateness and individual appropriateness (Bredekamp, 1987).

Age appropriateness—Human development research indicates that children undergo universal, predictable sequences of growth and change during the first nine years of life. These predictable changes occur in all domains of development: physical, emotional, social, and cognitive. Knowledge of typical development of children within the age span served by the program provides a framework from which teachers prepare the learning environment and plan appropriate experiences (Bredekamp, 1987).

Individual appropriateness—Each child has a unique pattern and timing of growth as well as an individual personality, learning style, and family background. Both the curriculum and adults' interactions with children should be responsive to individual differences. Learning results from the interaction between the child's thoughts and experiences with materials, ideas, and people. These experiences should match the child's developing abilities while challenging the child's interest and understanding (Bredekamp, 1987).

The content of the curriculum, teaching methods, classroom materials, and adult interaction should be responsive to the age and individual differences of the children. Teachers individualize by respecting the present developmental stage of each child and the unique approach that each child brings to the learning experience and by planning a range of appropriate activities to ensure each child's success.

Child-Centered Learning

Thoughtful teacher planning ensures that activities are relevant to each child. A child acts on his interests when he chooses a particular activity and individualizes that activity at his own developmental level. By planning flexible and interesting activities and by carefully observing children during the activities, the teacher can change and adapt materials and activities as needed. Most activities are conducted in small groups to maximize the opportunities for individualization. When children learn at their own pace, the classroom becomes a dynamic and changing environment with materials and experiences designed to correspond to children's individual interests and developmental stages.

Family Participation

Families are the primary educators of children and have the greatest influence upon them. Families desire the best for their children and want them to be successful and productive citizens. Families must, therefore, be seen as partners who play a critical role in the child's educational process. In the Step by Step Program, families reinforce and expand classroom learning, and the teacher builds on the interests and learning that occur at home. The reciprocity between home and school reflects a mutual respect between parents and teachers.

Step by Step is a two-generation program. It promotes family participation in many ways: family members assist in classrooms; they are actively involved in decision making through parent advisory committees; and they contribute information for the teaching team about the developmental needs and strengths of their children. Teachers and parents share the responsibility of working together to develop communication, mutual respect, and acceptance of differences. Communication between the teaching team and families takes many forms: notes, conversations, meetings, conferences, parent support groups, and home visits.

Democratic Practice

The Step by Step philosophy promotes democratic behaviors among young children and their families. Educating young children in a manner that encourages individuality, critical thinking, initiative, questioning, choice, independence, decision making, respect for diversity, and individualization will lead to a generation of citizens equipped to live in democratic societies. Including children with disabilities in the mainstream of society is an expression of democracy. School communities must not only create opportunity for inclusion for children with disabilities; they must and will grow to appreciate and celebrate their inclusion.

How This Manual is Organized

This manual follows the experiences of the three children—Peter, Ali, and Anna—whose stories are based on the real lives of children and their families. Throughout, we will learn about their teachers and the challenges they encounter as they develop inclusive, child-centered classrooms. The manual is divided into three sections:

Part I: Creating Inclusive Classrooms. Chapter One describes the factors that contribute to the development of inclusive classrooms in early childhood education programs. A brief history of the inclusion movement in education helps readers understand the vital roles that families, teachers, and advocates for persons with disabilities have played in establishing inclusive educational practices.

Part II: Meeting Individual Needs. Chapters Two through Four discuss the central role that family participation and shared decision-making play in the design and implementation of educational programs for children with disabilities. Fundamental components of meeting individual needs are discussed: individualized assessment, developing an individualized education plan (IEP), adapting the classroom environment, and planning instruction. Examples of assessment methods and individualized education plans are included.

Part III: Facilitating Learning in Inclusive Classrooms. Chapters Five through Ten provide specific examples of curriculum adaptations and instructional strategies by developmental domains. Chapter Eleven is a reference and resource guide for teachers.

Terminology

The child-centered approach avoids the medical model or categorical approach toward educating children with disabilities. As used in this manual, the term *special needs* refers to an individual's need for specific educational planning due to the presence of a disabling condition or developmental delays. The terms *children with special needs, children with disabilities,* and *children with developmental delays* are used interchangeably to refer to a distinct group of children: those from birth through age eight who require specialized instruction, tools, techniques, or equipment in order to grow and to learn. Chapter Eleven defines the disabilities.

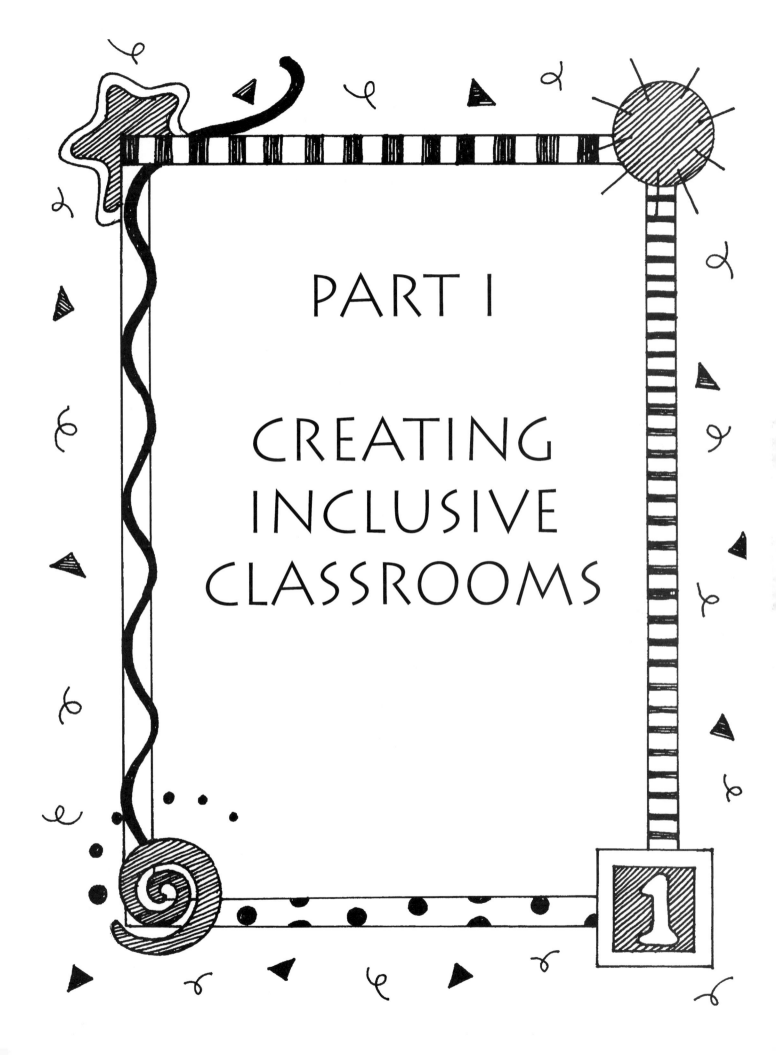

PART I

CREATING INCLUSIVE CLASSROOMS

1

CHAPTER ONE

FOUNDATIONS OF INCLUSIVE CLASSROOMS

1. FOUNDATIONS OF INCLUSIVE CLASSROOMS

Chapter Overview
- The Basic Principles of Child-Centered, Inclusive Classrooms
- The Evolution of Changing Attitudes
- A Brief Historical Overview
- The Benefits of Inclusion for Children, Families, Teachers, and Communities
- Strategies for Establishing Inclusive Classrooms
- Meet the Children and Their Teachers

The Basic Principles of Child-Centered, Inclusive Classrooms

In both democratic societies and child-centered classrooms, each individual is regarded as unique and as having a valuable contribution to make. In a true democracy, each citizen is treated in an equitable manner and has fair access to participate fully in all aspects of community life. The extent to which persons with disabilities have an opportunity to participate as members of society is an indicator of democracy (see Chapter Eleven for an overview of kinds of disabilities). When children with disabilities are educated alongside children without disabilities, in a practice known as inclusion, children are offered an equal opportunity to be recognized on the basis of merit, regardless of their cognitive, physical, social, or emotional challenges. In inclusive classrooms, children become aware of the range of human potential, which helps them to develop sensitivity and an appreciation for the human experience.

Child-centered programs are founded on beliefs that are consistent with democratic ideals. These beliefs include the following:

- Individualize school experiences for each child.
- Provide children with opportunities for making good choices that encourage further learning.
- Engage children in active learning.
- Form relationships with families and encourage their direct involvement in their child's education.

In child-centered early childhood education programs, teachers and administrators are committed to work with families to reinforce the beliefs that:

- Children are more alike than different, regardless of their ability.
- Children are part of families and communities.

5

- Children learn best from each other in communities that support normal life experiences.
- Children thrive in settings where their needs are considered and met in an individualized manner.

Today, child-centered programs are found throughout the world. These programs are designed to meet individual children's needs and to foster democratic ideals and principles. In these child-centered classrooms, children are encouraged to make choices, to think critically, and to be creative, imaginative, and resourceful. They learn to take responsibility for their decisions and to help each other.

Child-centered, inclusive early childhood programs foster the potential of every child. As teachers in these programs strive to meet each child's individual needs, they model acceptance of human diversity, demonstrate the value of human relationships, and show through their actions how human problems can be solved when communities work together and people support each other.

The Evolution of Changing Attitudes

Over the past several decades, early childhood programs around the world have begun to include children with disabilities. The effort to create inclusive schools—which all students, irrespective of talent, ability, socioeconomic background, or cultural origin, may attend—has gained momentum and public acceptance.

In the early 1980s, in order to focus world attention on the need to promote equalization of opportunities and full inclusion in society for persons with disabilities, the United Nations proclaimed the "Decade of Disabled Persons." Members of the United Nations recommended action steps to advance the goal of full inclusion in world society.

6

These steps included:

- establishing national coordinating bodies on disability-related matters
- promoting legislation to remove barriers that prevent individuals with disabilities from participating in society
- promoting public awareness about disabilities
- improving the accessibility and availability of communication systems for individuals with disabilities, such as text telephones and closed-captioning on televised broadcasts
- providing education for all children with disabilities that meets their specific needs, including inclusive education
- improving job training and employment opportunities for individuals with disabilities
- preventing the causes of disability
- developing rehabilitation services, assistive devices, and self-help organizations
- increasing cooperation between countries and regions where services to individuals with disabilities need development.

Many nations have responded by acting on these recommendations. In the face of numerous and compelling societal needs, they are developing inclusive classrooms to meet the educational needs of all their children. These countries have learned that by maintaining high expectations and providing meaningful access to school life, most children with disabilities are able to attain challenging standards and to achieve more than society has historically expected. Still, much remains to be accomplished in providing high-quality and effective education to young children with developmental delays and disabilities.

A Brief Historical Overview

Before the nineteenth century, the care and treatment of children with disabilities was primarily custodial. Children remained at home with family members who cared for them or were institutionalized. Often, children with disabilities were perceived as a burden to their families. Families had nowhere to turn for assistance in caring for them.

In 1800, Jean-Marc Itard, a French physician, developed unique teaching techniques in the first recorded attempts to educate children with disabilities. Followers of Itard brought his techniques to the United States, where they established an organization dedicated to the scientific study of cognitive disabilities.

In the 1830s, schools for the deaf and the blind were created in the United States. These first schools provided education for individuals with disabilities in segregated, specialized programs created to serve the needs of a specific disabled population. Schools for the deaf used sign language, finger spelling, and alternative systems of communicating. These large institutions, often located hundreds of miles from a child's home community, boarded young children.

In Russia, a system of formal special education was initiated after the Russian Revolution of 1917 (Malofeev, 1998). The state paid for a child's maintenance away from home and away from regular schools that were not equipped to handle children with special needs.

During this time, the sociocultural theories of L. S. Vygotsky and other Russian scholars were formulated. It would be another fifty years before Vygotsky's theories would reach the West. When his works eventually became available, they began to have a profound worldwide impact on the education of children with disabilities.

Vygotsky described the detrimental effects of social isolation on persons with disabilities. He concluded that creating a special social environment away from a child's family and friends in effect produces a "second disability"—one of society's own making (Vygotsky, 1978). Children with disabilities are profoundly affected when their basic social needs are neglected.

In the early 1900s, Maria Montessori, an Italian physician, became concerned about children living in poverty in Rome. She worked to provide children with organized, predictable security in her "Children's House." She believed in respecting a child's individuality, allowing children to make activity choices, and encouraging children to solve problems. Her belief was that young children needed to develop skills necessary for caring for themselves. She was an advocate on behalf of children who many believed were beyond hope of educating (Cook, Tessier, and Armbruster, 1987).

Increasingly, in Europe, the United States, Australia, and Canada, parents urged educators to include their children with disabilities in classrooms in their local schools. They were aware of the inadequate number of appropriate school programs for their children and had a growing desire to reduce the stigma of segregation due to disability. Families wanted to keep their children with disabilities in their own homes where they could be valued family members.

Beginning in the 1950s, parents and advocacy groups in America won a series of significant court cases based on U. S. Constitutional protections. Children with disabilities began gaining access to regular education classes based on both legal appeals and legislation. Many of these children adjusted and succeeded where, for so long, it was believed they could not.

During the mid-1960s, Project Head Start in the United States was started as a comprehensive program of education and health care for preschool children and their parents. By 1972, Project Head Start was taking steps to include children with disabilities in its classrooms. Head Start became an early model for serving children with disabilities and their families.

In 1975, the U. S. Congress passed landmark legislation that provided for the use of federal funds to assist states and school districts in making "free, appropriate public education" available to students with disabilities. For very young children, this law placed special emphasis on the family unit as an important part of any early education program.

In the United States, young children with disabilities can now receive an inclusive education that, along with therapeutic services, helps them grow and develop to their potential. Children with disabilities go to local preschools and elementary schools and participate in community activities. Older individuals with disabilities have graduated from vocational schools, high schools, and colleges. Adults with disabilities have the potential to work, pay taxes, and enjoy the opportunities available throughout society.

The Benefits of Inclusion for Children, Families, Teachers, and Communities

Inclusive early childhood education programs offer children with disabilities an opportunity to observe, imitate, and interact with typically developing children. In other words, children with disabilities can develop social relationships the way that most children do—through experience. The benefits of inclusion also extend to typically developing children and to families, teachers, and communities.

Benefits for Children

Both children with disabilities and typically developing children benefit from inclusive education practices. For a child with disabilities, being a member of a classroom with typically developing peers means having peers who can be role models for communication and age-appropriate social skills.

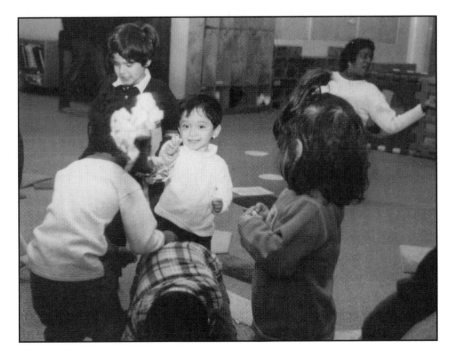

Increased social interaction helps children develop friendships and positive social relationships and establishes a supportive social network (Snell and Vogtle, 1996). Cognitive benefits range from increased alertness to improved motivation and learning.

Successful inclusive and normalized experiences in the early years give children with disabilities the foundation for continued inclusive experiences throughout life. By attending a community-based program, a child has the opportunity to acquire the skills necessary to function successfully and independently in the community as an adult.

Children without disabilities also benefit from inclusion. They develop an understanding of the challenges that individuals with disabilities face. They become sensitive to the needs of others and are better able to accept differences. They learn that all individuals can overcome considerable challenges and achieve success.

Research has shown that students without disabilities who are educated in inclusive settings have demonstrated improvement in their attitudes toward people unlike themselves. They are more likely to take on increased social responsibility and show greater social self-confidence (Staub and Peck, 1995).

Benefits for Families

Parenting can be a challenging task, even under the best of circumstances. Parenting a child with a disability puts a greater demand on families. When a son or a daughter attends an inclusive local school, families of children with disabilities report feeling less isolated. They describe feelings of relief. Their family experiences become more like those of other families, rather than increasingly different.

The convenience of having a child attend a local program is an advantage for many families. Parents who might otherwise need to provide continuous care in their home for their child with disabilities are able to work in the community. Parents may have other children attending the same community-based program; they become more involved in their children's education when their children attend the same school. Parents then develop friendships and a support network with other parents.

All parents worry about their children's future. This concern is intensified for the parents of a child with a disability. Active participation in their child's educational program lessens this worry. Parents of children with disabilities find that they benefit from their participation on their child's educational planning team. Being a part of a "team" gives them the support they need and allows them to cope with their child's daily needs knowing that they are not alone. When parents, teachers, and specialists collaborate, each team member's contribution to the group enhances the group's effectiveness and ensures success for the child. Successful team experiences in the early years have empowered many parents to become strong, lifelong advocates for their child.

Inclusion also benefits families with children without special needs. These families have opportunities to develop meaningful new relationships. They learn about individual differences and how families cope with providing for their son or daughter with disabilities. Families have discovered new ways to help one another, which has the effect of strengthening communities.

Many parents of children without special needs have rallied community support for families of children with special needs. Parents have been instrumental in getting local governments to provide access to public buildings, transportation, and services. Some parents have organized respite care, recognizing that families of children with disabilities need an occasional break from the daily care of their child. As more members of a community become familiar with the challenges of raising a child with disabilities, communities become better able to generate needed support.

Benefits for Teachers

Teaching in inclusive classrooms requires a broad knowledge of child development. With experience, teachers in inclusive classrooms become more skilled at observing variations in learning styles. They become more confident in assessing individual strengths and determining specific areas needing support. Teaching children with and without disabilities helps teachers appreciate the staggering variation in learning styles, individual strengths, and specific learning needs of all children.

Teachers develop skills in identifying mild to moderate learning issues in children who are struggling with learning. They are more cognizant of the benefits of further assessment and evaluation. As the teacher's skills in providing individualized teaching expand, she becomes more comfortable with children's needs. She learns new instructional techniques as she plans and works with other teachers and specialists in implementing individualized education plans (IEPs). (See Chapter Four for an in-depth discussion of IEPs.)

Benefits for Communities

Children who become participating, productive members of a community contribute to rather than rely on their community for support. When children go to school in their local communities, their presence helps everyone to understand the needs of special populations.

Inclusive schools may offer long-term financial benefits to communities. Educating young children with disabilities in the same setting as their typically developing peers is usually less expensive than creating and funding alternative school placements. Communities conserve their educational resources by limiting the need for segregated, specialized programs. In addition, children who receive appropriate intervention when they are young may require a reduced level of services—or none at all— as they continue through school and later in life.

Society loses whenever a segment of the population cannot participate in community life. Children who learn to live and play in a diverse group become competent, independent, working adults, sharing their skills and talents with others. Communities benefit when individuals with disabilities contribute in meaningful ways to the ongoing welfare of society.

Strategies for Establishing Inclusive Classrooms

Establishing inclusive programs can be a challenge for teachers, school administrators, and families. The discussion that follows identifies the most common concerns and some strategies that inclusive programs have found helpful to address these issues. These are grouped in three sections: employing successful administrative and management strategies, developing a mission statement and outlining goals, and reducing fears by addressing concerns.

Employing Successful Administrative and Management Strategies

One of the most important lessons that schools have learned is that, before undertaking the establishment of inclusive classrooms, parents and educators need to come together to discuss the concerns that parents and educators have about inclusion. This type of discussion can forestall many problems that ultimately are due to lack of information about impending changes.

School administrators are critical to the success of inclusive schools. School leaders must develop school resources, make decisions, meet challenges, and prepare school faculty and staff for change. The change toward inclusive practices must be led with clear vision and actions that are consistent with the school's philosophy (O'Brien and O'Brien, 1996). In situations where school leaders have wavered or made poor decisions, or no decisions at all, real change has not occurred.

All those involved in the process of creating inclusive classrooms will need extra support. Teachers need training and education. Parents require information, support, and firm, unwavering guidance when challenges arise. The children in the classroom, both those with disabilities and those without, will need extra attention. The clear messages of a strong and compassionate leader will help promote successful inclusive experiences.

Drawing from the experiences of schools that have adopted inclusion practices, the following are some specific administrative and management strategies for creating an inclusive program:

- Establish a site-based inclusion committee, including administrators, teachers, teacher assistants, parents, and specialists. Everyone who has a stake in the process should have a part in the planning. The inclusion committee should:
    - develop a mission statement (See sample mission statement on page 14.)
    - identify reasonable and available resources for training teachers and parents
    - give teachers and parents opportunities to comment on collaborative planning and on the management of resources, both human and financial
    - provide systematic support for staff using a team approach to problem solving
    - recognize and build upon all successes.

- Establish educational planning teams to assess children's learning needs. The teams should be multidisciplinary and include parents as partners and vital members.

Team members should exchange information informally, openly, and honestly. Problems that are encountered are team problems to be solved together.

- Establish a parent resource center in the school. If possible, arrange for a parent volunteer to be in the center a certain number of hours a week to take phone calls from parents and community members, talk with teachers, and maintain a collection of reading materials on the subject of inclusion.

- Appoint a school staff member to serve as an inclusion facilitator. This staff member supports and encourages the successful participation of the children with special needs, acts as a liaison to families and specialists, develops materials for curriculum adaptations, helps to identify individual goals and objectives for students, and establishes links to community resources and information. The inclusion facilitator can help teachers use effective teaching strategies. (See Chapter Five for examples of teaching strategies.)

Additional strategies that are important to consider but that may not be feasible in every community include the following:

- Teachers should be permitted to volunteer to have children with special needs placed in their classrooms. When teachers have a choice, they, like children and parents, have greater control over the situation, which often results in their assuming greater responsibility for making sure that changes take place successfully.

- Administrators should consider reducing total class size in response to the specific needs of a group.

- Support services, such as the services of instructional aides and therapy services, should be assigned in an individualized, differentiated, and flexible way to meet the varying needs of teachers and students.

Developing a Mission Statement and Outlining Goals

Schools are busy places where human needs must be met hourly, daily, and year after year. Teachers and school personnel work long hours and, in many places, receive less than adequate compensation for their work. Sometimes, to help teachers and administrators recognize their common purpose of educating young children, it is helpful for school staff and community members to sit down together to develop a mission statement, to list goals that support the implementation of the mission, and to write out an action plan for implementing those goals.

A mission statement for educators in inclusive programs should reflect the beliefs of those working in the program. It should state in simple terms the group's beliefs about how children learn and how children and families should be served. Such a mission statement regarding inclusion will:

- help school communities define their purpose
- provide educators and community members with the opportunity to communicate with each other about their goals for young children's education
- establish a benchmark for assessing how well the school is achieving its stated mission.

Because the principles of inclusion do not apply only to students with disabilities, it is important to recognize that meeting diverse student needs will help schools to become more effective for all students. A mission statement that clearly addresses the school's child-centered philosophy will provide a point of focus when challenges arise and barriers to success must be overcome.

A Sample Mission Statement

We believe that all children—regardless of level of ability, gender, and race—are entitled to a quality educational program that recognizes, values, and encourages the development of skills and competencies that will be needed throughout their lives. The implementation of this mission will include the following program features:

- Child-centered instruction that encourages the development of children's critical thinking skills through choice making and active learning
- Activities and environments that encourage children to both discover and solve problems
- Opportunities to make meaningful contributions to routine activities that enhance the development of children's independence and autonomy while at the same time encouraging a sense of responsibility for community, country, and the environment
- Use of creative, imaginative, and resourceful methods for thinking and learning while meeting individual children's educational needs
- Focus on strengthening friendships and cooperation among children, adults, and families
- Establishment of partnerships with families so that schools and communities work together in a caring, supportive relationship.

After the inclusion committee agrees on a mission statement, it draws up a list of program goals, which should include the following:

- *Support families in achieving their own goals.* Inclusion is most likely to be effective if it is consistent with family goals and priorities.

- *Promote child engagement and mastery.* A key goal of inclusion is to help children learn to interact with others and be successful in school.

- *Promote development in important areas.* These areas include cognitive, motor, communication, play, social, and self-care skills, as well as self-esteem and self-control.

- *Build and support social competence.* Social competence is especially important for children with special needs because unaddressed deficits in social skills may remain lifelong areas of need.

- *Facilitate the generalized use of skills.* Children need to be able to transfer skills learned in one setting to others.

- *Provide and prepare for normalized experiences.* Children with disabilities can continue to learn and grow in normalized settings throughout school and community life.

- *Prevent future problems or disabilities.* Many young children with special needs are at risk for future learning problems, although their difficulties may not be immediately obvious. A child with delayed communication skills in infancy, for example, may later demonstrate specific learning disabilities as an older student (Bailey and Wolery, 1992).

Reducing Fears by Addressing Concerns

Some parents and teachers may express concerns that the needs of children with disabilities may not be adequately met in inclusive classrooms. Other parents and teachers worry about the needs of typically developing children in inclusive classrooms. One of the biggest fears about inclusion is that schools may fail: students with and without disabilities will learn less, students with disabilities may experience social rejection, and the job of teaching will become too complex. School administrators often fear increased costs and the possibility of parental protest.

A growing body of evidence indicates that when schools approach inclusion as a complex change that is worth pursuing, the above-mentioned fears are not realized (NAEYC, 1997). What has proven most successful is to have a plan in place to deal with concerns and problems as they arise. The following elements should be included in such a plan:

- *Establish flexible student-to-teacher ratios.* Although experience with inclusion has not established an ideal number of children with disabilities to include in a classroom, many schools have found that two or three children with mild to moderate disabilities integrate well into the classroom. Decisions about the composition of specific classes should be made after considering:

    - the individual needs of the children with disabilities
    - the characteristics and needs of the children without disabilities
    - the attitudes and skills of the classroom teachers
    - the degree to which support services are available
    - the total ratio of adults to children.

15

- *Coordinate with parents.* Program administrators and teachers should meet with a student's parents before including the child in a program. Teachers initially learn about a child's strengths and needs from the child's parents. Parents share vital, practical information about their child and his or her disability. For example, they may share specific information related to the child's routine medical care.

- *Facilitate transition from home to school.* Some programs have found it helpful to have a new child visit the classroom for a short time prior to the child's enrollment. Such visits, which can take place before or after the regular program day, often relieve the initial concerns of the child, parent, or teacher. Home visits by the teacher are also extremely helpful for establishing positive relationships in a relaxed setting. Some children may benefit from participating in a shortened school day as they gradually acclimate to the school routine. A parent's presence in the classroom may be required until the child becomes comfortable in the program.

Meet The Children and Their Teachers

Throughout this manual, the reader will have an opportunity to meet three different children with special needs and their teachers.

The Children

Peter is a small, active four-year-old, with a glowing smile. His darting eyes seldom miss any opportunity for adventure. He never seems to stop running, climbing, and jumping. He tries hard to play with other children, but his efforts to share toys and wait for his turn often result in emotional outbursts and tears. Peter's father, a widower, has tried everything to help his son to slow down. He says that Peter has trouble sitting even for a few minutes to listen to a story, despite his love of picture books. Peter often cannot locate his shoes, coat, or toys. He never forgets a face but has a hard time remembering names. While Peter is eager to go to school with his older brother and sister, his father is not sure he is ready.

Just before *Ali*'s second birthday, his mother and father began noticing changes in their son's behavior. He stared indifferently in the midst of activity all around him. He stopped learning new words. He would spin round and round for long periods of time. Within six months, Ali no longer knew the names of family members, pets, or neighbors. Ali's parents suspected that he was having difficulty hearing. Ali's doctor conducted a thorough examination based on the information that Ali's parents related about the changes in their son's behavior. The doctor found that Ali's blood contained extremely high levels of lead, a toxic substance. Lead may be present in paint on the walls of older homes. There is also the possibility of environmental exposure in the drinking water or air or from crops grown in contaminated soil. Treatment for Ali involved removal of the lead from his body using medications. The doctor also diagnosed the presence of a seizure disorder. Explaining that Ali's seizures might be the result of his exposure to the lead, the doctor prescribed medication that would calm the seizures. The doctor advised

Ali's family that he should participate in every aspect of normal daily experiences. With the help of the medication, Ali would be able to relearn the names of family members. The doctor encouraged Ali's parents to use pictures and simple hand and finger movements to help Ali communicate and continue to learn. The doctor added that Ali would benefit from going to school with children who were developing normally; they would be models for Ali to learn from.

Anna has soft blonde curls, large sparkling eyes, and a cheerful disposition. When she was nine months old, her parents recognized that her development was not as even as her older siblings' had been. Anna ate and slept well, smiled at family members, and made beginning babbling sounds. She was able to hold her head up and was just beginning to roll over. She did not demonstrate the ability to move all her limbs equally; for example, she made kicking movements with only one leg, and reached for and held toys with only one hand. A series of visits to the doctor and a specialist determined that Anna had cerebral palsy. At three and a half years of age, Anna has just begun standing without support. She makes a few sounds that her family recognizes as her "words" for her favorite toys and foods. She is very responsive to others and appears to understand much of what she hears. Her parents hope that Anna can attend the same nursery school her older brother and sister attended.

The Teachers

Eva has taught young children for more than 20 years. She is a dedicated teacher who thoroughly enjoys her work. She particularly excels in providing children with creative musical experiences. She is known for her skill in developing the children's spontaneous joy and excitement for dance and singing. Eva has learned from her program administrator that the school is considering including children with disabilities. She has a good relationship with her administrator and trusts her leadership. Privately, however, she wonders if she is skilled enough to teach children with disabilities. She has trouble imagining how music activities will be conducted with children in leg braces or with children who are deaf. She worries that she will no longer be recognized for her teaching skills and experience.

Vlad has received the news about the possibility of including children with special needs with great joy mixed with some sadness. One of his younger brothers was born with Down syndrome. Vlad's brother never had the opportunity to go to school, because no program for children with disabilities existed when he was of school age. His brother still resides with Vlad's elderly parents. Vlad and his other brothers and sisters look after their parents and brother. Vlad recognizes that many persons with disabilities have great untapped potential. He is very excited to be teaching in a school that is considering reaching out to include individuals with disabilities and cannot wait to begin.

This is *Lena's* first year of teaching. She has experienced challenges, as well as successes, in her work with a group of 20 four-year-olds. Her teaching assistant, who is many years older than Lena, has openly questioned Lena's decisions about letting the children play in mud and make pretend mud pies. Lena initially had difficulty establishing control of a small group of boys, who challenged her when she tried to set limits on their behavior. When she learned about the school's plans to begin including children with disabilities, she felt overwhelmed. "How will I ever meet all the demands of teaching?" she wondered. She feels some resentment about the expectations placed on her, and she wonders if she should look for another job in a different field.

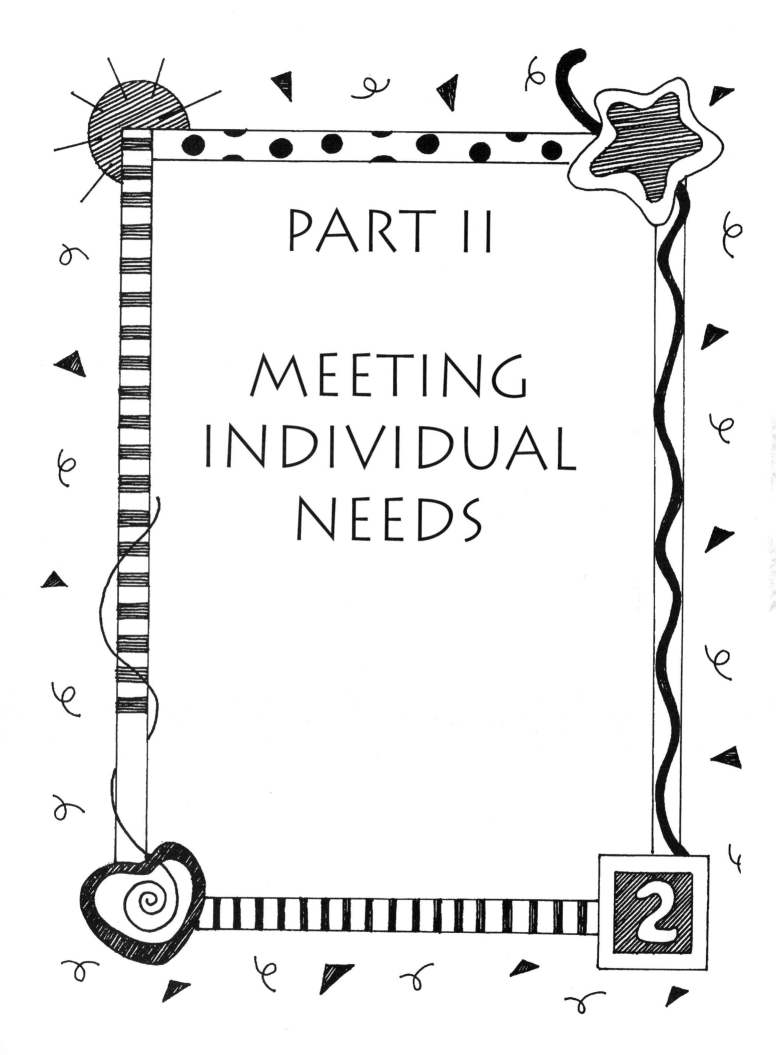

PART II

MEETING
INDIVIDUAL
NEEDS

CHAPTER TWO

FORMING PARTNERSHIPS WITH FAMILIES

2. FORMING PARTNERSHIPS WITH FAMILIES

Chapter Overview
- The Philosophy of Parents as Partners
- Communicating with Families
- Providing Support to Families
- Fostering Family Involvement
- Building a Supportive Team

The Philosophy of Parents as Partners

Child-centered practices are founded on the belief that the family is the child's first and primary teacher. Early childhood teachers respect the learning that occurs in a child's home and build on the interests of children and their families. As early childhood programs expand their scope to include children with special needs and their families, the goal of providing family services takes on renewed importance.

Family interests, priorities, and concerns are central to the philosophy and practice of sound programs serving young children, especially those with disabilities. Parents of children with disabilities will develop strong relationships with their child's teachers and become partners with the school in designing and implementing a child-centered education for their child.

Understanding the Individual Needs of Families

Families of children with disabilities are ultimately responsible for their children for the rest of their lives. One of the most important roles educators can fill is to help families believe in their own strengths and resources so they can cope with the challenges they face. Families vary considerably in their needs, resources, and priorities. Some families need more support than others, so no one model or guide can be successful for all. Each family has unique strengths and needs.

Many families will look to the school to provide them with information about care for their child with disabilities. They may need information about services for their child both while the child is in the early childhood program and in the future. A child's transition from early childhood programs into primary school programs is of particular concern to families, and they are likely to turn to the school for support at that time. Ultimately, schools will go beyond simply helping families to empowering them so that they are not dependent on professionals for decisions regarding the care and future of their child with special needs (Dunst, Trivette, and Deal, 1988).

Services to the family of a child with disabilities should be available when a child enters a program. When the child is older, services become more costly, and may be needed for a longer period of time to adequately address a child's needs. Early intervention helps a child while skills are developing, instead of after, when habits are established and more difficult to change.

Educational programs can affect parents' behavior and the outcomes they expect for their children. Parents seek information and practical methods for teaching their child important skills or managing their child's behavior. Teachers can demonstrate such methods to parents in the classroom, during home visits, or at parent-teacher meetings.

It is important that the school offer family members a variety of ways to communicate with school personnel. Some parents prefer a written format; others prefer face-to-face conversations. As communication increases, parents feel more competent and their children are likely to show increased levels of competence and self-esteem. Families report that they feel a reduced sense of competence and lowered feelings of control when institutions make decisions for them or do not communicate with them. Most families will share personal information in order to gain access to the services they need. In the case of families who deny that their child needs services, the school must continually encourage their participation by communicating nonjudgmental, factual information about their child.

Communicating with Families

Teachers know that talking with family members is an effective way to learn more about their children. Developing a positive and trusting relationship between school personnel and a family also promotes the family's overall sense of support and empowers the family to make decisions. To foster these relationships, teachers need certain qualities and skills, all of which the teacher can develop over time with diligent practice and understanding. This section will describe some of the important qualities and skills necessary for forming supportive relationships with families.

A Foundation for an Effective Relationship

The teacher qualities needed to build a foundation for an effective relationship with parents are (1) respect, (2) a nonjudgmental attitude, and (3) empathy (Beckman, Frank, and Newcomb, 1996).

Respect

Because families are the most important teachers in their children's lives, they warrant consideration and particular attention from professionals. Professionals can show their concern for topics that are difficult to talk about regarding a child. For example, parents who experience difficult behaviors with their child may initially be reticent to discuss their feelings of anger, frustration, and resentment. A professional willing to acknowledge the parents' feelings becomes a welcome source of support.

Nonjudgmental attitude

A nonjudgmental attitude requires thinking positively and openly about families regardless of their personal qualities. When teachers remain nonjudgmental, they encourage families to value their own decisions without feeling pressured to adopt the teachers' opinions. A parent may become alienated if a teacher disapproves of the way the parent manages his or her child's life.

Empathy

The ability to be sensitive to the family's situation and communicate understanding of the situation demonstrates empathy to the family. Teachers can determine whether they are effectively demonstrating empathy by observing the way a family responds to them. Those families that seem comfortable sharing personal matters with teachers are feeling the teachers' empathetic communication. Family members who are less open in sharing their concerns are less likely to be feeling the empathetic efforts of the teacher.

Communication Skills

Once teachers understand the qualities necessary to develop partnerships with families, they can begin to further develop their communication skills by using the following techniques:

- *Employ active listening.* The teacher listens to family members, respects their views, and offers support. In this way, the teacher gains an understanding of how the family members view themselves, their child, and their circumstances.

- *Ask questions.* The teacher asks questions to elicit information, expands conversations, and clarifies. Using a balance of both open-ended and close-ended questions allows the teacher to obtain different types of information. Open-ended questions promote free-flowing discussion. For example, "What is challenging for your child?" or "What makes your child happy?" are questions that invite an expansive discussion. Close-ended questions elicit brief answers: "Do you have other children?" or "Does your child ride a bike?" The teacher should note the family's style of interaction and pacing of answers. By adjusting questions to the family's style, the teacher conveys a respectful attitude toward the family.

- *Reflect and clarify.* The teacher makes comments that let the parents know they have been heard and understood. The teacher restates the situation and clarifies the points that remain.

- *Reframe.* The teacher asks the parents to look at the situation in a new way and explore different ways of problem solving. For example, if parents describe their child's difficult behavior, the teacher may help them realize that the child is not being difficult—he is simply unable to complete the task.

Strategies for Effective Communication

Families of children with special needs are frequently overly anxious about their child's success on a daily basis. They may be extremely relieved to learn of the small steps toward success that are occurring regularly. Teachers, therefore, should take advantage of natural, informal occasions to talk with family members.

Discussions at drop-off and pick-up times

The classroom schedule must allow for a relaxed beginning and end of the day. The first and last half-hour of the day should be free time, when children and their families can play and work together in the classroom. At the beginning of the day, families should bring their children inside and help them get organized. Be sure that one member of the teaching staff greets family members and offers them an opportunity to share and receive information about the program and their child. As families become more comfortable during the course of the program, encourage them to stay and help: to provide administrative support, bring snacks, fix toys, or help the teacher prepare for the day's activities.

The afternoon pick-up is a good time to report on the day's activities, tell families about successes, and remind families of meetings or events. This informal time allows families to talk with other parents, ask the staff questions, request a meeting, play with their children, or read to a group of children. It is not a the time to discuss concerns or problems, since the children and other parents are present.

Notes and notebooks
Sending a short, informal note home with a child facilitates communication. The note should address a specific accomplishment, new skill, or behavior. It might also thank families for some contribution to the program. Encourage families to send notes back to the teaching team. Notes from home are particularly effective if the teachers are working on a specific goal with the child and the family is reinforcing it at home.

For ongoing communication, notebooks that travel between the school and home are a good idea, especially if family members have limited time or do not have phones. In the case of a child with specific needs or problems, notebooks ensure continuous communication and can alert both the teaching staff and family members to successes or changes. This technique is most successful if used at least once a week, and works best for families who are comfortable putting their thoughts and ideas in writing.

Bulletin boards
Bulletin boards show families what activities are going on at school and can include information of general interest, such as notices of meetings or articles about child development. Bulletin boards can also display children's art, stories about field trips, or photographs of children's family members. The schedule for the day, sign-up sheets, and instructions for volunteers can be posted. Information on the bulletin boards may repeat or reinforce information mentioned in other forms of communication, such as newsletters or notes to parents.

It is important to make the bulletin boards bright and cheerful and to update them frequently. Changing the bulletin boards can be a revolving job assignment for the teaching staff. Be creative; let the bulletin board communicate the atmosphere and activities of the classroom. For example, if a father is an artist, ask him to come to the classroom and draw or paint with the children, then post the artwork on the bulletin board.

Tips for Using Bulletin Boards

- Place information at an average adult's eye level.

- Change at least some of the information on the board regularly.

- Remember that everyone likes to see pictures and names of themselves and their children.

- Display children's work.

- Keep information brief.

- Ask families to contribute to the bulletin board.

- Post personal messages that acknowledge family contributions, such as a thank-you note to a parent who has helped on a project.

- Assign two people to create bulletin boards. It's easier and more fun.

Newsletters

A biweekly or monthly newsletter helps ensure that all the families in the program receive consistent information. The intent and topics of the newsletters may vary. Some newsletters describe the events and activities that are happening in school and suggest ways to reinforce those activities at home. Others use a thematic approach (see Chapter Six) and discuss activities and ideas that pertain to that theme. Some newsletters have various recurring features such as current events, things to remember, or articles on child development. Items in a newsletter may include:

- announcements of meetings, trips, or other events
- requests for materials or help with a project
- community information
- current focus of classroom activities, such as a current theme or a specific skill that the children are learning
- suggestions for activities at home
- thank-you notes to volunteers or requests for volunteers.

Newsletters should be short and easy to read. It is more effective to send out brief newsletters regularly than long ones infrequently. Newsletters should include names of children in the program and family members as often as appropriate, making sure everyone is mentioned over time.

Providing Support to Families

Sharing Information

Some of the tasks that a teacher performs involve giving information to and receiving information from parents, organizing meetings with them, and reviewing educational options for their children. If the teacher can complete these tasks—and at the same time be aware of the family's personal concerns—she will be a valuable support to the family.

Simply providing useful and pertinent information to families about their child is very supportive. Families view teachers as important sources of information; therefore, teachers should feel comfortable discussing the child's disability and information about how to teach and interact with the child.

Teachers will not be able to provide all the information that families of children with disabilities need. Teachers must sort out the information they know from the information they must seek. Not having information readily available should not be viewed as a professional weakness. What is necessary is to help families find people who do have the information or to brainstorm ways of solving a problem.

Reaching into the Community

No one program will be able to meet all the needs of a family with a child with disabilities. Staff members of inclusive programs must contact other service providers and strengthen bonds with organizations throughout the local community such as religious institutions, other schools, and civic and professional groups. These efforts will foster a comprehensive and integrated response to the needs of families requiring support. This community-wide approach is also a way of maximizing scarce financial resources and avoiding duplication of agency efforts.

Facilitating Transitions

Careful planning and thoughtful actions help to alleviate the stress that accompanies the transition between home and school life. The major transitions in early learning environments—from home to an early childhood program, to infant-toddler programs, to preschool programs, to kindergarten—require significant adjustments for all young children and their families (Wolery and Wilbers, 1994). Families of children with disabilities have concerns that are compounded by their children's additional needs.

Preparing children with disabilities for successful transitions involves collaborating with a child's family and with the teachers and service providers in the child's new and previous programs. Teachers should nurture a child's functional skills—self-help, social, and independence and group participation—to facilitate inclusion in new programs.

- *Self-help skills.* Children with disabilities typically have a more difficult time acquiring self-help skills such as toileting, hand-washing, dressing, and eating because of the complexity of those tasks. Teachers and parents must consider the individual child and their own priorities when setting goals for self-help skills. Perhaps the family is most interested in having their child establish toileting skills rather than eating skills. The teacher can work to meet these goals within the new program.

- *Social skills.* Children with disabilities will benefit by learning skills for interacting with other children and adults. Using eye contact, expressing needs, asking questions, sharing, and taking turns are a few examples of skills that promote positive social interactions. The teacher can lower the social barriers among all the children within the classroom by planning activities that encourage friendships between children. (See Chapters Five and Six for activity ideas.)

- *Independence and group participation.* Independence and active group participation are essential skills for a child to have if he or she is to experience successful inclusion in an early childhood program. Children with disabilities need natural opportunities to practice their skills within the context of day-to-day classroom activities. By using clear, concise language, adhering to a classroom routine, and adapting activities for individual children, teachers can assist children to acquire independent and active participation skills.

Teachers can also make transitions go smoothly by reassuring the parents and providing specific information about the new opportunities the school provides for their child's growth and development. In addition, the teacher can facilitate the transition by taking the following steps:

- *Explain the child's disability.* As families come to realize their child's disability, they will need to hear honest information about the disability. The teacher should try to deliver the information to both parents at the same time, avoiding the use of any educational or medical jargon. Many families need to hear the information several times and to hear it explained in many different ways. Though families may agree that they understand the information presented, they may think of new questions or concerns at a later time.

- *Listen to the family.* Parents are the child's most important caregivers and teachers; therefore, classroom teachers need to acquire valuable information from the family. The ability to help parents to supply this information involves many of the communication skills described on pages 25-27. For example, teachers who listen to parents and ask key questions are learning about the unique needs of the child and planning for a comfortable transition to the next educational level.

- *Help families gather important records.* Parents can provide the teaching staff with information such as health records, medical information, and assessments. The school staff should give families a list of information that will be helpful in establishing a child's educational plan.

- *Encourage the family to visit the classroom.* A family's visit to their child's classroom provides reassurance that their child's needs are being met and gives the family a sense of belonging and a sense of trust in the professionals working with their child. Whenever possible, the teacher, principal, and any other service providers should meet with the family before or after the classroom visit so that their concerns can be addressed. An important goal of the classroom visit is to give the family a sense of belonging in this new setting.

Fostering Family Involvement

Families in the Classroom

One of the best ways to foster family involvement is to invite families into the classroom. These experiences give parents strategies for working with their children at home. Making effective use of parents when they arrive in the classroom is the responsibility of the Step by Step staff. Some parents may automatically join in the classroom activities; others will need some help.

The teacher can facilitate a positive experience for family members who participate in classroom activities by following the suggested practices listed below.

- Select an activity that can be demonstrated easily. Give parents a brief explanation of the purpose of the activity and the steps involved in completing it.
- Have parents work with small groups of children (no more than two or three children).
- Encourage parents to relax and be playful in the activity. A relaxed atmosphere will promote risk-taking among the children, who will then get more out of the activity than if they simply "obey orders."
- De-emphasize winning. It is the *process* of learning that is important in early childhood, not the end result.
- Talk to parents about managing children's behavior. Give parents specific strategies to use for positive results.

Hundreds of activities go on daily in a preschool classroom. Families who work with the children on a volunteer basis should not be expected to know exactly what to do. Let them know that when they help in the classroom, they can always ask the teacher if they are uncomfortable or do not know how to handle a situation. The specificity of the instructions will depend on the comfort and skill of the family member coming to the classroom and the activity he or she will help with.

It is useful to provide some general guidelines for helping parents feel comfortable, competent, and productive while working in the classroom. A short list such as the one below can be given to parents or posted on the bulletin board.

General Information for Families in the Classroom

• Get a feel for the classroom climate—noise level, activity level, teacher interaction, etc.

• Participate in group activities. Sit with the children.

• Give children enough time to do things for themselves before you offer to help or solve a problem.

• Feel free to ask the teaching team questions when you feel it is necessary.

• Do not interpret children's artwork, block building, or wood work by giving it a title. Ask children what they call it. Have them explain it to you.

• Do not discuss the individual children with other adults, their parents, or other family members. If you have comments, concerns, or questions, ask the teaching team or director.

• Do not discuss children's behavior in front of them.

• Tell your ideas and suggestions to the staff so they can use them in the classroom.

• Have a clear understanding of classroom management and of the teacher's expectations for dealing with behavior problems.

• Enjoy yourself.

When the family member arrives in the classroom, the teacher can hand him or her a personalized brief note, such as the one that follows, with specific directions for the activity of the day.

Good Morning Mrs. Brown,

When the children arrive, greet them by name and talk to them about their morning. Tell them that you will be visiting them today. Help them remove their coats and put them away. Don't do it for them, but help them as they need it.

Today, we will be sorting objects by colors. Please take these children one at a time [give list of names] and work with them on the sorting activity. Show the child the objects on the manipulative table and ask him or her to find others that are the same color. Praise them for the colors they can match. If they cannot match the color after a few attempts, show them which ones match and then ask them to try again.

Please help us set up the art activity by taking out the markers, paper, scissors, and glue from the storage shelf. Sit with the children and talk to them about what they did today.

Thanks for helping us. We really appreciate it.

Here are additional ways to show your appreciation to family members who help out in the classroom:

Showing Appreciation to Family Members

- Thank family members by name, and remember to mention their child's name as well.

- Plan meaningful activities for the families to do. Show them what you expect them to do, and ask if they have any questions. Also ask them what they would like to do. Give them choices.

- Be prepared to invest time in training parents in the classroom. Show helpers around, explain things, introduce them to the staff, and indicate where they will work.

- Arrange for a place for helpers to sit and relax and store their personal belongings.

- Supply enough food so the helpers can eat with the children.

- Make teaching staff available to answer family members' questions and give them directions when they arrive.

- Create a section in the newsletter that highlights family members' activities.

- Send notes home talking about families who have come to the center or contributed to the program.

- Award plaques or certificates of recognition.

- Hold celebrations to honor everyone who made the program successful.

- Be supportive of parents' efforts. Thank them and thank them again. Encourage them to bring their spouses. Include activities that fathers may feel more comfortable with (e.g., building outdoor equipment or playing in the block area). Specifically invite them. Grandparents may also be willing to help. Ask them what they would like to do.

Conferences with Parents

Parent conferences occur for various reasons. At the beginning of the year, teachers will meet the parents and introduce themselves and the program. Later they will talk about progress that is being made, discuss areas that need extra attention or support, create a plan to ensure the best possible learning environment and program for the child, and discuss concerns raised by either the teacher or parents. Conferences should be scheduled at specific intervals during the school year:

- A conference can take place before school begins to make initial contact with the family and to give the child a chance to explore the classroom. The teacher outlines the objectives of the program, shares expectations for the child and parents, and answers any questions that the parents or child may have. The teacher also asks questions of the parents to gain useful information about the child.

- A conference can be held several months after the year has begun (during the fall and spring) when the children have settled into the classroom and have adjusted to each other. The teacher lets the parents know how the child is doing and gives some follow-up information about the program. The conference is an occasion for a teacher to hear concerns from the parents or for the teacher to express concerns about the child at school.

- A conference can be held at the end of the year to review the child's individualized education plan, set new objectives for the following year, and pass the plan to next year's teacher. It is also a good time to suggest activities that keep the children actively learning during the summer.

Teachers can prepare for parent conferences by asking themselves the following questions:

- Is the purpose of this conference to generally discuss a child's adjustment to school or the progress the child has made?
- Will we be reviewing goals previously set and setting new ones?
- Is there a specific issue I want to discuss with the parents?

At the end of a conference, the teacher should ask herself:

- What information did I convey?
- What did I hear?
- What was my reaction to parent comments?

Home Visits

Visiting children and their families at home should occur two to three times a year. When a teacher conducts a home visit, she establishes a rapport with the family in their natural setting. The teacher can also learn about the family's culture, style of interaction, special skills, interests, and talents (Coughlin, Hansen, Heller, Kaufman, Stolberg and Walsh, 1997). Home visits are successful when teachers follow these protocols:

- Schedule a visit at a convenient time for the family. Give the family a clear purpose for the visit and keep to the allotted time.

- Encourage parents to share their thoughts and concerns at this time. Avoid talking in front of the children about his or her disability. If such discussion is needed, schedule it for another time and let parents know the day and time well in advance so that they can arrange for someone to watch their child.

- Plan to demonstrate several activities. Showing parents how to work with their child helps to enhance the learning that occurs at home.

- Draw the parents' attention to the child's individualized education plan (IEP) if one has been developed. (See Chapter Four for information on IEPs.) Help parents understand the connection between the learning activities occurring in the classroom and the learning goals written on the IEP.

- Maintain confidentiality. Confidentiality is necessary to develop trust. Families have the right to their privacy and teachers have a professional responsibility to keep private information confidential.

- Be open-minded. Focus on the things that are relevant to educating the child, especially the family's positive efforts and successes. Successful practices at home can be adopted at school. Listen to and ask about effective techniques that the family uses. Try to avoid negative judgments.

Parent Support Groups

Parents who have a child with special needs benefit from meeting and talking with other parents who have children with disabilities. Many parents are in need of information about their child's specific disability, school educational services, medical resources, transportation, and so forth. Parent support groups offer parents an opportunity to share information, give and receive emotional support, and work as a team to address common concerns (Ripley, 1993).

The function of a parent group will depend on the group's needs and goals. Parent groups might distribute information, create a family resource center, invite speakers to talk on specific topics, or set up respite care and baby-sitting services—all the while providing social opportunities for the members.

The impetus for starting a parent support group should come from the parents. A small group of interested parents should consider the following questions:

- What are the primary purposes of the group?
- Who will join the group?
- What schools, disabilities, age groups, and geographical areas will it include?
- How will parents communicate with each other?
- Where will the meetings be held?
- How often will the group meet?
- Should children be involved in the meetings?

After discussing these questions, the group can arrange for the first meeting. Below are some guidelines for setting up the initial parent support group meeting:

- Determine who will conduct the first meeting. Select a leader or establish a small group to divide the tasks into manageable parts.

- Create an agenda for the meeting. Ask parents to introduce themselves. Then they can talk about future organizational issues. A guest speaker may be invited to discuss a pertinent topic. Keep the purpose of the meeting in mind so that the meeting satisfies the goals established on the agenda.

- Select a place for the meeting. Look for a convenient location that can accommodate the expected number of people. Whenever possible, select a place that is accessible to persons with disabilities.

- Provide advance information about the meeting. Notification of the meeting can be made in newsletters, brochures, newspaper articles, or by telephone calls. Notices should be placed in schools, doctors' offices, libraries, or any other locations where future members might see them.

Establishing a sense of community should be an important goal of all parent support groups. Having a safe place where parents can feel comfortable laughing and crying as well as discussing similar concerns will enable them to feel more support and less isolation. Ultimately, parent support groups should seek to strike a balance between social and educational needs.

Maintaining Confidentiality

Families have the right to be assured that any personal information they reveal, whether orally or in writing, will be held in confidence by staff. The parents of children with disabilities necessarily have more information to contribute about their children's needs than other parents, and much of it is apt to be sensitive. Teachers can be guided by the following principles of confidentiality:

- Parents should be the primary source of information about themselves. Information sought from them should be limited to that which is essential for helping their children.

- Parents and other volunteers should be prohibited from reviewing records other than those of their own children.

- Children's records and family records are open to staff and special consultants only to the extent necessary to provide services.

- Families are told about information that will be shared with other staff and the reasons for doing so. (Staff may use a signed consent form that includes how information is to be shared, and with whom). When in doubt about releasing information, obtain permission from a family member. The only exception to this procedure is in instances of suspected child abuse and neglect.

- On a yearly basis, with input from parents and staff, decide what information will be collected, how it will be used, and with whom it will be shared.

Source: Head Start, Social Services Training Guide.

Parents as Co-Decision Makers

The direct involvement of parents in decisions affecting their child with disabilities is essential. Many families enter a program with established connections to specialists, community services, and sources of information and can be important resources to the school and to other families. Through these connections, schools and specialists learn of new opportunities to establish partnerships. Parental input must be included in decision-making regarding:

- screening, assessment, and diagnostic activities for their child (Assessment is discussed in greater detail in Chapter Three);
- identification of their child's strengths and the areas needing educational support;
- establishment of specific goals and objectives for each school year;
- determination of the services their child will receive and any support the family wishes to receive; and
- decisions that are made as a result of year-end evaluations of their child's progress.

Building a Supportive Team

Teachers, parents, and students have consistently stated that the most important ingredient of a successful inclusive program is their collaboration with one another and with specialists (Stainback and Stainback, 1996).

Specialists with specific training and skills in supporting the development of children with disabilities have much to offer educators who are working to create inclusive programs. Speech and language therapists, physical and occupational therapists, psychologists, neuro-behavioral psychiatrists, social workers, and nutritionists each have specific areas of expertise that contribute to the success of inclusive classrooms.

When collaborating, it is important to view all participants involved as helping and supporting one another. If participants assume traditional roles in a group—with some people always acting as helpers and some people always being helped—the contribution that collaboration can make to inclusive education will be limited.

The make-up of the teams will vary, depending on the child and the nature of his or her disabling condition. Teams should always include the child's parents and teacher, but may also include other caregivers and specialists. Guidelines for effective team collaboration among educators, parents, specialists, and others include the following:

- Involve all key players so that collaborative decisions and activities receive widespread support and recognition.
- Establish a team leader who is recognized by every member, is willing to take risks, and is capable of facilitating change. Often the teacher, or another Step By Step professional, will act as the team leader.
- Establish a shared understanding of how the team will collaborate and what the expected outcomes will be for the family and their child with special needs.
- Encourage each team member to take responsibility for participating on the team.
- Establish open communication at the outset, maintain open communication continuously, and recognize that disagreement among team members is a part of the process of team collaboration. Establish ways to deal with conflict constructively.

Support networks should be devised within schools so that everyone who is involved in the inclusion process can be helpful to each other. Space, authority, control, and knowledge should be shared. School staff, including bus drivers, cooks, art and music teachers, secretaries, and administrators, should be familiar with the ways that they can provide support. Use of existing resources and assets reduces the need to develop outside resources.

All the support that a child receives should be focused on empowering him or her to gain independence in living. A danger exists that so much support will be provided to a child that he or she will become unnecessarily dependent on that support.

Some people understand the requirements of sharing, others may have a fear of relinquishing control, and some individuals are not yet ready to reveal personal information that is pertinent to a student's need for support. Showing respect for teachers, students, their families, and specialists requires time, energy, and thoughtfulness.

CHAPTER THREE

OBSERVATION AND ASSESSMENT

3. OBSERVATION AND ASSESSMENT

Chapter Overview
- The Importance of Observation
- Planning for a Formal Assessment
- Parents, Teachers, and Specialists as Assessment Partners
- Conducting the Assessment
- Ethical Responsibilities in Assessment
- Using Assessment Results
- Chart of Normal Development

The Importance of Observation

Observation Is Fundamental in Child-Centered Programs

From the first day of school, teachers greet students and their parents, engaging them in meaningful and personalized relationships. Over time, observations of the child can reveal patterns of behavior, learning preferences, mastery of specific skills, and the child's overall developmental progress. The primary purpose of observing a child is to gather information that will enable the teacher to structure classroom experiences to best meet the child's needs and support the child's continued development.

Teachers conduct observations in many ways, using a variety of techniques and recording methods. The most natural method for teachers is to observe children in actual situations in which they play, work, and learn (McAfee and Leong, 1994). Such observation is a unintrusive way to gain needed information about a child. Professionally, observational measurement is widely accepted as appropriate for use with young children (Goodwin and Driscoll, 1980). It yields descriptions of children's behaviors and quantitative measures of their actions.

Meaningful observation can begin when meeting the child for the first time. Teachers must be cautious about drawing conclusions in isolation from others who know the child well. However, initial observations are the first step in establishing good relationships with the child and the child's family. Here is an example of how a teacher can use the first meeting with a child to begin to understand and plan for that child.

Peter's father is looking for another school for his son. The teachers at his present school advise him that Peter may have a behavior problem that interferes with his ability to learn like other children. His teachers say that Peter is not a "bad" boy, but he is so active that they are concerned for his welfare.

After looking for many weeks, Peter's father has found a school where children with behavior problems are included in regular classrooms and where they also get help for their problems. Although Peter is very active, his father is hoping he will settle down as he gets older.

The teacher, Eva, greets the family at the classroom door. She smiles warmly and extends an enthusiastic greeting. She tells Peter's father how pleased she is that he could come. She says she has many toys ready for Peter to take a look at. Peter, meanwhile, has already wiggled out of his father's arms and is investigating a half-full watering can on a nearby shelf. To reach the watering can, Peter has climbed onto a table and pulled the can down. The can falls from Peter's outstretched arm, and, before anyone has time to react, water spills onto the table, a chair, the floor, and a nearby rug. Peter's father is startled. He reproaches Peter, saying, "Son, what have you gotten into already?"

Eva reassures the pair that, after all, it's only water and water will dry soon enough. She helps Peter wipe up the spilled water and then shows Peter how to refill the watering can at a sink. She guides him as he carries the watering can to a nearby plant. He very carefully wets the soil, all the while talking about flowers growing in his grandmother's garden. This story leads to another about the fruit trees in his grandmother's back yard. Soon Peter's attention is drawn to something across the room.

Peter runs toward an animal cage and bumps into a table, knocking over a chair and several small toys. Reaching the object of his interest, Peter flings open the cage door without hesitation and puts his head and hands through the opening. A small rabbit inside quickly retreats to the safety of a nesting box. Peter continues his pursuit of the frightened rabbit as Eva, without using any words, quickly crosses the room and closes the cage door.

Peter looks at Eva for the first time. Eva realizes that for Peter, actions speak much louder than words. Sitting face to face, so that Eva can maintain Peter's focused attention, she uses short phrases to convey a message: "No hands on the cage door. Get Eva. Eva can open the door. Eva can get the rabbit for you." Eva uses simple hand gestures as she speaks. Peter tries to get out of the chair. Eva places her hands firmly on his knees. She says, "Wait." She asks Peter to repeat what she has said. He begins to repeat what Eva has told him. He needs her help to remember each part of the message. When Peter has finished, she opens the cage door and lifts the rabbit out. She places the animal in Peter's lap, telling him he mustn't move. Peter does exactly as Eva asks. He remains quiet and entirely absorbed in petting the rabbit for more than ten minutes.

After Peter and his father have left, Eva records her observations and reflections of Peter's first visit.

The Children's School

Child: *Peter M.*   Date: *12/15/98*   Time: *3:30 PM*

Observer: *Eva Z.*   Setting: *The classroom*

Others present (adults, family, and peers): *Peter's father*

Peter's father arrived carrying Peter. Peter was alert and fascinated by his surroundings. Within minutes he spotted the watering can and went right for it. He climbs well, but because he moves so fast, he topples things over when he doesn't intend to. Peter provided lots of information on a topic related to his interest: his grandmother's garden that he related to the use of the watering can. He remained calm and interested in watering the plant until another novel activity caught his eye. Without any words, he darted straight for the rabbit. He applied no caution and never looked at his father or me. His father remained quiet. He deferred to me in dealing with Peter's behavior. Peter responded to clear, concise directions. I used Sign Language for "wait," "stop," "help," and the pronouns "me" and "you" for emphasis. Peter watched my hands intently and repeated my words when asked to. He appeared to thoroughly enjoy holding the rabbit. He petted her gently and spoke calmly to her. He used complete sentences and took turns in conversation when talking about his grandmother's garden and the school rabbit.

Reflections:

Peter moves very quickly. He appears to have good physical skills. Twice he remained focused for an appropriate amount of time during his visit, but he transferred his focus very rapidly. Does he see adults as helpers? Or does he completely rely on his perceptions and inner motivations? He communicated about things that interested him, but needed gestures to help him attend to and make use of my words. He made little use of language to organize his actions or express his needs. He responded to gestures and signs. He linked exploratory activities to previous experiences. How is Peter's father managing his active son? He seemed sad. I wonder if he would like some guidance and support. I wonder if Peter behaves differently when other children are present.

Observation Is the Foundation of Assessment

Over time, teachers come to know each of their students as individuals. Observations of children with special needs can help a teacher discover the ways that a child with disabilities is similar to typically developing children. Through observation, the teacher can also identify behaviors that may need further assessment by a specialist. Perhaps most importantly, through observation, the teacher can immediately appraise a child's response and actions. As a child shows mastery of a specific skill, subsequent adjustment of curriculum and instruction will contribute to hastening the child's developmental progress (Vygotsky, 1978). Thus, by keeping current with a child's developing skills and abilities, teachers can adapt instruction. They can also confirm and validate what they know about children and report information accurately to parents.

Because students' needs change during the time they are in a program, it is important for teachers to maintain ongoing observations. Observing a child continuously during placement is referred to as ongoing or continuous assessment (Hills, 1992; McAfee and Leong, 1994), and is the responsibility of the teacher. Sometimes, however, it is necessary to conduct a more formal assessment of a child, one in which parents and specialists participate and in which specific activities and instruments are used. How to conduct a formal assessment—and what to do with the information that is the result of the assessment—is the subject of this chapter.

Planning for a Formal Assessment

Assessment is a comprehensive process of gathering information about a child in each of the developmental areas. That information is then used to determine the child's strengths and any areas that need support to develop and grow. The goal is to investigate thoroughly an individual's current level of functioning so that appropriate educational placement and planning can be determined (Bagnato and Neisworth, 1991).

Assessment activities used with children who have special needs must be more comprehensive, focused, and precise than those used with typically developing children (Wolery, Strain, and Bailey, 1992). They must be comprehensive so that a child's capabilities and all areas of potential need are accurately considered; they must be focused so that the contributions of various team members will provide a detailed picture of the child's current level of performance; and they must be precise so that the child's unique patterns of functioning—his or her knowledge, attitudes, and interests—can be described in an individual profile, or summary report, which will be prepared at the conclusion of the assessment.

When planning for the assessment of a child, it is important to consider which activities to assess; what the setting will be; and whether other children or people familiar with the child, such as the parents, will be present. Young children are difficult subjects to assess accurately because of their high activity level and distractibility, short attention span, wariness of strangers, and inconsistent performance in unfamiliar environments. These elements need to be considered when selecting assessment activities and summarizing the assessment data.

Other factors that may affect a child's performance include cultural differences and language barriers, a child's limited prior exposure to play materials and activities, and a child's level of interaction with other children. Consequently, assessment of young children requires sensitivity to the child's background and knowledge of testing limitations and procedures with young children.

Parents, Teachers, and Specialists as Assessment Partners

In assessment, adults familiar with the child gather information from a variety of tasks over a sustained period of time and in various settings for the purpose of making educational decisions about the child (McAfee and Leong, 1994). Because single-discipline evaluations provide a "snapshot" from a limited perspective, assessments involving specialists from more than one discipline are recommended. Assessment should be an ongoing, collaborative process of systematic observation and analysis (Greenspan and Meisels, 1994). A single test, person, or occasion is not a sufficient source of information to be considered valid (Neisworth, 1993).

All parents hope that their child's teacher will recognize their child's strengths and support their child's growth in every way. Early childhood educators readily acknowledge the central role of families in the development of their young children. Paying close attention to a family's wishes for a child with disabilities can directly enhance the family's effect on their child's development (Hanson and Lynch, 1989). A teacher's effectiveness in creating successful learning experiences for a child with disabilities is improved when a partnership between teachers, specialists, and the child's parents is developed.

Parents may need to be reassured that teachers have their child's best interests in mind during the assessment process. They may have concerns that assessment information will be used to limit their child's access to education, rather than to help define the best way to provide an education for their child. Educators can speak with parents about these feelings and reassure them that their child's strengths will lead the interpretation of assessment information.

The assessment, therefore, should not be considered a measure of a child's incapacity or of the way a child cannot fit in with other children of the same age. It is not intended to sort out children to determine whether they are ready for school. It is not designed to assign a child to a group of other children who perform similarly on assessment items. It is not about passing or failing test items.

An assessment of a young child is quite unlike the testing methods that have been traditionally used for older children. The purpose of assessment of young children is to develop an educational plan. It is a process of gathering information that assists teachers, parents, and specialists to work together on behalf of a specific child. Assessment results are the tools that teachers, parents, and specialists use to plan individualized, child-centered curriculum and adaptations for children with disabilities.

Conducting the Assessment

Obtaining the Parents' Permission

Written parental permission for assessment should be obtained before any assessment activities begin. Written permission sets a certain standard of professionalism: ethical consideration of privacy will be maintained at the same time that those knowledgeable about the child are still able to communicate freely with one another.

Here is a sample parental permission letter.

Dear _____:

The teachers and staff of The Children's School are pleased to join with you in the assessment of and potential individualized planning for your child. We have found that successful collaboration or joint partnerships between families and other professionals who are knowledgeable about your child increases our ability to meet your child's educational needs. We frequently gain helpful insights and support from specialists in related professions working on behalf of children and families. Our work together maximizes the potential for your child's growth and development.

We understand that written reports and assessment materials are to be considered confidential. We assure you that any information shared between you, professionals, and the faculty and staff of our school will be handled with the utmost consideration for your child's right to privacy.

Sincerely,

Program Administrator

PERMISSION TO RELEASE INFORMATION and PERMISSION TO COLLABORATE

We give permission to the faculty and staff of The Children's School to review any pertinent information provided by us on behalf of our child, _____.

We give our permission to the following persons to communicate with one another on behalf of our child.

_____ Administrator, The Children's School

_____ Faculty, The Children's School

_____ Speech and Language Pathologist

_____ Occupational Therapist

_____ Physical Therapist

_____ Psychologist

_____ Psychiatrist

_____ Date _____

_____ Date _____
Parent Signatures

Determining the Observation Setting

Multiple observations across a variety of settings provide a more complete picture of a child. Young children are more likely to display their skills in speaking and in understanding what they hear when they are speaking with familiar people, such as their parents or other family members. Further, children feel more comfortable talking about objects and toys they have seen, touched, and played with before. Assessment of young children with disabilities should also be conducted in the child's native language (Meisels and Provence, 1989).

Involving parents in the process of assessment has many benefits for the child, the parents, and the child's teachers. The young child feels more secure when a parent is nearby (Greenspan and Meisels, 1994). Parents have so much knowledge about what their child can do well and the ways that their child needs help to develop and grow. Grandparents, siblings, and other people familiar to the child can also contribute valuable information to the assessment. Observing the child interacting with extended family members in various community settings should be considered.

Conducting the Parent Interview

When parents come to a school interview at the beginning of the assessment process, they have, in most cases, already provided specific and essential background information about their child on a school enrollment form. This information includes previous schools, family composition, custody arrangements, health history, ongoing health concerns, and the existence of allergic conditions. Care should be taken so that parents are not asked to share such personal information repeatedly. One school representative should be responsible for gathering from the family information that will be helpful in understanding the child. This practice helps to build a working relationship with the parents and makes good use of the parents' time.

Collecting background information about a child with disabilities occurs in a parent interview because the parent always retains the right to provide the information he or she feels is necessary. Parents appreciate having a choice of ways for them to provide the school with information. Some enjoy writing responses to the school's questions in addition to a face-to-face meeting. Others would rather speak directly to someone from the school.

Parents may need guidance in providing information that will be most helpful. Be sensitive and respectful, but elicit their help. They know the child best and they will soon understand that you regard them as a partner in the process of helping their child. Communication with parents is a two-way process. Let them know how helpful the information they share with you will be and that it will benefit their child directly. Provide them the opportunity to ask questions of you as well.

Information to be collected as an assessment process begins can include the following:

- Who is the child—what is his or her history?
- Who are significant persons in the child's life?

- What are the child's developmental accomplishments?
- What are the child's physical skills?
- What social and emotional skills has the child mastered, including play skills?
- What are the child's communication skills?
- What are the child's cognitive abilities?
- What kinds of activities interest the child the most?
- What are the areas in which the child needs support (e.g., communication, social and emotional development, play skills, physical growth and development, and problem-solving and thinking skills)?
- What remedies and resources are available to the educational team? What materials and equipment? What human resources?
- What methods used by the child, the family, and the teachers help the child (e.g., direct interaction, modeling, prompting, and providing accommodations and adaptations)?
- When does the child do well and when does he or she need support (e.g., at mealtimes, bedtime, outdoors, in solitary play, or in cooperative play with others)?
- Where, or under what conditions, is the child successful and where does the child experience difficulty (e.g., at home, in the neighborhood, at family events, in large or small groups, or at school)?
- How do the child's interests and motivation for learning influence his or her ability to learn? Do those interests involve the participation of others? Do the interests fit in with school activities?
- How does the child show what he or she knows (e.g., by speaking, demonstrating, singing, or showing)?

Parents have the right to choose whether, when, and how behaviors, attitudes, beliefs, and opinions are to be shared with others. As noted above, parents should be asked to give their permission before any direct assessment is conducted. Parents should also be asked their permission before any information is released or shared with another teacher, specialist, school, or program administrator.

Share information about children only with people who have a need and a right to know. Never make spoken or written statements about a child to anyone unless you have the parent's permission to do so. Keep written notes, checklists, or other records in a place where they are not visible to adults or other children who might casually read them. Place private information in an appropriate file and discuss the contents only on a professional basis. Files should be located in a locked place in the school office. Less sensitive information, including portfolios of children's work products, can be kept in the classroom.

Collecting Assessment Information

Information about the child is drawn from a variety of people, including those who live with the child, the child himself, and specialists who work with the child.

Interviews

Persons likely to be interviewed can include the child's parents, grandparents, a baby-sitter, and any specialists who have known the child or have provided the child with treatment. A medical professional may submit a written report or may be interviewed by telephone.

Specialists

Specialists contribute to an accurate profile of a child's current accomplishments and needs. Medical or mental health practitioners might not be directly involved in the assessment process, but they may work with the family during that time. Mental health practitioners—such as psychologists, in particular—can provide information on testing, legal requirements, and the merits and limitations of assessment methods. Mental health practitioners need to be familiar with the different assessment methods, their limitations, and current assessment trends and the reasoning for using them.

Other specialists who can offer substantial assistance during assessment are physical and occupational therapists, audiologists, speech and language therapists, and educators who have specialized training in working with persons with disabilities. In recent years, changes in the assessment materials and methods used with young children with disabilities have occurred. The current emphasis is on child-centered approaches. Such approaches evaluate the "total child" rather than a specific area. Specialists delve into the domain related to their specialty, but they consider the influence of all domains and they work in collaboration with other team members to determine eligibility for services and the best means of providing support.

Assessment tools

Recorded observations and other assessment data preserve information and become a part of the child's personal profile. Thorough, accurate, recorded information is essential to assessment, as it will be shared with everyone involved in the assessment.

Many options are available for recording assessment data:

Descriptive records

Descriptive records are "pictures" that are written, drawn, photographed, or taped (McAfee and Leong, 1994). Sometimes referred to as "running records," these descriptive records are detailed, containing a continuous written record of everything said or done during an assessment session. Behavior is recorded as it is observed. This type of record can be used to document verbatim responses in interviews or a child's behaviors and responses to elicited activities. This method of recording information takes more time and attention than any other method and should be used only when another adult is free to supervise any other children present.

Here is an example of a running record that shows Ali's behaviors during ten minutes of activity center time in Vlad's classroom. Vlad's program administrator recorded the observations so that Vlad and his instructional assistant remained available to the children.

The Children's School

Child: *Ali*   Date: *11-12-98*   Time: *9:30 AM – 9:40 AM*

Observer: *Program Administrator*   Setting: *Vlad's classroom*

Others Present: *The instructional assistant, 14 of the other 15 classmates*

Ali is engaged in active, sensory/exploratory play at the watertable. Two other classmates are also engaged in play at the watertable. Ali is pouring water from a cup onto a plastic baby doll. He bends over to look in the doll's eyes. Ali says to the doll, "No soap in eyes, baby. No worry." Ali picks up a bar of wet soap floating in the watertable. He rubs the soap on a washcloth and begins scrubbing the baby's legs. He looks at one of the other children pouring water through a waterwheel toy. Ali says, "Me want it." He looks out across the room. Ali sees Vlad helping another child hang a wet painting to dry. He calls in a loud voice in Vlad's direction, "Me want it! Me want it!" Vlad finishes hanging the painting and walks toward Ali. Ali repeats his message several times. The other child grabs the toy and holds it close to his chest.

Vlad bends down near Ali. He speaks calmly and firmly, using hand signs as he speaks, saying, "I want a turn." He looks toward Ali and repeats, again using simple signs, "Say, I want a turn." Ali watches Vlad, but says nothing. Vlad says, "1-2-3, I...." He makes the hand sign for "I" and waits for Ali to begin. Ali is still watching Vlad. He looks at the other child with the toy. He looks back at Vlad. Vlad makes the hand sign for "I" but doesn't say "I." Ali makes the hand sign for "I" and says "I." Vlad signs and says, "want." Ali says, "want." Vlad signs and says "a turn." Ali signs and says, "a turn." Vlad repeats the whole sentence: "I want a turn." Ali says, "...want turn." Vlad turns to the child holding the toy. He asks the child if Ali may have a turn. The child nods his head yes and offers the waterwheel to Ali. Vlad signs and says, "Thank you." Vlad asks the other child if he would like the baby. The child says yes and the two boys continue playing. Vlad stands and surveys the rest of the room. He stays near the watertable for a few minutes more.

Anecdotal, or narrative, records

Anecdotal, or narrative, records are detailed, story-like descriptions of what occurred during an observation. This method requires a minimum of equipment. It is best to make narrative records as the information is collected. Caution should be used in interpreting anecdotal records because a recorder's memory may not be reliable. Following Peter's visit to Eva's classroom, Eva recorded her observations of the visit in a narrative manner (see page 43).

Diagrams, drawings, and photographs

Visual representations can preserve important details of products and processes that would otherwise require lengthy written records. These methods are used to record information that cannot otherwise be saved, such as a child's block-building.

Lena, Anna's teacher, records information about one of Anna's block-buildings:

The Children's School

Child: *Anna S.*   Date: *10/13/98*   Time: *10:00 AM*

Observer: *Lena*   Item: *A Block-building*   Materials: *Unit blocks and accessories*

Notes: *Anna is a self-starter when it comes to block-building. She readily looks for and selects the size and shape of block that she needs for her structure. She added the small family dolls to her building. She took nearly twenty minutes to complete her structure to her visible satisfaction. She became distracted four times by other children's activities taking place nearby, but she returned to her building each time without adult redirection. She got her teacher's attention by gently tugging on the teacher's skirt and pointing to her building.*

Audiotapes and videotapes
Audiotapes and videotapes can capture complex activities and provide authentic evidence of skills and abilities, particularly physical skills and oral language. Tapes preserve a child's part in a presentation or in active play (solitary or in association with others), interactions between a child and a specific material or other individuals, and the teacher's or parent's behavior with the child. It is true that because audio- and videotapes retain a tremendous amount of information they can take an excessive amount of time to review. They are, nonetheless, marvelous records over time and are frequently enjoyed many years later.

Checklists
Checklists record the presence or occurrence of specific behaviors. They are often teacher-made or produced by individual schools for ease in recording expected behaviors during the school year. A checklist is a practical and flexible way of documenting many types of behaviors. Checklists do not describe how a child performs a

skill, and thus, they are not comprehensive in describing a child's strengths and areas of need. Nonetheless, checklists are useful to teachers for maintaining information and records that can be used as a basis for further inquiry or screening.

Below is an example of a checklist that shows Ali's skills throughout the school day:

The Children's School

Child: *Ali*   Date: *12/18/98*   Time: *All day*

Observer (s): *Vlad*   Setting: *The Four-Year-Olds' Classroom*

Observation of Skills Across the School Day

Arrival	• Greets teachers and friends • Uses stairs with alternating footsteps • Hangs up outerwear and school bag • Chooses an activity • Initiates play activity	*Waits to be spoken to* *Yes* *With reminders* *Needs help to vary choice* *Needs help to vary activity*

Activity Centers	• Enjoys many activity centers
	• Maintains interest in self-selected activities for 15-30 minutes
	• Uses materials to create original products
	• Seeks interaction with several other children
	• Constructs with blocks, manipulatives, woodworking
	• Engages in various levels of play:
	   * Exploratory/sensory play
	   * Plays parallel to other children
	   * Plays interactively with other children
	   * Takes on a variety of roles in imaginative play
		Water, art, cars, and trucks
		5-10 minutes
		
		Makes one project many times
		
		Yes, seeks others
		
		Plays with vehicles in block area
		
		Very much so
		Yes, enjoys this
		
		Initiates this, but is not sure of next step
		No

Clean-up Routine	• Stops activity upon familiar cue • Puts toys away in appropriate places • Cooperates and works with others • Follows sequence of expectations once familiarity of routine is established	*No* *With guidance* *Not during clean-up* *Not yet*

Circle/ Meeting Time	• Anticipates gathering together • Participates in songs and finger plays • Participates in movement and group games • Maintains own space for 10-15 minutes during group activities • Focuses attention on peer or adult speaker • Contributes to discussions	*Yes* *With great enthusiasm* *Yes, requires help with directions* *For 5 minutes* *This is difficult* *With guidance*

Bathroom	• Independently washes hands
	• Turns faucet on and off
	• Uses soap, rinses hands
	• Dries hands with towel
	• Toileting
	    * Adjusts clothing
	    * Uses toilet
	    * Wipes self, if necessary
	    * Follows sequence routinely, independently
		Yes
		Yes
		Yes
		Doesn't like the feel
		
		Is emerging
		Needs help, sits briefly
		Not yet
		Not yet

Snack	• Takes seat and socializes with others • Passes food to others • Enjoys a range of foods and beverages • Follows eating routines, manages pouring and serving • Asks to be excused	*Yes* *With help* *Has a good appetite* *Not yet* *Not yet*
Outdoor Play	• Enjoys running, climbing, and riding wheel toys • Digs in the sand • Uses swings, slides, and overhead bars • Plays interactively and imaginatively with others while outdoors • Kicks and throws a ball with accuracy • Jumps down from one foot height • Participates in animal care and gardening activities • Observes and comments on natural events, weather, and seasonal changes	*Good climber, no wheel toys yet* *No, doesn't like the texture* *Loves these* *Follows others* *Not yet* *No* *Animals scare him* *With prompting*
Dismissal	• Assists in gathering belongings for dismissal • Says good-bye to peers and adults • Greets family and shares information about the day	*No* *Yes* *Greets family with excitement; not sharing info yet*

Frequency counts

Frequency counts are useful for examining the rate or change in the rate of frequently occurring behaviors. Behaviors can be recorded during classroom activities informally.

Date	Frequency of Behavior: *Tripping, knocking over materials, running through classroom* For: *Peter*	Total
1/5/99	ЦНГ III	8
1/6/99	IHI HHI II	12
1/7/99	ЦНГ	5

Time samples

A time sample records how long a child or a group of children does something. This recording method is useful for examining how long a child or group of children remains engaged in a specific behavior. Using a watch or a stopwatch, the observer records the stop and start times or the total number of minutes a child spends in the targeted behavior.

Date	Activity	Total Length of Time
10/20/98 10:30 AM - 11:10 AM	*For Anna* *Activity choice: doll play* *Painting at the easel* *Eating*	*24 minutes* *1 minute* *Sat at table with the other children for 15 minutes, ate less than 2 minutes*
10/21/98 10:30 AM - 11:10 AM	*For Anna* *Activity choice: doll play* *Painting at the Easel* *Eating*	*15 minutes* *5 minutes* *Sat at table with the other children for 15 minutes, ate less than 2 minutes*

Rating scales

Rating scales are designed to quickly record the evaluation, or judgment, of a child's behavior. They can be used to gather the evaluations of others besides teachers, such as parents and specialists, and have been helpful to educational teams in determining a child's behavior in a variety of settings. They are limited in their use, however, since they are solely evaluation-based. Also, because rating scales are interpreted differently by different users, and some raters may not be sure how to interpret a scale, caution should be used in interpreting their results.

Eva asked Peter's father to fill out this rating scale. She used this method for several reasons: she wanted to find out more about Peter's behavior in settings outside the classroom, and she hoped that the rating scale itself would help Peter's father to focus on some of the behaviors Eva wanted to discuss at the assessment interpretation meeting.

Behavior	Rating			
Remains focused in play for 10 minutes	Never N/A	Sometimes	Usually	Always
Remains undistracted in the presence of other interesting stimulation	Never N/A	Sometimes	Usually	Always
Transitions from one activity to the next with ease	Never N/A	Sometimes	Usually	Always
Makes a plan for play and follows through on plan	Never N/A	Sometimes	Usually	Always
Responds to adult direction or redirection	Never N/A	Sometimes	Usually	Always

Criterion-referenced measures (charts of normal development)

Criterion-referenced measures are designed to compare a child with a set of developmental or growth standards. These measures are available commercially. They have been compiled by using established information of growth and age standards, such as those developed by Bayley (1968) and Gesell (1940). The items on the measures are arranged and sequenced by chronological age; by area of development, such as cognitive or physical skills; or by curriculum area, such as drawing or block-building.

The skills are referenced to the approximate age at which the typically developing child demonstrates the skills. For young children, ages are usually expressed in terms of year and month. One measure lists an item "3.0 – 3.2 years, uses noun and verb plurals." This means that when children have had opportunities to develop language, they use noun and verb plurals between three years and three years, two months of age, without additional teaching or intervention. In other words, in the course of a child's developing language skills, that skill normally occurs at that time.

Most parents and professionals don't need to refer to a criterion-referenced measure for information about benchmark skills. They know by experience that young children generally walk around their first birthday, they eat most foods by age three, and they lose their first teeth by the time they are six. However, when designing support for children who are not following a typical developmental path, parents and professionals may want to refer to what has been observed and recorded by professionals who have studied child development. This information is available by referring to a criterion-referenced measure or to charts of normal development, such as the one that appears in this manual on page 63.

When used for a child with special needs, a criterion-referenced measure or chart of normal development should be interpreted cautiously. The goal of assessment is to determine a child's strengths and areas needing support. Referring to the ages when specific skills should have developed is not directly helpful in planning the instructional program for a child with special needs. The purpose is not to compare the child with other children. The purpose is to acknowledge success that is recognizable and to design support that has a basis in the progression of child development.

It is useful, however, to discover what the child can do and to plan what steps to take so that the child can reach the next sequential targeted skill in that developmental area (if it is one that is appropriate for the child to achieve). In such use, criterion-referenced measures help identify the sequence of skills a child will need to reach a targeted goal. When larger goals are broken down into interim skills, progress can be more readily recognized as each skill is mastered. Little steps lead to larger strides.

The reason for using a criterion-referenced measure is to document a child's developmental success with assurance. It is also used as the basis for identifying the support services that a child and family need. Finally, use of a criterion-referenced measure means that time will not be squandered in pursuit of goals that are beyond the capacities of all children, let alone those with special needs. When criterion-referenced measures or charts of normal development are used, children are more likely to be efficiently taught (Cook, Tessier, and Armbruster, 1987).

Norm-referenced tests
Norm-referenced tests offer the most standardized information for observation. While norm-referenced tests are usually not helpful in planning individualized education programs for children, they are useful when comparing a child's performance with that of a larger group of children who are the same chronological age. For young children,

norm-referenced tests are most useful for screening and classification, while criterion-referenced measures identify what to teach (Smith, 1983).

Ethical Responsibilities in Assessment

Follow School Policies and Procedures

Schools rarely have written policies about observation of students, and so teachers must use professional judgment when observing students and recording their observations. A student's and family's right to privacy is crucial. Many schools do have policies clarifying the parents' role in all school-related decisions based on an assessment of their child, and teachers may be required by a school to report assessment results in a manner that assures families of their central role in the assessment process. Adhering to school procedures is an important part of the assessment process. Parents, specialists, and other professionals will want to know that teachers and schools maintain high standards for student privacy.

Remain Fair and Impartial

Collect facts about a child's skills and behaviors without distorting the information by allowing personal feelings or prejudice to enter into one's observation. When personal background, experiences, and feelings strongly influence the interpretation of a child's behavior, then objectivity is greatly minimized. Awareness of personal beliefs is the first step in remaining fair and impartial. Since negatively pre-judging a child may significantly reduce the ability to meet the child's needs, teachers, parents, and specialists will want to help each other to remain fair and impartial.

Motivations and intentions are important aspects of a person's ability to succeed in school and in later life. However, when assessing young children to determine strengths and areas of need, it is important to limit interpretation of a child's possible motivations, feelings, beliefs, attitudes, or desires. Record facts. Learn to distinguish between the description of behaviors that are occurring and the interpretation of what has occurred. Record descriptions of actual events. Allow for time and the input of additional information, possibly from other knowledgeable sources.

Description: Peter runs toward an animal cage, bumping into a table, knocking over a chair and several small toys.

Interpretation: Once again, Peter didn't wait and ask permission. He ran ahead to get what he wanted. He's always rushing around and causing trouble.

The interpretation of assessment results is separate from the process of collecting information. Interpretation occurs after all information has been collected. Because young children are developing and changing daily, many times the interpretation of assessment results is deferred so that ongoing observation can continue.

Here is an example of a communication sample collected by the instructional assistant during snack time in Vlad's classroom:

Name: Ali   Age: 4 years, 4 months   Date: 10-9-98
Time: 11:00 AM
Place: Classroom snack table
Activity: Participating in snack time
Recorder: Elena
Communication Sample:

Ali: "More. Some more."

Vlad: "Ali, would you like some more juice?"

Ali: "No. More. More cak – zes."

Vlad: "I am passing the crackers. Would you like some crackers, Ali?"

Ali: "More cak – zes."

Avoid the Use of Labels

For many years, medical and educational labels have been used to describe an individual's disability. Children were labeled, for example, "mentally retarded," "emotionally disturbed," or "learning disabled." These labels grew out of educational practices based on a medical model of evaluation, diagnosis, and rehabilitation.

Current practice, however, avoids the use of a label to describe or diagnose a young child. There are many reasons for this change in approach. Labels often do little to assist families, teachers, and therapists to determine the specific goals and accommodations that maximize an individual's success. In addition, negative expectations may be inappropriately associated with an individual as the result of a specific diagnosis.

Labels can lead to long-lasting, negative effects. They also inadequately represent the matters of concern about a child, and they convey little of a child's strengths. Today, educators of children with disabilities are shifting from labeling and treating children by category to intervening early and comprehensively without concern for labeling at all. It is hoped that early detection and intervention will effect developmental progress to such an extent that the need for any educational support will be minimized.

Be Sensitive to the Influence of Diversity on Assessment

Children are a part of the greater society, and many live in communities that are made up of diverse races and ethnicities. A dominant language often coexists with many other languages. Additional factors such as socioeconomic conditions, war, disease, and natural disasters affect the lives and living conditions of children. Families may reside in remote, rural areas or in densely populated urban ones. Children may reside within an extended family with many people, or they may live with one parent. Prior school experiences and access to medical care and treatment vary in the lives of children. Each of these factors influences a child's assessment.

To minimize the discontinuities between children's lives in their homes and their experiences in schools, teachers need to heighten their awareness of the effects that diversity has on the assessment process. Materials and procedures, or their adaptations, should be culturally appropriate and unbiased at the same time that they accommodate the child's sensory and response capabilities (Neisworth, 1993).

Using Assessment Results

Select, Organize, and Summarize the Assessment Material
At the conclusion of the assessment process, the program administrators help the teachers select, organize, and summarize the assessment materials for a child. All children who are assessed will have some materials that are fundamentally the same (previous school records, enrollment records, parent interview, narrative notes on home and classroom visits, etc.). Because of the children's individual characteristics and the characteristics of their families, however, some of the assessment materials are different for each child. Family goals are also considered when selecting assessment materials.

Assessment materials for Peter included:
* previous school records
* enrollment records that include information about Peter's family and the results of a current physical examination by a pediatrician
* parent interview
* narrative, or descriptive, observation notes of Peter's initial visit to the classroom
* a time-sample record taken during Peter's first week at school
* a frequency count taken during Peter's first week at school
* a rating scale, with multiple input from knowledgeable sources from different settings.

Assessment materials for Anna included:
* enrollment records that include information about Anna's family and the results of a current physical examination by a pediatrician and other physical specialists
* parent interview
* narrative, or descriptive, observation notes of the visit to Anna's home
* narrative, or descriptive, observation notes of Anna's initial visit to the classroom
* diagram of Anna's block-building with a peer
* photographs of Anna contributed by her family
* results of a developmental checklist, with multiple input from all knowledgeable sources.

Anna's teacher, Lena, gathered information about Anna by watching her interact with her family and her surroundings. Lena used ongoing, developmental, and unstructured observation. She gathered information about a variety of tasks over a sustained period of time and in various settings for the purpose of making educational decisions about Anna (McAfee and Leong, 1994). She recorded examples of Anna's development in each of four domains: social and emotional, communication, physical, and cognitive development. She also interviewed adults who knew Anna well. She recorded her observations on narrative record-keeping forms.

Lena discovered that Anna's greatest educational needs existed in two domains: communication and physical development. Anna did demonstrate some strengths in each domain, however, and she possessed some age-appropriate skills in the cognitive and social and emotional domains. Anna consistently showed great motivation to learn. She was happy to try each activity and performed particularly well when she was with other children. She was comfortable with adults and used adaptive skills—gestures, focused attention, and physical prompting—to communicate her wants and needs to others. She often pulled on Lena's skirt to get her attention.

Lena began to understand that assessment is a part of the intervention process, not just a means of measurement. Because Lena's observations were based on a home visit and the family's visit to the classroom and playground, they were useful in writing appropriate goals and objectives for Anna.

Assessment materials for Ali included:
- enrollment records that include information about Ali's family and the results of a current physical examination by a pediatrician
- parent interview
- narrative, or descriptive, observation notes of the visit to Ali's home
- narrative, or descriptive, observation notes of Ali's initial visit to the classroom
- several communication samples collected at school, at home, and at Ali's grandmother's home, including two audiotapes taken during mealtime at home and snack time at school
- results of a developmental checklist, with multiple input from all knowledgeable sources.

Once all the assessment materials are prepared, a meeting is planned to share the information and discuss interpretations. The teacher schedules a meeting at a time and place convenient to the children's parents. The parents are encouraged to invite any knowledgeable sources, such as the child's pediatrician or specialists, where applicable, to attend and contribute to the meeting. To facilitate the meeting process, assessment materials and results are given to meeting participants prior to the meeting.

Make Recommendations for Educational Planning

After a discussion of the assessment results, the meeting participants make specific recommendations for the child. They identify the individuals who will be actively supporting the child; those persons will schedule another meeting to develop written goals and objectives for the child and family. The individualized educational planning meeting will be scheduled as soon as possible. Meanwhile, the child enters the school program so that the assessment and planning process does not impede the normal flow of his or her life.

Recommendations for Peter

Develop an individualized education plan for Peter to include:
    Individual goals and objectives
        Social and emotional domain
        Communication domain

Strategies for behavioral management at home:
    Support for Peter's father to develop appropriate techniques to manage Peter at home

Team members for Peter will include:
    Peter's father
    The school administrator
    The teacher

Recommendations for Anna

Develop an individual education plan for Anna to include:
    Individual goals and objectives
        Physical domain
        Communication domain
        Social and emotional domain

Specialists will support Anna at school:
    Physical specialist
    Speech and language therapist

Team members for Anna will include:
    Anna's parents
    The school administrator
    The teacher
    Her physical therapist
    A speech and language therapist

<u>Recommendations for Ali</u>
Develop an individual education plan for Ali to include:
      Individual goals and objectives
            Cognitive domain
            Physical domain
            Communication domain
            Social and emotional domain

Team members for Ali will include:
      Ali's parents and grandmother
      The school administrator
      The teacher

Employ Developmental Guidelines

It is important to remember that in every classroom there is a wide variance of developmental differences in every classroom. Children are unique in the rate at which they pass through their developmental stages, yet they all fit within the broad range of developmental patterns. There are patterns in physical maturation, language acquisition, social behavior, and cognition and thinking (Wood, 1997). Children with disabilities have characteristics and needs similar to those of typically developing children. Meeting the individual needs of all children in a classroom requires that a teacher understand normal child development and recognize what a child can already do and what the child needs help learning to do (Bailey, Cryer, Harms, Osborne, Kniest, 1996).

Using the Chart of Normal Development as a resource will help guide a teacher in recognizing where a child stands in his or her development. Additionally, the chart can be useful to plan instructional activities for an individual or small groups of children and to make curricular choices for the whole group.

Step By Step Developmental Progress Record

Child's Name _____

M = Mastered (in ink with date), D = Developing (in pencil with date), No notation = not seen at this time

SOCIAL AND EMOTIONAL SKILLS

Comments

Two Years
_____ Watches others play & may join in briefly
_____ Defends own possessions
_____ Makes a choice given two alternatives
_____ Shows independence by doing more for self

Two Years, Six Months
_____ Plays simple games such as "Ring Around the Rosie"
_____ Begins to play with another child, taking turns with
     one reminder
_____ Shows satisfaction in doing small tasks for others
_____ Knows gender identity

Three Years
_____ Shows preference for some playmates
_____ Initiates social interaction with another child
_____ Shares toys, materials, or food
_____ Asks permission to use things that belong to others
_____ Expresses a range of emotions through actions, words, or
     facial expression

Three Years, Six Months
_____ Waits or delays a want for 5 minutes
_____ Enjoys temporary attachment to one playmate

Four Years
_____ Shows pride in accomplishments
_____ May fabricate some, as imagination is developmentally dominant
_____ Resolves problems with peers using substitution, persuasion,
     or negotiation

Four Years, Six Months
_____ Shows confidence in attempting tasks
_____ Tells about recent experiences/events
_____ Prefers the companionship of other children rather than adults
_____ States reasons for another's feelings
_____ Carefully uses items belonging to another
_____ Terminates inappropriate behavior with one reminder

Five Years
_____ Has several friends, may have one special friend
_____ Praises, supports, or assists another child

Five Years, Six Months
_____ Seeks more autonomy
_____ Is frequently satisfied, shows ease in relating to others
     even when conflicts arise
_____ Verbalizes positive statements about uniqueness & abilities
_____ Independently makes friends with other children

Six Years
_____ Consistently problem solves in difficult social situations

PLAY & GROUP PARTICIPATION SKILLS

<u>Comments</u>

Two Years
_____ Helps adult put toys away
_____ Imitates actions of others
_____ Plays nearby other children in parallel play
_____ Makes eye contact with another when spoken to

Two Years, Six Months
_____ Engages in domestic make-believe play, imitating others
_____ Works with an adult for five minutes
_____ Uses a doll or realistic toy to support emerging pretend play
_____ Often tries new activities
_____ Participates in small group activities: singing, snack,
    listening to a story for 5 – 10 minutes
_____ Independently plays on own for 15 minutes

Three Years
_____ Uses blocks & other objects to construct simple enclosures
_____ Participates in a small group led by an adult for 10 – 15 minutes
_____ Begins dramatic play, acting out scenes: traveling, playing house,
    pretending to be animals
_____ Engages in solitary activities for 20 minutes

Three Years, Six Months
_____ Takes turns with increasingly less facilitation
_____ Works with others for 10 minutes
_____ Uses blocks or objects to construct more complex enclosures
_____ Routinely follows 3 classroom rules
_____ Puts toys away independently
_____ Plays with two or three children for 15 minutes

Four Years
_____ Performs simple, routine errands
_____ Plays a simple board game with facilitation
_____ Dramatic play is closer to reality, with attention paid to
    detail, time, and space

Four Years, Six Months
_____ Expresses verbal directions in play activities
_____ Takes turns in play without adult facilitation
_____ Assumes a role in make-believe play with others

Five Years
_____ Plays cooperatively with others involving group decisions, role
    assignments, fair play
_____ Carries out one daily chore with a reminder

Five Years, Six Months – 6 Years
_____ Plays competitive games
_____ Plays two or three board games
_____ Engages in independent work for 20 minutes
_____ Plays cooperatively with two or three others for 20 minutes
_____ States & routinely follows 5 classroom rules
_____ Crosses street safely
_____ Independently obtains & returns materials needed for task

PHYSICAL SKILLS Gross & Fine Motor

Two Years **Comments**

_____ Stands on one foot momentarily
_____ Jumps in place, 2 feet together
_____ Strings 4 large beads
_____ Turns pages singly
_____ Stacks objects from largest to smallest
_____ Builds a six or seven block tower
_____ Scribbles, seldom going off a large piece of paper
_____ Holds scissors and snips the edges of paper

Two Years, Six Months

_____ Jumps over 15 cm (6") high object, landing with both feet together
_____ Runs forward well, stopping & starting with ease, rarely falling
_____ Walks on tiptoe
_____ Walks up 4 – 6 stairs alternating feet
_____ Walks up to and kicks a stationary ball
_____ Throws a ball with both hands from overhead position
_____ Builds an eight-block tower
_____ Opens and closes scissors & begins to cut across paper
_____ Holds crayon with thumb & 4 fingers, not fist
_____ Rolls, pounds, squeezes, & pulls dough or clay

Three Years

_____ Stands on preferred foot for 5 - 10 seconds
_____ Stands on other foot momentarily
_____ Walks up and down stairs, alternates feet and holds railing
_____ Runs around obstacles
_____ Jumps forward with both feet four times
_____ Hops on preferred foot five times
_____ Hops on other foot one hop
_____ Kicks a ball with backward & forward leg swing
_____ Catches a bounced ball by trapping it to chest
_____ Pushes, pulls, & steers a wheeled toy or tricycle
_____ Uses a slide without assistance
_____ Builds a nine or ten block tower
_____ Copies a vertical line, a horizontal line, a cross
_____ Copies a circle
_____ Uses two hands together to accomplish a task
_____ Holds paper with one hand & uses scissors to cut a five inch
square piece of paper in two
_____ Forms balls, snakes, & cookies with dough or clay

PHYSICAL SKILLS Gross & Fine Motor

Four Years

_____ Stands on one foot for 10 seconds
_____ Walks forward on line with heel-to-toe for six feet
_____ Walks backward toe-to-heel
_____ Gallops
_____ Jumps forward ten times
_____ Jumps backward once
_____ Turns somersault/does a forward roll
_____ Does a coordinated kick with backward & forward leg
  swing, arm opposition, & follow-through
_____ Catches a ball thrown from 3 feet away with both hands
_____ Throws a small ball with one hand to person 4 – 6 feet away
_____ Builds an 11-block tower
_____ Draws a somewhat recognizable picture that is meaningful to
  the child
_____ Uses individual finger movements during finger plays
_____ Copies a square
_____ Prints a few letters

Five Years

_____ Stands on other foot for 10 seconds
_____ Walks a balance beam forward, backward, sideways
_____ Jumps backward two consecutive jumps
_____ Hops 2 meters on preferred foot
_____ Takes two or more coordinated steps prior to
  kicking a ball
_____ Catches a tennis ball with both hands
_____ Throws a ball with body rotation and a forward step
_____ Swings independently
_____ Handedness well established
_____ Prints first name
_____ Builds a 12-block tower
_____ Colors within lines
_____ Grasps pencil correctly between thumb & 2 fingers
_____ Picture of a person also includes hair, nose
_____ Copies a rectangle, triangle
_____ Cuts out simple shapes

Six Years

_____ Jumps rope
_____ Demonstrates 2 complex ball skills: dribble, bounce/catch,
  hit a ball with a bat
_____ Picture of a person also includes: neck, hands, mouth
_____ Copies a diamond
_____ Cuts out items such as paper dolls or pictures of animals

SELF-HELP SKILLS

Two Years

_____ Removes simple unfastened clothing
_____ Anticipates & communicates toileting needs
      fairly consistently
_____ Washes hands, may need assistance using soap efficiently
_____ Uses spoon, spilling little
_____ Drinks from a child-sized cup

Two Years, Six Months

_____ Puts on long-sleeved garment with help with fasteners
_____ Dries hands with assistance
_____ Uses toilet with assistance, has daytime control

Three Years

_____ Uses napkin, cleans up spills
_____ Pours well from a small pitcher
_____ Feeds self
_____ Gets drink from water fountain independently
_____ Puts on pullover garment
_____ Unbuttons & buttons large front buttons
_____ Puts on shoes or boots independently
_____ Uses toilet independently
_____ Attempts to wipe self when toileting
_____ Washes hands unassisted
_____ Flushes toilet
_____ Turns faucets on & off
_____ Knows which faucet is hot & which is cold

Four Years

_____ Removes pullover garments
_____ Dresses self without supervision
_____ Attempts to lace shoes
_____ Cares for all toileting needs
_____ Brushes teeth with supervision
_____ Wipes nose when needed

Five Years – 6 Years

_____ Ties shoes
_____ Dresses self completely
_____ Covers mouth when coughing or sneezing
_____ Brushes teeth unassisted

COMMUNICATION SKILLS Understanding & Speaking

Two Years
_____ Points to & names simple pictures
_____ Uses personal pronoun **me**
_____ Uses two word phrases
_____ Uses the words **my** and **mine** to indicate possession
_____ Understands & asks simple questions: **what** & **where**
_____ Understands **no**
_____ Makes negative statements: "Can't open it."
_____ Names mouth, eyes, nose, & feet
_____ Can repeat sentences of three and four syllables

Two Years, Six Months
_____ Responds to simple yes or no question related to visual information
_____ Uses 3 – 4 word phrases/simple sentences
_____ Uses possessive nouns
_____ Uses pronouns to refer to others
_____ Requests needs & wants
_____ Enjoys listening to simple storybooks for 10 – 15 minutes
        & requests them again
_____ Describes actions depicted in pictures
_____ Uses plurals, adding /s/
_____ Names body parts: hair, head, ears, hands, legs, arms, fingers,
        stomach, back, & toes

Three Years
_____ Uses simple 4 – 5 word sentences
_____ Uses personal pronoun **I**
_____ Answers **who** questions
_____ Uses negative phrases
_____ Uses past tense, tells about past experiences
_____ Asks & answers **why** questions
_____ Uses prepositions: in, on, under, & beside
_____ Carries out a series of 2 to 3 related directions
_____ Understands relationships expressed by if ..., then .../because
_____ Points to chin, thumbs, knees, neck, & fingernails
_____ Repeats one nursery rhyme & sings a simple song

Three Years, Six Months
_____ Asks questions: **what, who,** & **why** for information
_____ Relates experiences with some understanding of
        sequence & ending/closure
_____ Names chin, thumbs, knees, neck, & fingernails
_____ Names colors: red & blue
_____ Speech is understandable to strangers, still some errors

COMMUNICATION SKILLS

Four Years   <ins>Comments</ins>

_____ Understands some conjunctions
_____ Defines familiar nouns
_____ Asks **when & how** questions
_____ Asks definitions of words
_____ Follows 3 unrelated commands in proper order
_____ Points to chest, heels, ankles, & jaw
_____ Names colors green, yellow, orange, & purple
_____ Understands comparatives like pretty, prettier, prettiest
_____ Understands sequencing of events when told them

Four Years, Six Months
_____ Can describe differences in objects
_____ Can describe similarities in objects
_____ Names chest, heels, ankles, & jaw
_____ Names colors brown, black, pink, white & gray
_____ Talks about causality by using " and so,"
_____ Uses irregular verbs & nouns
_____ Demonstrates a variety of uses of language: gaining &
         giving information, expressing ideas & opinions

Five Years
_____ Uses five-word sentences
_____ Participates in conversation without monopolizing it
_____ Uses words related to sequence
_____ Uses tomorrow & yesterday
_____ Answers the telephone, takes a simple message, &
         delivers it
_____ Can repeat sentences of nine & ten syllables
_____ Routinely answers one question during a group activity of
         10 – 15 minutes

Six Years
_____ Uses six word sentences
_____ Relates experiences or shares items with a group of
         classmates
_____ Answers **when** questions
_____ Repeats sentences of eleven & twelve syllables

COGNITIVE SKILLS

Two Years

_____ Turns pages of a book individually
_____ Understands in/out, close/open, & front/back
_____ Points to big/little objects
_____ Explains use of common objects: chairs, cars, beds
_____ Shows: one more, just one, & many
_____ Matches red & blue items

Two Years, Six Months

_____ Matches green, yellow, orange, & purple items
_____ Knows why we have houses, pencils, & dishes
_____ Touches & counts 1 – 3 objects
_____ Responds to simple directions: "Give me the ball & the block."
_____ Has limited attention span, most learning is through exploration
_____ Uses 5 toys functionally

Three Years

_____ Understands empty/full & light/heavy
_____ Shows understanding of bottom/top, behind/in front of, & over/under
_____ Matches circles & squares with objects & pictures
_____ Matches brown, black, pink, & gray items
_____ Points to when requested: red & blue items
_____ Recognizes & defines a problem when one arises
_____ Intentionally stacks blocks or rings in order of size

Three Years, Six Months

_____ Names red & blue when pointed to
_____ Comprehends short/tall, thin/fat, short/long
_____ Comprehends less/more
_____ Knows the part of the day for specific routine activities
_____ Sorts objects into groups that are the same by one attribute:
    color, shape, or size
_____ Knows age
_____ Names or pairs objects that go together: "What goes with a cup?"
    Answer: "A plate (or bowl)."

Four Years

_____ Points to brown, black, pink, & gray when requested
_____ Names green, yellow, orange, & purple when requested
_____ Matches triangle, rectangle, & diamond
_____ Names circle & square when pointed to
_____ Comprehends slow/fast, few/many, thin/thick, narrow/wide
_____ Shows understanding of directional concepts: up/down, between,
    forward/backward, away from/toward, low/high, & above/below
_____ Classifies pictures of common objects: foods, dishes, people, & pets
_____ Knows what to do when a shoe is untied, when you are thirsty, &
    you want to go outside & it is raining
_____ Explains why we have: keys, refrigerators, airplanes
_____ Touches & counts 4 – 7 objects
_____ Sequences five daily activities & tell time of day for each activity

COGNITIVE SKILLS

Four Years, Six Months

_____ Names brown, black, pink, gray, & white when pointed to
_____ Points to when requested: triangle, rectangle, diamond
_____ Knows own street & town
_____ Retells 3 main ideas from a story

Five Years
_____ Names when pointed to: triangle, rectangle, & diamond
_____ Shows comprehension of directional concepts: center/corner &
     right/left
_____ Classifies numerals, things to read, fruits, & vegetables
_____ Explains what to do when you see a house on fire
_____ Explains why we have clocks
_____ Visually discriminates between two like or different: shapes &
     uppercase letters
_____ Recites alphabet: A – Z
_____ Matches uppercase letters: A – Z
_____ Points to uppercase letters when named: A – Z
_____ Names uppercase letters when pointed to: A – Z
_____ Visually discriminates between two like or different lowercase letters
_____ Matches lowercase letters: a – z
_____ Points to lowercase letters when named: a – z
_____ Names lowercase letters when pointed to: a – z
_____ Can recognize & read familiar words seen at school & in the
     community
_____ Explains the function of community helpers: doctors, nurses, firefighters,
     police officers, mail carriers, & dentists
_____ Knows where to go for community services: when sick, to buy food, to see
     animals like tigers & bears, & to buy medicine
_____ Prints first & last name
_____ Prints upper & lowercase letters
_____ Counts by rote to 20
_____ Recognizes numerals to: 1 - 20
_____ Demonstrates comprehension of: first, last, second
_____ Knows the position of the clock hands for daily activities
_____ Completes 4 opposite analogies: Ice is cold. Fire is _____ .
_____ Predicts a realistic outcome for a event or story
_____ Retells a story from a picture book with reasonable accuracy

COGNITIVE SKILLS

<u>Six Years</u>   <u>Comments</u>

_____ Explains what to do when you break something that belongs
      to someone else

_____ Explains what to do when you are offered candy by a stranger

_____ Explains the function of community helpers: teachers, farmers,
      mechanics, carpenters, painters, & storekeepers

_____ Knows where to go for community services: to borrow a book, to buy
      stamps for a letter, to get a haircut, to wash clothes, & to have a
      car repaired

_____ Visually discriminates between two like or different words

_____ Visually discriminates which of three symbols is different: shapes, uppercase
      letters, lowercase letters, & words

_____ Reads color words

_____ Reads number words: One, two, three, four, five, six, seven, eight, nine, & ten

_____ Reads common signs: GO, STOP, IN, OUT, BOYS, GIRLS, EXIT, ENTER,
      MEN, WOMEN, LADIES, POISON, WALK, WAIT, CAUTION, DANGER

_____ Reads simple pre-primers

_____ Establishes auditory discrimination for isolated letter sounds

_____ Isolates consonant sounds

_____ Matches initial letter sounds to pictures

_____ Isolates vowel sounds

_____ Prints age, telephone number, middle name & address

_____ Prints simple dictated words

_____ Prints simple sentences, one – four words

_____ Demonstrates number concepts: 8 - 10

_____ Counts by rote to 100

_____ Matches quantity with symbol/numeral: 1, 2, 3, 4, 5, 6, 7, 8, 9, & 10

_____ Demonstrates comprehension of: middle, third, fourth, & fifth

_____ Writes numerals in sequence from memory to 100

_____ Writes a numeral that follows a given numeral: 1 – 10

_____ On request writes numeral when dictated to 100

_____ Knows simple addition facts with sums to 20

_____ Knows subtraction facts with solutions to 10

_____ Can tell time to the hour

_____ Can tell time to the half hour

CHAPTER FOUR

DEVELOPING
INDIVIDUALIZED EDUCATION
PLANS

4. DEVELOPING INDIVIDUALIZED EDUCATION PLANS

Chapter Overview
- From Assessment to Educational Planning
- The Contents of an Individualized Education Plan (IEP)
- Anna's Individualized Education Plan

From Assessment to Educational Planning

Once the assessment is completed, everyone who has participated in the assessment—parents, teachers, and specialists—sits down together to interpret the assessment results and to decide what steps to take next. In most cases, that group of people will decide that an individualized education plan (IEP) should be drawn up for the child. An IEP is a formal, written document that describes in detail the education and related services the child will receive. A date is set for writing the IEP.

The people who later convene to prepare the IEP make up the "IEP team" (also called the "educational team.") Some of the same people who were on the assessment team will be on the IEP team—for example, the classroom teacher and the parents. Depending on the results of the assessment, some specialists may participate on both teams. An administrator will also be part of the IEP team. Team members collaborate as partners during the IEP meeting and jointly take responsibility for making decisions about the type and amount of support that is needed for the child to be successful in school. Once the IEP is drawn up, the team members are responsible for making sure that the plan is carried out. The fact that they work together is important. When a young child with disabilities is included in a regular school, effective collaboration is often a key element in the child's success (Hanson and Lynch, 1989).

The team is formed by the child's teacher or a school representative. This person assumes the role of team leader and coordinates the efforts of the team members, both during the IEP meeting and as the IEP is carried out. The team leader plans and schedules meetings, determines a location for meetings, and notifies each team member of meeting dates and times. The team leader also provides team members with requested information or documents as needed.

It is helpful to develop a list of the names, addresses, and telephone numbers of the members of the IEP team to facilitate communication among all members.

Educational Team Members for (child's name)

	NAME	ADDRESS	TELEPHONE
Parents			
School Administrator			
Classroom Teacher(s)			
Specialist(s)			

The Contents of an Individualized Education Plan (IEP)

The IEP document is developed by the team at one or more meetings. The team focuses on developing specific instructional strategies and all related services that will allow the child to access the regular education program successfully. A sample form that can be used to draw up an IEP is found on pages 81-86; a sample IEP with goals and objectives filled in (in this case, for Anna) begins on page 87. Basically, the IEP should include the following:

1. Identifying Information

The first page of an individualized education plan consists of basic identifying information, such as the child's name, age, address, telephone number, parents' name, child's areas of disabilities, and IEP and eligibility dates. It also is a place to record the names of the members of the child's IEP team.

2. Present Levels of Performance

Page two of the IEP provides a statement of the child's current educational level of development based on the data collected during the assessment process. This part of the plan describes what the child can do, including the child's strengths, and what the child's learning style is, particularly if one style is highly dominant over others. Specific statements of what the child is not currently doing, or areas needing support, follow the strengths. Parents' concerns regarding their child's educational progress should be addressed. The effect of the child's disability on his or her ability to access and progress in the regular education curriculum should be included. The IEP team works together to create the comprehensive level of functioning. The description of the child's current level of development must be as accurate as possible, for that is the foundation upon which the goals and objectives are built.

3. Goals and Objectives

Beginning on page three, the IEP team members set goals and objectives that will help the child to master the skills or behaviors they believe the child should attain. The written goals and objectives are based on the child's current level of functioning, which has been described on page two of the IEP. All related service providers who will be working with the child will participate in developing the goals and objectives.

Goals are statements of a desired result or achievement. They are expressed as positive statements that describe an observable behavior, skill, or event that will occur over the duration of the IEP. A well-written goal can be understood by anyone reading it.

Objectives are the intermediate steps necessary to achieve the goals. They are written in clear, simple terms.

Well-written goals will address who will do what, when, and how well.

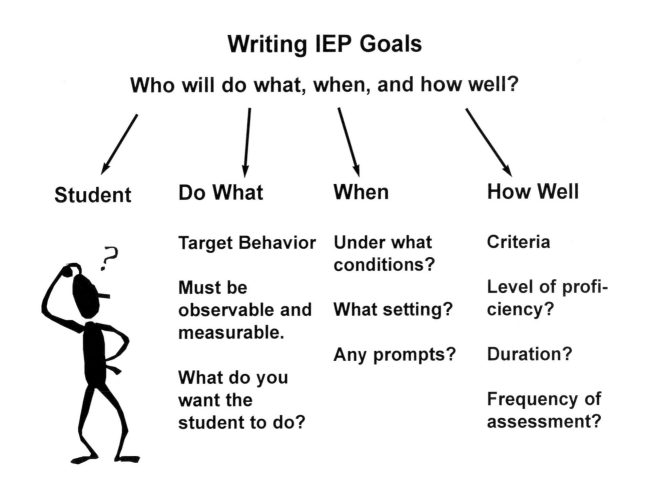

Writing IEP Goals

Who will do what, when, and how well?

Student	Do What	When	How Well
	Target Behavior	Under what conditions?	Criteria
	Must be observable and measurable.	What setting?	Level of proficiency?
	What do you want the student to do?	Any prompts?	Duration?
			Frequency of assessment?

M. Chamberlin

NOTE: A goal should be written for each major area of weakness identified in the current level of functioning—that is, academic areas, gross motor, fine motor, social/emotional, and speech and language.

An example of Anna's long-range goals with short-term objectives follows:

Information stated in the present levels of performance: Anna is beginning to walk steadily on flat ground. She waits to be carried up and down stairs.

Description of current skill area requiring support: physical domain

Long-range goal: Anna will walk up and down railed stairs, using a foot over foot pattern, without assistance in a variety of school environments during 80 percent of the opportunities over a nine- week period.

Short-term objective: Anna will walk up stairs using two feet per step, holding the handrail and an adult's hand.

Short-term objective: Anna will walk up stairs using two feet per step, holding only the handrail.

Short-term objective: Anna will walk up stairs using one foot per step, holding the handrail and an adult's hand.

4. Related Services
Related services include, but are not limited to, the following:
   audiology
   occupational therapy
   physical therapy
   psychological services
   speech and language services.

Service providers and teachers work together to integrate the related services into the regular classroom activities, thus avoiding fragmenting the child's educational program. Service delivery is most effective when it occurs within the regular classroom setting. There are times, however, when more intensive or specialized services are needed and can only be provided in a more individualized setting—for example, a child requires training on a specific piece of equipment that would be disruptive if used in the regular education setting.

The IEP team decides how many times a week the child should see the specialists and the duration of each service.

5. Classroom Accommodations and Modifications

Appropriate accommodations/modifications allow a child to access the regular education curriculum. The following areas should be considered when planning an appropriate program for a child with disabilities (see page four of the IEP):

- setting
- instruction
- directions
- behavior management
- organizational skills
- materials
- sensory needs.

6. Determining the Appropriate Program Placement

Following the development of the goals and objectives for a child, the IEP team must make a decision concerning the most appropriate placement for the child. The team considers where, or in what educational setting, the child's individualized goals and objectives can best be met. Two important factors must be considered when the team makes a placement decision: (1) the appropriate education program and (2) the program closest to the child's regular school in the local community.

An "appropriate education program" is one that can deliver individualized instruction and that has sufficient access to the related services the child needs to benefit from the inclusive school experience. When a placement decision is made, the final step is to write the "Program or Group Placement" in the space indicated on the first page of the plan.

7. The Dates the IEP Will Be in Effect

The suggested duration for the IEP is usually one year to maximize the child's growth and progress. However, any member of the IEP team (parent, administrator, teacher, etc.) may request a meeting at any time to write a new IEP or to add to the current IEP for any of the following reasons (this is not an inclusive list):

- The child has met the current goals.
- The child is having difficulty meeting the current goals.

- There has been a request to increase services.
- Questions have arisen regarding the child's current placement.
- The child is moving to a new school.
- The child's behavior is problematic.

Schools have the option of selecting when to write IEPs. Some schools write IEPs as the child enters the program and the IEP ends on the same date the following year. Others choose to write all IEPs during a specific time of the year (e.g., late fall or late spring). For example, if a child becomes eligible for special education services in October and is in a school that writes all IEPs in late spring, the initial IEP for that child is reviewed and rewritten the late spring of the current school year.

8. Documenting Progress and Evaluating Program Effectiveness
An integral part of the IEP process is the ongoing assessment and collection of data that will be used to determine the child's educational progress.

Assessment/data collection methods include, but are not limited to the following:

- work samples
- observations
- checklists
- anecdotal records
- criterion-referenced tests
- norm-referenced tests.

During the course of the year, the teacher and any service providers evaluate the child's progress and determine whether the plan is an effective one. Progress is shared with the parents. If any member of the IEP team requests a progress review, an IEP meeting is arranged prior to the annual review date.

The date and progress are recorded directly on the IEP, indicating the mastery level of the annual goal. An example of a reporting system is listed below:

- M = student has mastered this annual goal
- SP = student has made significant progress toward achieving this goal within the duration of this IEP
- IP = student is making insufficient progress toward achieving this goal within the duration of this IEP
- NP = the student has made no progress toward meeting this annual goal
- NI = this annual goal was not introduced.

An IEP may be created in many different formats or layouts. The value of the plan lies not so much in the actual document but in the action that the plan sets in motion. Consistently implementing the IEP with day-to-day effort and documentation is the best means for achieving success for the individual student. In this way, the use of an IEP supports accountability.

Individualized Education Plan (IEP)
[Name of School]

Child_____ Date of Birth _____

_____

Parent or Guardian _____ Telephone _____

Address_____

_____

Area(s) of Disability _____

Eligibility Date _____ Grade _____

IEP Dated from _____ to _____

Program or Group Placement _____

IEP Meeting Participants _____

Student	Date	Participant/Relationship to student	Date
Parent	Date	Participant/Relationship to student	Date
School administrator	Date	Participant/Relationship to student	Date
Teacher	Date	Participant/Relationship to student	Date

Summary of Special Education and Related Services:

Services	Frequency	Setting	Dates of Service Delivery

I AGREE with the contents of this IEP. I have had an opportunity to be involved in the development of this IEP. I have received a copy of this IEP.

_____
Parent or Guardian Signature   Date

I DO NOT AGREE with the contents of this IEP. I have had an opportunity to be involved in the development of this IEP. I have received a copy of this IEP.

_____
Parent or Guardian Signature   Date

81

INDIVIDUALIZED EDUCATION PLAN
[SCHOOL NAME]

CHILD'S NAME

PRESENT LEVELS OF PERFORMANCE

(Describe the child's educational levels based on assessment data and classroom performance. Summarize data/strengths and weaknesses in the areas of social/emotional, physical, and cognitive development, communication.)

INDIVIDUALIZED EDUCATION PLAN
[SCHOOL NAME]

CHILD'S NAME

ANNUAL GOAL:

SHORT-TERM OBJECTIVES	Assessment	Date and Progress
	Work samples	
	Observations	
	Checklists	
	Anecdotal records	
	Criterion-referenced test	
	Norm-referenced test	

ANNUAL GOAL:

SHORT-TERM OBJECTIVES	Assessment	Date and Progress
	Work samples	
	Observations	
	Checklists	
	Anecdotal records	
	Criterion-referenced test	
	Norm-referenced test	

INDIVIDUALIZED EDUCATION PLAN
[SCHOOL NAME]

CHILD'S NAME

CLASSROOM ACCOMMODATIONS /MODIFICATIONS

Check as appropriate: Preferred Learning Style

☐ Auditory ☐ Visual ☐ Multisensory
☐ Kinesthetic ☐ Tactile

Setting	☐ Preferential seating ☐ Individual ☐ Small group
Instruction	☐ Frequent/immediate feedback ☐ Incorporation of learning styles ☐ Peer tutoring ☐ Cooperative learning groups/pairs ☐ Other _____
Directions	☐ Directions given in a variety of ways: __ Oral __Written __ Demonstration/model __ Cue student's attention ☐ Other _____
Behavior	☐ Frequent breaks ☐ Movement opportunities ☐ Clearly defined limits/expectations ☐ Proximity/control ☐ Quiet time ☐ Advantageous seating ☐ Wait time for compliance location ☐ Positive reinforcement ☐ Choices/alternatives
Materials	☐ Manipulatives ☐ Braille materials ☐ Adapted alternatives ☐ Pencil grip/slant board ☐ Other
Organizational Skills	☐ Individualized schedule written for student ☐ Other
Sensory Needs	☐ Monitor student's use of: __ hearing aids __ glasses __ auditory/FM equipment __ assistive technology equipment ☐ Other
Other	_____ _____ _____

Anna's Individualized Education Plan

Based on the interpretation of the information collected during Anna's assessment meeting, Anna's educational team, including her parents, teacher, and school administrator, agree that Anna will receive special education services, including occupational and physical therapies and speech/language services.

Anna's educational team meets, and together they write a draft copy of her present level of performance and goals and objectives. Once the draft is written, an IEP meeting is held at Anna's school. Anna's parents, her teacher, a school administrator, a physical therapist, an occupational therapist, and a speech and language clinician are present. At the meeting, the following information becomes a part of the IEP document:

- A paragraph is added to the end of the "Present Level of Performance" regarding her parents' concerns.
- The speech and language clinician shows Anna's parents one type of augmentative communication device, "Cheaptalk", that the teacher and the clinician will use in the classroom with Anna. (This device allows Anna to request help, ask for more of something, or make a comment when she presses a button with a picture on it.) The use of picture symbols facilitates communication. Cheaptalk is listed on the "Classroom Accommodations and Modifications" page of the IEP.

After reviewing the goals and objectives stated in Anna's IEP, the team writes a summary of special education and related services on the first page of the IEP:

- Anna will begin speech and language services at school. She will receive two 30-minute sessions each week. Sessions will take place in the classroom while Anna is interacting with other children during activity center time and also in an individual session. The clinician will model techniques for Anna's parents and teachers to promote better coordination of services between home and school.
- Anna will begin occupational therapy twice a week at school. One session will take place in the classroom and the other will be held in the indoor gymnasium where specialized therapy equipment is located.
- Anna will begin physical therapy twice a week at school. Both sessions will occur outside of the classroom in the indoor gymnasium, outside on the playground, and within the school environment.

The team decided that the IEP would be in effect for one year. Anna will receive all services at her local school.

ANNA'S INDIVIDUALIZED EDUCATION PLAN

PRESENT LEVELS OF PERFORMANCE

(Describe the child's educational levels based on assessment data and classroom performance. Summarize data/strengths and weaknesses including areas such as social/emotional, physical development, communication, cognition, and behavior.)

Anna is a 3-year, 7-month-old girl who attends kindergarten. Assessment indicates that she was found eligible to receive special education services as a child with physical disabilities and speech and language deficits in March 1999.

Current testing results (formal and informal) include:

Developmental Inventory:	Cognitive: 36 months
	Gross Motor: 11 months
	Fine Motor: 32 months
	Communication: (receptive) 20 months
	Communication: (expressive) 9 months
	Social/Emotional: 24 months
Motor Scales:	Fine Motor: 1st percentile
	Grasping: 4th percentile
	Hand use: 2nd percentile
	Eye hand coordination: 2nd percentile
	Manual dexterity: 1st percentile

Anna's parents have expressed concerns about their daughter's limited communication skills and her social interactions. They worry that the other children in her class will make fun of her.

Anna's physical limitations and her language deficits affect her ability to access the regular education program without modifications and adult support.

Areas of strength:	Areas of weakness:
• Gross Motor Improved movement in all extremities Increased muscle tone in extremities Improved ability to use gross motor skills at school Is beginning to take steps using a railing	• Gross Motor Unable to sit on the floor Limited ability to use playground equipment
• Fine Motor Ability to snip with scissors Interest in coloring/painting activities	• Fine Motor Difficulty using hands and arms Poor grasp
• Receptive/Expressive Language Improved skill in following simple one-step directions Beginning to use sounds to express displeasure	• Receptive/Expressive Language Limited verbalizations Difficulty making needs known
• Cognitive Is beginning to demonstrate under-standing of shapes Enjoys listening to stories Completes a set of stacking rings Points to four colors upon request	• Cognitive Unable to demonstrate understanding of concepts such as big/little, less/more, short/tall, etc.
• Social/emotional Enjoys peer and adult interactions Is beginning to make choices regarding activities Exhibits a friendly disposition	• Social/emotional Uncomfortable with unfamiliar adults and peers Unable to transition without signifi-cant support

INDIVIDUALIZED EDUCATION PLAN
SCHOOL NAME

CHILD'S NAME *Anna*

ANNUAL GOAL: *Communication – Anna will communicate her needs using picture symbols, vocalizations, and mechanical devices 80% of the time with no more than 3 adult prompts per person.*

SHORT-TERM OBJECTIVES	Assessment	Date and Progress
• Uses gestures, such as pointing, to indicate a need • Uses Cheap Talk to indicate "more", "finished", and "help" • Uses picture symbols to express needs and make choices • Attempts vocalizations paired with pictures	Work samples (Observations) Checklists (Anecdotal records) Criterion-referenced test Norm-referenced test	SP 5-15-99

ANNUAL GOAL: *Fine Motor – Anna will demonstrate use of bilateral hand skills when completing a variety of fine motor activities during 80% of opportunities 4 out of 5 days sampled in each report period.*

SHORT-TERM OBJECTIVES	Assessment	Date and Progress
• Builds structures using a variety of different size blocks • Uses left hand to anchor while drawing with right hand • Holds paper and snips with adapted scissors • Manipulates play dough, finger paints, and thera-putty with both hands	(Work samples) Observations Checklists (Anecdotal records) Criterion-referenced test Norm-referenced test	SP 5-15-99

INDIVIDUALIZED EDUCATION PLAN
SCHOOL NAME

CHILD'S NAME *Anna*

ANNUAL GOAL: Social / Emotional — Anna will participate in activities with her peers 5-10 minutes in duration with decreasing) adult support based on weekly observations.

SHORT-TERM OBJECTIVES	Assessment	Date and Progress
• Initiates greetings • Sits with one other peer to play with manipulatives • Participates in simple turn-taking games • Independently initiates an activity with a friend	Work samples (Observations) (Checklists) Anecdotal records Criterion-referenced test Norm-referenced test	SP 5-15-99

ANNUAL GOAL: Cognitive — Anna will sort a variety of objects by three attributes), 4 of 5 trials) over 3 consecutive data collection points.

SHORT-TERM OBJECTIVES	Assessment	Date and Progress
• Finds identical object from an array of 3 objects • Recognizes same and different attributes of objects • Sorts objects by color (2-3 colors) • Sorts by shape (2-3 shapes) • Sorts objects by color, shape, size	Work samples Observations Checklists (Anecdotal records) (Criterion-referenced test) Norm-referenced test	SP 5-15-99

INDIVIDUALIZED EDUCATION PLAN
SCHOOL NAME

CHILD'S NAME *Anna*

CLASSROOM ACCOMMODATIONS /MODIFICATIONS

Check as appropriate: Preferred Learning Style

☐ Auditory   ☑ Visual   ☐ Multisensory

☐ Kinesthetic   ☐ Tactile

Setting	☑ Preferential seating ☐ Individual ☑ Small group
Instruction	☑ Frequent/immediate feedback ☐ Incorporation of learning styles ☐ Peer tutoring ☑ Cooperative learning groups/pairs ☐ Other _____
Directions	☑ Directions given in a variety of ways: ✓Oral ___Written ___ Demonstration/model ___ Cue student's attention ☐ Other _____
Behavior	☐ Frequent breaks ☐ Movement opportunities ☑ Clearly defined limits/expectations ☐ Proximity/control ☐ Quiet time ☐ Advantageous seating ☐ Wait time for compliance location ☑ Positive reinforcement ☐ Choices/alternatives
Materials	☑ Manipulatives ☐ Braille materials ☐ Adapted alternatives ☐ Pencil grip/slant board ☐ Other
Organizational Skills	☐ Individualized schedule written for student ☐ Other
Sensory Needs	☐ Monitor student's use of: __ hearing aids __ glasses __ auditory/FM equipment __ assistive technology equipment ☐ Other
Other	*Cheap Talk* *Picture Symbols*

90

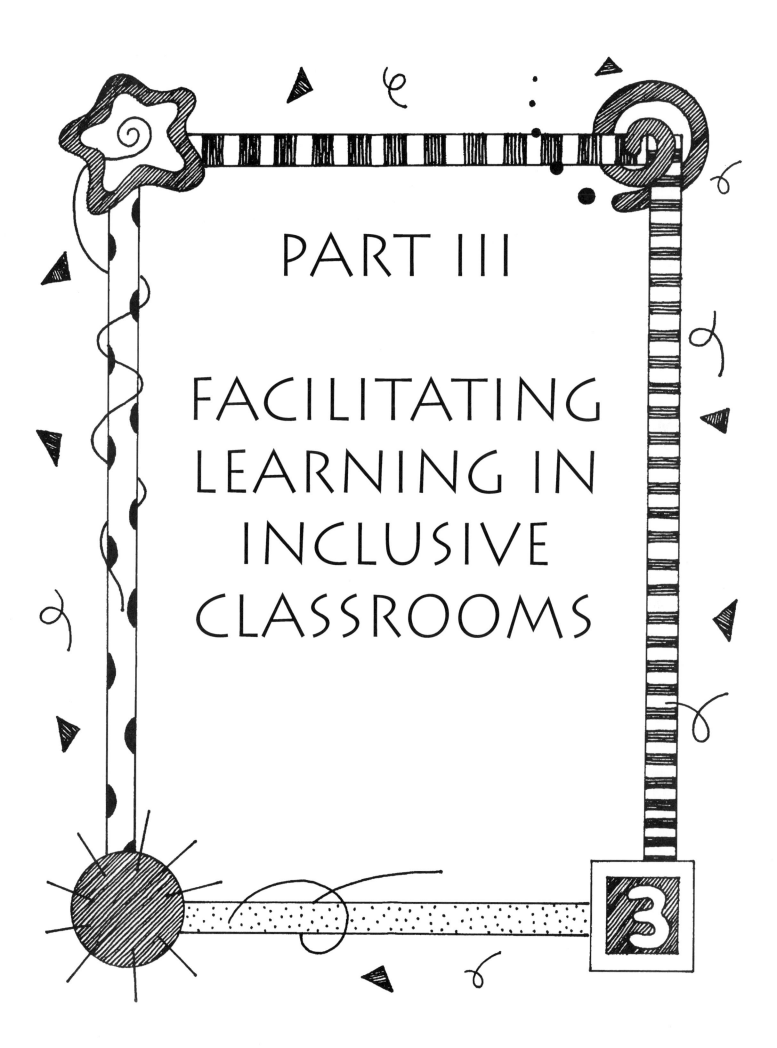

PART III

FACILITATING LEARNING IN INCLUSIVE CLASSROOMS

Chapter Five

Adapting the Classroom for Children with Disabilities

5. ADAPTING THE CLASSROOM FOR CHILDREN WITH DISABILITIES

Chapter Overview
- Classroom Strategies
- Accommodations for Peter
- Arranging and Furnishing the Classroom
- Building a Caring Community

Classroom Strategies

Every child deserves opportunities to play and learn in enriched environments, guided by supportive adults who are knowledgeable about early childhood environments. This chapter presents a variety of classroom adaptations and teaching strategies that will encourage all children to flourish.

Create Activity Centers

Inclusive early childhood classrooms are arranged in well-defined areas known as activity centers. In the activity centers, teachers place a wide array of materials that allow for variation in the individual learning styles and developmental abilities. After observing each child carefully to determine his or her learning needs, teachers plan instructional activities to accommodate a range of developmental levels. Children who are adequately challenged will be confident when exploring new ideas and activities. Children for whom expectations are above or below their level of development may lose interest, become bored, restless or frustrated (Coughlin et al., 1997).

Activity centers, which permit children to make choices during daily blocks of time, support the following basic curriculum assumptions that facilitate all children's learning:

- An integrated, holistic curriculum informed by children's interests and needs supports the children's overall development. Subject matter and skill and concept development are woven into children's interactions with materials, peers, and adults.

- An emphasis on all aspects of a child's growth and development—including first- and second-language development, the impact of culture on learning, and attention to diverse learners with varying abilities—is fundamental to planning, implementation, and assessment in early childhood education.

- Play is a critical component of all early childhood settings, and it is a powerful integrator and generator of knowledge. Through play, children develop divergent thinking, abstract thought, problem-solving ability, and concept-formation and language abilities, in addition to social, emotional, and physical skills and abilities.

95

Use Structured Activities

Teacher-structured activities, sometimes referred to as large and small group activities, are interspersed throughout the program day. During these times, the teacher leads the group through songs, fingerplays, discussions, or exercises. These activities contrast with the exploratory, self-guided nature of outdoor play and indoor activity center times. Teachers formally plan for these times. Often, there is a relationship between what is presented by the teacher during these times and the thematic curriculum. In a thematic curriculum, teachers plan related activities and experiences for a specific period of time, such as over two or three weeks. (Thematic curriculum is discussed in greater detail in Chapter Six.)

Children with developmental delays and special needs often make good use of teacher-structured instruction, generally because of the positive relationships they establish with adults who help them. But there are children for whom structured activities pose quite a challenge; they might not, for example, be able to maintain focused attention to the group or perhaps they have not yet developed the skills of listening to language and making use of what they hear.

Children with special needs will require teacher-structured instruction that is presented in a variety of ways and at different times during the school day. It is important to observe children to determine their ability to comprehend information presented in a group situation. A child may benefit from priority seating at group time, use of visual aids to accentuate focused attention to the group topic, or shorter, perhaps more frequent, periods of individualized or small group instruction.

Some children with developmental delays and special learning needs will require teacher-structured activities related to skills that other children seem to have acquired quite spontaneously. For example, although children generally have no difficulty in learning to point, children with perceptual-motor delays or cognitive limitations may need instruction in learning to point in order to show someone what they want or need. When asked to "Show me the apple," the child is trained through modeling and repetition that the question will require a response and that the child can use a finger to point to his or her response. In this way, the child has a nonverbal means of indicating a choice or showing comprehension.

During activity center time, teachers can target specific skills they wish specific children to be introduced to and to practice. The teacher may encourage a child who is manipulating play dough to point to the cookie cutter, the rolling pin, or the plate. Because this guided play, or brief teacher-structured activity, takes place during the time when children choose activities, it makes good use of spontaneous play.

Children frequently become aware of their teacher's play facilitation. They are likely to join in the relaxed atmosphere of supported play. They will often imitate teacher behaviors, thereby extending learning opportunities for their peers. Guided play should never be forced. It should remain fun and functional.

Teacher-structured learning during activity center times also encourages a child to make functional use of new skills in a variety of contexts. Pointing accurately to a picture in a book, showing a friend a new pair of shoes by pointing, or showing the gerbil's tail to a visitor in the class by pointing demonstrates generalized use of a new skill in multiple contexts.

Employ Naturalistic Teaching Strategies
When teachers use naturalistic teaching strategies, they help a child to develop new skills and practice previously acquired skills. Teachers use natural teaching strategies within the context of everyday events and activities that are motivating to children— for example, mealtime, play, and toileting. The following are examples of important naturalistic teaching strategies:

- *Modeling* calls for the adult to provide the word or words necessary as the child focuses on a particular object or event. For example, if the child hands the adult a container of bubbles, the adult would say, or model, "open." By following the child's lead during play activities, the adult builds on the child's topic of interest.

- *Expansion* adds information to what the child is already doing or saying. If the child hands the bubbles to the adult and says, *"Open,"* the adult says, *"OK, I'll open the bubbles."* When commenting or using parallel talk, a form of expansion, the adult talks about what the child is doing—for example, *"You're stirring the batter"* as the child performs the task. With associative strategies, the adult pairs a word with a motor task, such as saying the word *"hop"* as the child pretends to be a bunny hopping around the room.

- *Observing* children helps the teacher to select materials that are reinforcing and of high interest to children. Lena observed that Anna likes salty foods, such as pretzels.

At snack time, Lena planned to elicit the correct vocabulary from Anna, knowing a pretzel would help her to recall and pronounce the word.

- *Incidental teaching episodes* allow the teacher to facilitate the learning in the context of naturally occurring events. An example would be the child who stands looking at the toy car placed out of reach on a shelf. Instead of immediately giving the child the toy, the teacher, with a puzzled expression on her face, waits for the child to initiate a request. Upon making the attempt at communication, the child is given the car. If no attempts at communication are made, the teacher then provides a prompt such as, *"What do you want—the car or the blocks?"* This technique of prompting and offering a choice—as opposed to direct questioning (*"What do you want?"*)—allows the child to experience success in attempts to communicate.

- *Scaffolding* is a strategy in which the teacher provides a bridge between what the child can and cannot do by providing the necessary prompt and cues. The teacher must first be aware of the child's abilities. Then, by modeling and prompting at a level slightly higher than the child's, the adult enables the child to perform more independently at higher levels. For example, when reading "The Three Little Pigs" to the child, the adult might prompt the child with a question such as *"Uh-oh, it's the wolf again. What do you think he's going to do?"*

Scaffolding can also promote self-help skills, such as placing a cup on the table after drinking. The teacher provides the visual cue of a small container lid secured to the table; the teacher then tells the child to place the cup on the lid, as opposed to dropping or throwing the cup on the table.

Promote Social Interactions

In the inclusive environment, children with disabilities have daily opportunities for social interaction with their typical peers. Simply placing children in a program is not enough. Teachers must actively facilitate interactions among children with disabilities and their typical peers. This may be accomplished in a variety of ways. For example, through the use of labels with children's names, teachers can prearrange seating during activities such as circle and snack. Teachers can pair verbal children with less verbal children or can encourage typical children to interact with specific children. Some children enjoy being a facilitator, or helper, and assisting other children. Other children may simply take a liking to certain children.

Teachers will want to consider these personality characteristics when pairing children for small group activities. Teachers can support the development of friendships by offering activities in which children actively consider each other. During circle time, for example, typical children can be encouraged not only to choose an area to play in during activity center time, but also to invite a friend to accompany them. That sort of prompt may be especially beneficial for children who have difficulty making choices or initiating activities independently.

Children with disabilities should also have the opportunity to assist their typical peers whenever possible. Some children with disabilities may demonstrate strength in a particular area, such as visual acuity. As a result, they may be quite efficient in putting puzzles together. During clean up, the teacher could arrange for this child to assist a typical peer in making sure the puzzles are completed and put away. Whenever possible and appropriate, the teacher should encourage children to assist each other rather than always seek adult assistance.

The use of unstructured group activities is one way to foster social interactions among children. During music and movement activities, for example, children with disabilities can be paired with typical children. Pairs of children can participate in the song "Row, Row, Row Your Boat" by holding hands and rocking back and forth while seated on the floor. This strategy may be beneficial for children who prefer assistance from peers rather than adults. It may also help passive children who are reluctant to participate. Using commands such as, *"Give a friend a high five,"* or *"Shake a friend's hand"* are ways to modify "Simon Says."

Group socialization procedures (a) provide a systematic process of encouraging social interactions, (b) teach children social behaviors under diverse conditions, and (c) build a context for class discussion of individual differences and the importance of friendship.

Use Different Grouping Strategies

Throughout the majority of the school day, teachers design activities that offer children opportunities to work in small groups, pairs, and independently. The following gives examples of grouping strategies to use in the classroom:

* *Cooperative learning groups*—In groups of two, three, four, or more, children play cooperatively in an activity area. They share materials, plan, experiment with ideas, change plans, and settle on a sequence of play that satisfies them.

Lena is concerned that Anna often plays alone when the children are outside. Aware that Anna has difficulty maintaining the physical pace of the other children, Lena identifies the sandbox play area and the swings as two areas where Anna could become involved in a cooperative group. With Lena's support, Anna starts digging and filling buckets with sand. Every day she enjoys swinging with other friends. Once these outside play relationships became established, the children, including Anna, developed a favorite play activity: taking turns riding in and pulling each other in the wagon around the playground.

- *Child partners*—Two children engage in an experience that sustains their focused involvement. Examples of paired activities might include painting, making play dough creations, putting a puzzle together, building with blocks, or taking on roles in dramatic play. This is often a spontaneous play experience, but can also be planned through teacher facilitation.

Once Peter has become successful in solitary play experiences, his teacher, Eva, begins to plan activities for him and one other child. Eva tells Peter that she would like to play with him for a few minutes. They sit at a table and put towers together and simple vehicles with plastic building blocks. Eva invites another child to join them. Eva remains beside Peter as the other child joins in, but she begins to decrease her direct involvement with the blocks while maintaining her proximity and expressing her interest in what Peter and the other child are doing. After several successful episodes of facilitating Peter's success in playing alongside another child, Peter demonstrates progress in spontaneously playing with others without direct adult involvement.

- *Individual instruction*—This may be adult-to-child, or child-to-child; one individual guides another individual's experience. The teacher's role is to demonstrate and model, followed by observing the child's response. The teacher may determine that the child would benefit by learning the sequential parts of a task that lead to skill mastery. Another child may need opportunities to repeat practice of a skill, or the elements of a skill, in order to master it. Some children require individual instruction in knowing when to apply the use of a newly acquired skill.

Peter had many physical skill strengths. He steered wheel toys speedily around the playground, ran swiftly, climbed with agility, and slid down poles. But Peter could not jump rope, which was a favorite activity of the children at Peter's school. Eva observed Peter's reluctance when challenged to learn new skills. With individual teaching, away from the other children, Eva showed Peter the sequential steps of jumping rope. With practice, Peter was able to join the other children and jump rope with them.

- *A child engaged in independent activities*—Solitary learning can be observed when a child is engrossed with materials or experiences. When teachers encourage individual activities, they give children choices and help them gain independence through their own exploration.

Use School Routines for Learning

In inclusive classrooms, an organized daily schedule and consistent routine enhance children's learning opportunities. Systematically structuring group transitions from one activity to the next also is critical for many children. Scheduling decisions are based on the type of program, the age of the children, the length of the school day, and other aspects specific to individual programs.

Establish predictable routines

To determine the sequence of daily activities, teachers must be sensitive to the individual differences between children and their special needs and preferences. For children who travel long distances to school, a snack or meal may be the best activity to begin the day. For another group, vigorous outdoor physical activity may prepare the children for purposeful indoor activity center play. Very young children will benefit from making a close connection with their teacher upon arrival. Older children will be anxious to meet and begin socializing with their friends. In each setting, teachers must consider their individual circumstances and address these in developing their daily schedules.

For many children, and very often those with special needs, activities need to follow an orderly and predictable sequence. Regular routines are satisfying rituals that give children a sense of competence and security: the child knows what to expect and enjoys relying on the knowledge of what to do. Changes in routines may be especially difficult for very young children and for children with developmental delays.

Use routine activities to support skill mastery

Routine activities are good times to introduce labels and tasks designed to promote concept development. Use of picture charts to symbolize the parts of the day helps build visualization, memory, and communication skills. During outdoor play or activity center times, some children benefit from individual choice charts so that they can make informed choices and so that adults can help them to vary their play choices. During snack or meal times, communication boards or charts help children focus their attention on building mealtime vocabulary and appropriate social patterns.

Breaking a simple task, such as washing hands, into its components helps a child learn the task and perform it without teacher assistance. Picture cards that depict turning the faucet on, lathering the hands with soap, rinsing the hands, turning the faucet off, drying the hands, and placing the used paper towel in the trash can be mounted on the wall in the bathroom. Such visual depictions of predictable sequences provide good opportunities for all the children to follow. This activity supports the development of left-to-right

progression in visual tracking for reading, the development of sequential memory, and the emergence of symbolic thought.

An example of a daily schedule with picture symbols:

Sample Daily Schedule for Three- and Four-Year-Olds		
	7:00-10:00	Arrival, Breakfast, Morning Activity Time. Children arrive, are greeted by the teacher, and offered breakfast. As they finish, they can choose an activity center to begin their work.
	10:00-10:15	Group Activity Time. One large or two small groups meet with the teacher. Children who are busy at work may choose to continue working and not participate in the group activity.
	10:15-10:30	Snack and Clean-Up Time
	10:30-11:30	Outdoor Play
	11:30-12:30	Wash up, set tables, and have lunch.
	12:30-12:45	Group Story or Individual Book Time
	12:45-2:15	Rest and Quiet Time
	2:15-3:15	Afternoon Free Time. Children choose among the activity centers.
	3:15-3:30	Snack and Clean-Up Time
	3:30-4:30	Outdoor Play
	4:30-4:45	Group Activity Time. One large or two small groups meet with the teacher. Children who are busy may choose to continue working and not participate in the group activity.
	4:45-5:30	Quiet Activities

An example of an activity choice board:

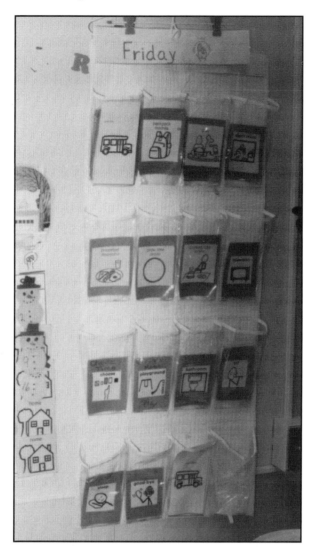

An example of a picture sequence:

An example of a snack or mealtime communication board:

Plan transition times

The underlying principle of smooth transitions is that each child moves individually, at his or her own pace, from one purposeful activity to the next. Individual differences among the children in the class will have an impact on the whole group's ability to transition from one activity to another. Teachers must plan for these times, providing support where it is needed and increasing the responsibility for children who are ready to take it on.

Smooth transitions are the result of planning, knowledge about each child, and adult attention. When children with disabilities are included in the classroom, transition times require additional planning and adult attention. Children may need more time to clean up the activity centers in preparation for the next program activity or when walking from one area of the school to another. Considering and assisting others at these times are excellent lessons to draw from these experiences.

Accomodations for Peter

The long-range goal for Peter is to gain increased control over his own behavior. Peter's father and his teacher, Eva, begin by preparing his environment. Extraneous noise in the classroom and at home will be minimized. Peter's concentration improves when he is given a protected, quiet place to play. Eva puts a soft rug and some large pillows in the corner. She tells the children that the corner is a place for quiet play. Peter often chooses to go there independently.

Limiting Peter's use of toys and materials that have many small pieces contributes to his ability to manage the play space around him. He does better with fewer pieces that cause less frustration. Eva divides some of Peter's favorite manipulative building materials into several smaller amounts and puts them in boxes. Using one box of toys at a time helps Peter produce a variety of different constructions out of similar materials. His creativity and imagination are more apparent. Even Peter begins to recognize his success with small manipulative materials.

Eva shows Peter the daily schedule in pictures to help him understand the sequence of daily events. He is soon independently referring to the daily schedule when he needs to know what will come next in the day.

Whenever Peter succeeds—at brief interactions with other children or extended periods of concentrated effort—Eva recognizes his efforts. This helps Peter understand the behaviors his father and teacher are hoping he can develop, and it strengthens Peter's relationship with Eva. He begins to view her as someone to get help from. Once Eva has established this relationship with Peter, she tries to engage Peter in play with one or two other children at a time. She stays nearby, ready to lend assistance when Peter needs her help.

Arranging and Furnishing the Room

The Physical Space

As noted above, the inclusive early childhood classroom is arranged into activity centers that focus on the interests and developmental abilities of all young children. Activity centers such as blocks, dramatic play, art, sand and water play, outdoor play, cooking, science, and manipulative toys are fundamental to quality programs and highly appropriate for all children, including children with disabilities. This environment maximizes opportunities for children to interact with the materials and each other and to increase their capacities for independence.

Basic Furniture and Equipment

The basic furniture and equipment used in early childhood classrooms is the same furniture and equipment necessary for educating many children with special needs. However, individual children may require specific adaptive pieces of furniture or equipment. In planning with a child's family, school administrators and teachers can discuss the requirements for individual children within their school space.

As a general rule, children with visual and hearing impairments, children with orthopedic impairments, and children who are medically fragile will have personalized adaptive equipment that teachers must become familiar with. Hearing aids can be routinely checked to ensure their proper functioning. Glasses must be cleaned and properly protected. Orthopedic aids may possibly be removed for specific activities, for periodic massage, or for ease and comfort in dressing and undressing. The school should acquaint all staff members with the specific requirements of each child's care.

Schools can support the feeling of belonging by providing many adaptive pieces of equipment or furniture for use by many individuals. Providing a range of seating options allows for choice and meets a wider range of comfort levels. A range of seating options might include:

- chairs with arms or sides
- soft seating, such as bolsters or beanbag pillows
- benches, which can be adapted for use as a floor "desk"
- options for floor sitting, which include support for weak trunk and back muscles.

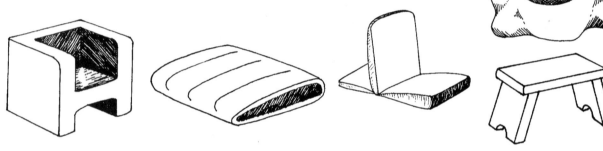

Work surfaces should be presented both horizontally—for example, at tables or desks—or vertically—on chalkboards, slant boards, easels, or walls. Here, ease of access and independence is the primary goal. In some cases, visual impairments may also be a consideration. Again, meeting an individual's needs is of primary importance, so observation of successful functioning will require teacher attention.

Adults must ensure that the sizes of furnishings and materials available in classrooms are appropriate for the individual children who are included. Children's feet should rest on the floor when they are seated in a chair. A worktable should cross a child's chest at, or just above, the waist. Hooks, washbasins, toilets, and drinking facilities that can be reached and child-operated allow children to help themselves. Children with impairments can learn to take care of many of their own special needs at individually appropriate times.

Adaptations for Learning

To have a successful inclusive program, the teacher will need to consider the following elements:

- *Time*—Be aware of the length of time a child can maintain focused attention to tasks. At the beginning of the year, it may be helpful to keep play periods short so that the children experience a sense of success. End play periods when children become distracted or tired. Two or three short periods of play per day are often better than one long one. As children become more skillful and comfortable in play, play periods can be lengthened.

- *Comfort*—Determine the activity center where a child will be most comfortable and relaxed. For example, a child may be more comfortable sitting on the floor than standing beside a table. After the child has multiple, happy experiences in comfortable surroundings, help the child become familiar with a wider variety of activity centers, toys, and materials.

- *Distractions*—Observe the children to determine the effects of environmental distractions. Some children react more favorably to facing a plain wall than to sitting in the middle of a room. Other children like being in the midst of the action. Consider individual learning styles and help create a favorable learning environment for the child.

- *Noise*—Busy classrooms should have a wonderful "hum," rather than a disturbing roar. Many children prefer playing in environments that are quiet. Some children have difficulty focusing their auditory attention when other sounds compete for their attention and so should be seated near the main speaker in group meetings and gatherings. Some children find it difficult to focus on the task at hand if they are working near a window or door.

- *Lighting*—Children should have an abundance of fresh air and natural lighting. Their developing visual systems benefit from exposure to natural lighting; prolonged exposure to unnatural lighting sources, such as televisions and computer screens, is not desirable. Indoor lighting should be soft lighting or with spotlights on the play areas to help a child to focus better.

- *Material selection*—Teachers need to consider selecting toys and materials that foster child development in each of the four domains of development: social and emotional, physical, communication, and cognitive. The open-ended nature of clay, play dough, paints, and building blocks makes these materials ideal for use for all children.

Building a Caring Community

In a school where diverse students are being educated through differentiated teaching methods, adults need to support each other in creating effective teaching strategies. For that to happen, a nonthreatening atmosphere should exist. Adults will want to be valued for their talents and skills and to feel supported in their efforts to implement new teaching methods. They will need time and energy to try new techniques. They will benefit from the opportunity for reflection and discussion, so that they can evaluate the effectiveness of their interventions.

Teachers understand that it makes very little sense to use a single method to teach all children. Children have varying strengths, needs, and styles of learning. Teachers must employ a wide array of approaches if all children are to be successful in inclusive classrooms. In particular, they should consider the following approaches, which have been shown to be highly effective in inclusive schools: active rather than passive learning, an emphasis on cooperation instead of competition, and the development of critical thinking skills rather than a dependence on rote learning (Benjamin, 1989).

ADAPTATIONS FOR LEARNING—INDOORS

①

②

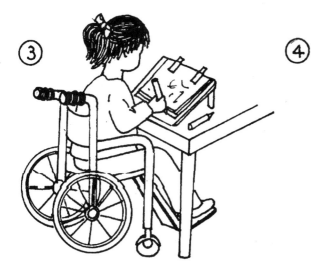

③

④

⑤

⑥

Illustrations accompany diagram on p. 110.

INDOOR ACTIVITY AREA

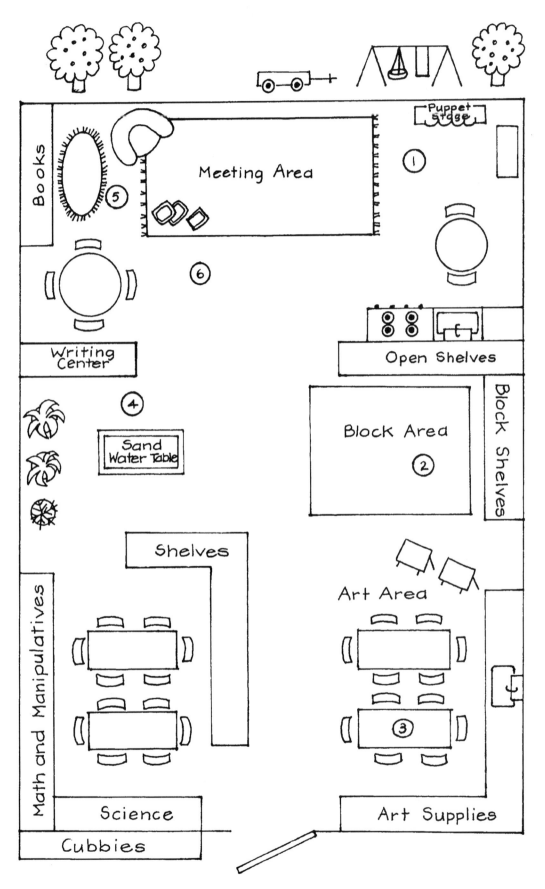

ADAPTATIONS FOR LEARNING—OUTDOORS

Illustrations accompany diagram on p. 112.

OUTDOOR ACTIVITY AREA

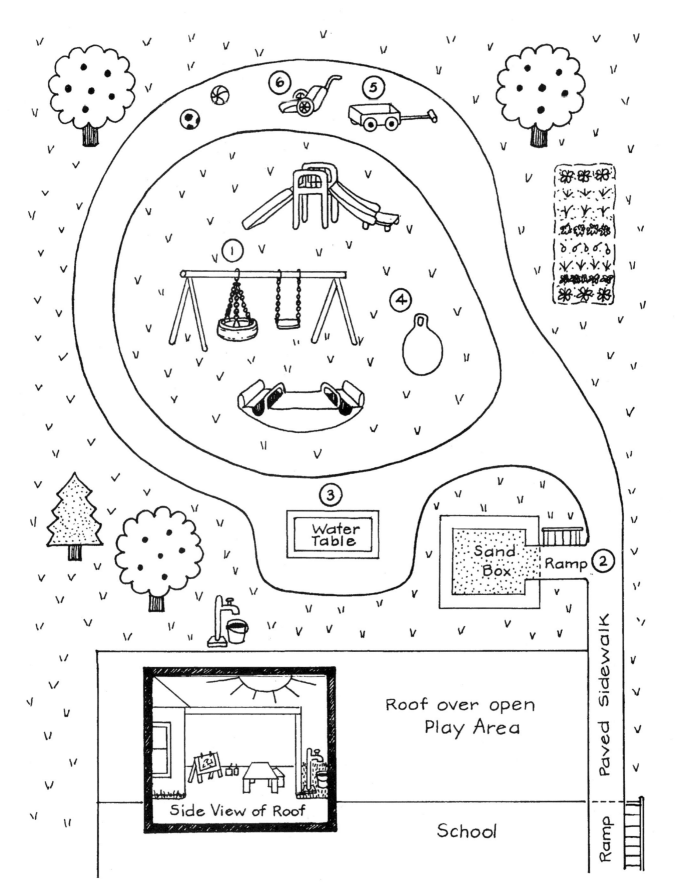

Water Table

Sand Box

Ramp

Paved Sidewalk

Roof over open Play Area

Side View of Roof

School

Ramp

CHAPTER SIX

PUTTING IT ALL
TOGETHER:
THEMATIC
INSTRUCTION

6. PUTTING IT ALL TOGETHER: THEMATIC INSTRUCTION

Chapter Overview
- What Is Thematic Instruction?
- Advantages of the Thematic Approach in Planning for Children With Disabilities
- The Importance of Planning a Wide Range of Activities Related to a Theme
- Linking Thematic Units to Planning for an Individual
- Planning Instruction for All Students

What is Thematic Instruction?
Curriculum that is developed around a central theme promotes young children's thinking, especially their formulation of conceptual thought. In the early years, children develop conceptual ideas by noticing and remembering characteristics of their experiences. They organize their experiences by two kinds of features: (a) invariant, or what always happens, and (b) optional, or what occasionally occurs. With age and experience, children develop event and conceptual knowledge continuously by making predictions, engaging in exploration, revising their predictions, and drawing conclusions.

The younger the children, the more the activities should be event based. When teachers organize curriculum thematically, they provide many opportunities for children to organize their conceptual thinking. The children relate the curriculum to their life experiences, incorporating regional and cultural variations. In this way, the teachers and the children create curriculum together, absorbing what each member brings to the classroom experience.

Thematic project work and curriculum help children to generalize conceptual processes. When a theme is encountered many times, in many ways, throughout the school day, children come to rely on the manner in which they take in information. They have multiple opportunities to practice the development of basic skills. They explore materials during hands-on learning activities and gather authentic information during field trips related to the central theme. Themes help children organize knowledge so that they remember it and access it readily.

Factors Essential to Theme Development
- Theme topics should have a direct relationship to children's interests, experiences, and general thinking-skill levels.
- The theme should be reflected throughout the daily program and the daily routine.
- A curriculum theme should be reflected in the choice of materials available in the classroom. There should be puzzles, books, props for the blocks, and water and sand table toys that are all related to the project theme.
- A theme can be ongoing for a minimum of one week.

- The decision to discontinue work on a certain theme can be made when the class has a sense of completion or a new interest.
- The class can return to a project at a later time (Katz and Chard, 1989).

Young children learn about their families and those of other children using the "Who am I?" theme. The chart that follows depicts the integration of social/emotional, communication, physical, and cognitive skills taught through this theme. A lesson plan for using "Me" boxes follows.

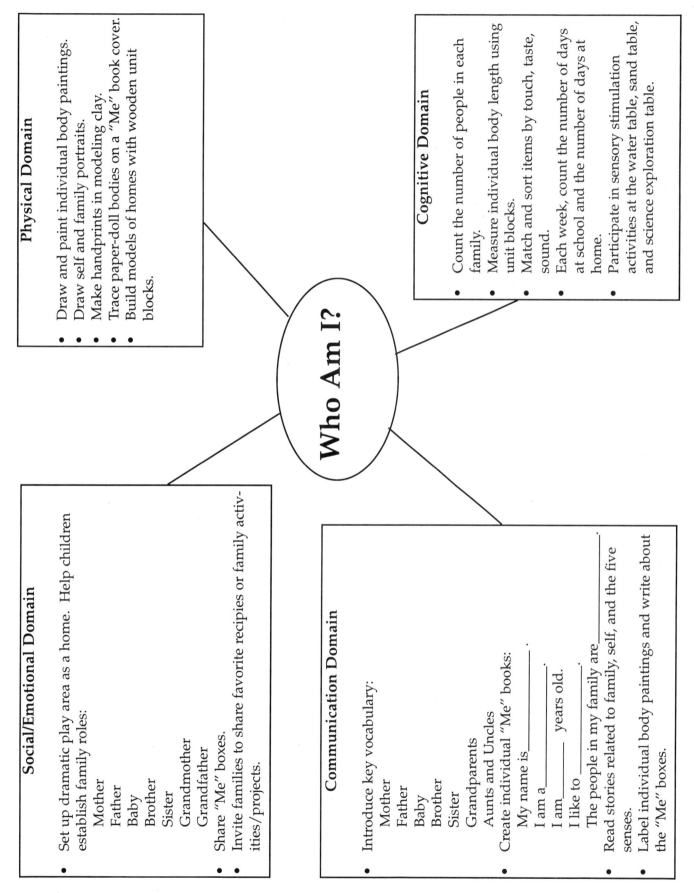

Who Am I?

Physical Domain

- Draw and paint individual body paintings.
- Draw self and family portraits.
- Make handprints in modeling clay.
- Trace paper-doll bodies on a "Me" book cover.
- Build models of homes with wooden unit blocks.

Cognitive Domain

- Count the number of people in each family.
- Measure individual body length using unit blocks.
- Match and sort items by touch, taste, sound.
- Each week, count the number of days at school and the number of days at home.
- Participate in sensory stimulation activities at the water table, sand table, and science exploration table.

Social/Emotional Domain

- Set up dramatic play area as a home. Help children establish family roles:
  - Mother
  - Father
  - Baby
  - Brother
  - Sister
  - Grandmother
  - Grandfather
- Share "Me" boxes.
- Invite families to share favorite recipies or family activities/projects.

Communication Domain

- Introduce key vocabulary:
  - Mother
  - Father
  - Baby
  - Brother
  - Sister
  - Grandparents
  - Aunts and Uncles
- Create individual "Me" books:
  - My name is _____.
  - I am a _____.
  - I am _____ years old.
  - I like to _____.
  - The people in my family are _____.
- Read stories related to family, self, and the five senses.
- Label individual body paintings and write about the "Me" boxes.

117

Lesson Plan for "Me" Boxes

Small or Large Group Activities: To make and share personal collections of things that tell about a person's life, family, interests, and favorite activities.

Concept: Everyone is special. While we are all unique individuals, we have characteristics and personal interests in common.

Preparation: Send a newsletter to the children's parents to introduce the curriculum unit and help their child collect a few personal items from home. Place the items in a shoebox or other small box for safekeeping. Ask parents to help their child practice what they will share at home. The children will later have the opportunity to share their "Me" box with their classmates.

Learning Objectives:
To use language to describe
To explain concepts
To identify objects and people by name
To express feelings
To find similarities and differences among objects and people
To discuss personal information with others

Materials Needed:
A shoebox or other small box
A parent letter or newsletter
Personal items from home
A place to store and display the box collections in the classroom

The Instructional Activity: The children will want to share, talk about, and discuss their "Me" boxes many times. These can be spontaneous small group activities during activity center time or a large group activity during a class group meeting time.

Advantages of the Thematic Approach in Planning for Children with Disabilities

Children with special needs who are in inclusive classrooms benefit from the thematic approach. A unifying theme and a curriculum that supports the theme give every child opportunities to experience the theme firsthand and time to practice the skills needed to make functional use of the thematic material.

Many children with special learning needs require "over teaching, over time" in order to acquire and retain new knowledge, skills, and vocabulary (Mandell and Gold, 1984). The thematic approach gives children exposure to experiences that are directly related to the theme. As the theme receives continued

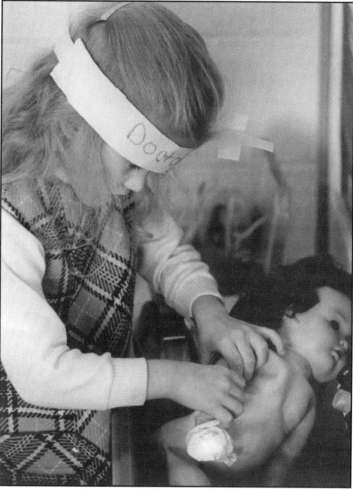

focus, children are encouraged to present their personal knowledge of the theme. Teachers provide individualized support for the internalization of knowledge. Concept development is presented through multi-modalities—for example, block-building, working with clay, responding to music, participating in motor experiences and field trips, and using new vocabulary—all of which relate to the project theme.

Individual differences exist in all children in their problem-solving predispositions, interests, skills they bring to concrete tasks, preferred modes of representing things, abilities to move easily through a particular sequence, and the degree to which they are initially dependent on extrinsic reinforcement from the teacher. Thus, as Bruner (1966) notes, "if a curriculum is to be effective in the classroom, it must contain different ways of activating children, different ways of presenting sequences, different opportunities for some children to 'skip' parts while others work their way through those parts, different ways of putting things. A curriculum, in short, must contain many tracks leading to the same general goal" (p. 71).

The metaphor of scaffolding (Wood, Bruner, and Ross, 1976) is useful for illustrating the process of teaching that generates autonomy among children and permits them to absorb subject matter at varying rates at any one time. This concept, derived from Vygotsky (1978), emphasizes that adults ideally gauge the amount of support and challenge necessary for children's optimal growth. Adults take the initiative to supply supports when children are younger and gradually decrease those supports to allow children to become more autonomous as they mature. In turn, that new autonomy brings with it expectations and challenges that need new forms of scaffolding.

When children engage in group project work, teachers have more time to offer various forms of assistance to individual children. Scaffolding cannot take place during direct instruction to a group. It is a personalized method of responding to a specific learner's needs. All people produce more with assistance than they can alone, but the overall direction of the growth of the child is toward independence.

Vygotsky's "zone of proximal development" (1978) lies between what the child can currently accomplish independently and what the child can learn to do in a supportive environment. Bruner (1966) described the support a teacher can provide in the way of scaffolding, but Vygotsky also pointed out that the supportive capacities of other children, the style of program delivery, and the equipment and materials available to the group all have important effects on the success of teaching and learning.

For children who experience information processing difficulties or concept development problems, it is very important to generate themes from their preexisting knowledge bases.

Ali, for example, played each day in the water table. He knew how to use the available materials, understood the established rules, and participated well with others in exploratory play there. Vlad decided to use this activity center to support a new curriculum theme. Vlad replaced some of the available materials, such as the soap, washcloths, and baby dolls, with clear plastic tubing, siphons, and funnels. He put red food coloring in the water. The children used the new materials to explore concepts related to motion, force, and gravity. Initially, Ali was uncomfortable with the change of materials, but gradually he became interested in the novel materials and play. His previous knowledge and success in water play aided his ability to expand his playing and thinking.

Themes based on children's interests and life experiences ensure that the children can begin learning from the familiar. Teachers need to listen carefully to the interests of all the children in a classroom in order to design a curriculum that begins where the children are and moves cautiously into the unknown.

The ability to generalize or transfer what one learns at school to other settings is difficult for many children with special needs (Vaughn, Bos, and Lund, 1986). Practicing buttoning in a teacher-directed activity does not guarantee that a child can dress him- or herself at home. The thematic approach offers children the opportunity to role play or simulate real life experiences in the classroom and facilitates the transfer or generalization of knowledge or skills to home and community settings. Teachers who accept the challenge of designing "real-life" experiences add greatly to a child's personalization of what is learned in school.

Language is also more effectively learned when it is presented within a context than in isolation. Linkages occur through repeated usage and within functional experiences. Feedback should be directly related to experiences that may be repeated with "corrected" usage and consequences. Language facilitation can occur throughout the day and may be modeled by teachers and class peers. During child-directed activity times, teachers can encourage children to express their choices, share information, negotiate socially, solve problems, and make discoveries—all the while experimenting with and constructing language. Child-to-child communicative interactions give children opportunities to negotiate social situations, test communicative effectiveness, compare ideas, and initiate and sustain friendships. When the teacher uses the thematic approach, she provides a context for children to discover relationships between self, objects, and events using familiar topics.

The teacher's role during the child-directed portion of the day is that of facilitator and model. Teachers follow a child's lead and assist the child in accomplishing a goal. Consider the following example:

When Anna enters the dramatic play area, she puts on dress-up clothes and selects a baby doll for play. Anna is taking part in the same activities as her other classmates in the dramatic play area, even though she is unable to initiate and sustain an interaction with them. Lena, Anna's teacher, focuses on supporting Anna's interaction with the materials and the other children. She helps Anna develop short sequences of play based on Anna's experience and knowledge of family life and baby care. Lena's proximal support helps Anna organize and learn what is expected of her. She becomes better able to participate because of the support she has received from Lena.

Lena also demonstrates various strategies that Anna can use to initiate and maintain interactions with her peers. Lena offers one child an object to share, requests the assistance of another, and demonstrates positive methods of gaining still another child's attention. As Anna becomes engaged and more adept at using these skills, Lena's direct intervention is no longer required. The subsequent peer-peer interactions will become natural reinforcements, and Lena can provide intermittent reinforcements when necessary.

To establish the central theme in their classrooms, teachers gather resources and materials, plan for field trips, and invite guests who can share their expertise. Teachers monitor children's level of participation, noting their quality of functioning, variety of experience, level of challenge, and involvement with others. Teachers prepare individualized education plans using the information available on child development and different learning patterns. The scaffolding will vary with each individual's unique learning style, capacity to learn from previous experiences, and general disposition. A child's success in a learning experience has a great deal to do with the presentation of curriculum and the methods used to support him or her as a learner.

The Importance of Planning a Wide Range of Activities Related to a Theme

Inclusion, it should be noted, does not automatically ensure a child's learning success. Teachers must design opportunities for children with special needs to experience what they need to learn. Teachers plan natural learning situations. Activity centers provide the springboard for these situations. They are already set up and designed for specific activities that children enjoy and benefit from; adding theme-related props, toys, and materials to them for a theme-related curriculum heightens their use as natural instructional classroom areas. Teachers and children are free to change the materials as they delve deeper into a topic. Classroom teachers can collaborate with resource teachers, specialists, and a child's family to reinforce understanding of the subject matter. They can also reinforce understanding at music time and story time and during outside play and motor activities.

For example, before the "Who Am I?" theme starts, a newsletter to families tells them that the curriculum will focus on the children and their sense of themselves. Parents are encouraged to send in photographs of their child. Families respond by sending in baby photos and pictures of grandparents and brothers and sisters. These are displayed in the classroom so all the children can see and discuss them. Families are also encouraged to visit the school to share a favorite family story, meal, or family tradition. Anna's father makes potato pancakes one morning at school. Her grandmother attends another day and reads a story to the class. All the children gain knowledge of themselves and each other during these shared experiences.

When the "Who Am I?" theme is being carried out, teachers make sure that there are props in the dramatic play area that support the theme. They add culturally accurate materials that reflect the lives of the children in their program. The puzzles at the manipulative activity center depict families. Art activities support the theme of identity and family. Each day, stories are read that relate to families, and the children learn songs and fingerplays that contain vocabulary and concepts related to the central theme.

Linking Thematic Units to Planning for an Individual

Thematic curriculum units such as "Who Am I?" are an effective way to develop curriculum and to implement goals and objectives for individual children. When activity center areas are linked to a theme, teachers can also link instructional planning to the areas they want to address for a specific child.

Linking instructional activities to Anna's individualized goals and objectives is shown below:

DOMAIN	GOALS AND OBJECTIVES	INSTRUCTIONAL ACTIVITY
Speech/Language/ Communication	<u>Goal:</u> Anna will demonstrate increased vocabulary and concept development.	Painting body Drawing family portrait Sharing "Me" box Sharing potato pancakes with family
Motor	<u>Objective:</u> Anna will demonstrate increased comprehension and expression of qualitative concepts (color, shapes, and size) in guided situations.	Sorting items
Physical	<u>Goal:</u> Anna will improve proximal stability and bilateral integration.	Assist in positioning Anna's body during cooking
Perceptual	<u>Objective:</u> Anna will effectively use one hand as a stabilizer and the other as a manipulator during bilateral tasks involving upper extremity weight-bearing.	Dressing-up
Social/Emotional	<u>Goal:</u> Anna will demonstrate independence and confidence in familiar surroundings.	Drawing group graph Sharing "Me" box
	<u>Objective:</u> Anna will try a new activity upon first examination.	Measuring Using Cheaptalk

123

Planning Instruction for All Children

Thematic curriculum units are one way for teachers to provide all children with possibilities for multiple skill development across domains and to support their individualized learning. Activities outside the theme also contribute to individualized learning. While cooking with a small group, for example, all children will engage in sensory experiences relating to the perception and discrimination of labeling smells, textures, and objects. Through the processes of mixing, stirring, chopping, and grating, some children will further develop their fine motor skills. Others will observe chemical changes that occur when ingredients are mixed, laying the foundation for beginning scientific reasoning. During this activity, the children share their own estimations, make predictions, and form conclusions. Through active participation, the children have individualized their own learning and practiced skills in a variety of domains.

Throughout the course of the day, teachers observe children during both structured and unstructured learning times and take notes on their development. They make instructional decisions based on their observations. After gaining a sense of each child's abilities, needs, interests, temperament, and learning styles, teachers create classroom activities that match the children's developing abilities.

Chapter Seven

Facilitating Social and Emotional Development

7. FACILITATING SOCIAL AND EMOTIONAL DEVELOPMENT

Chapter Overview
- Social and Emotional Development in the Young Child
- The Teacher as Facilitator of Social and Emotional Development
- Social and Emotional Development in the Child with Disabilities
- Instructional Activities that Facilitate Social and Emotional Development

Social and Emotional Development In the Young Child

Like all areas of development in children, social and emotional development occurs in predictable stages and sequences, but spans differing time periods for each individual. The healthy development of emotional and social skills depends on the child's abilities, but more significantly on the interplay of repeated interactions from the earliest moments of infancy between the child and the people who surround the child. From the first moments of life, the child begins to learn the skills of interdependence necessary throughout life.

When assessing the individual child's strengths and needs, it is necessary to review developmental milestones both before and after the child's chronological age. For the child with disabilities, such a review is even more important because this child is often at a less mature stage of development than his chronological age.

The Early Stage of Emotional and Social Development

In the earliest stage of emotional development, the infant forms a foundation of trust and attachment. The security of this attachment permits the child to move into a stage of autonomy and develop a sense of self. As the young child develops his sense of self, he explores his world. From his explorations, he becomes independent, which in turn encourages his imagination and creativity. Eric Erikson, the developmental theorist, outlined three stages of psychosocial development that he believes are necessary to the development of a healthy young child: developing a sense of trust, developing a sense of autonomy, and developing a sense of initiative (Cook, Tessier, and Klein, 1996).

The infant's first activities are instinctive and reflexive: grasping, sucking, and rooting. As cognitive and physical growth progresses, the infant smiles, vocalizes, and seeks attention through gestures. With increasingly mature development, the young child moves, speaks, and otherwise engages people into her young life. As the child moves into the preschool years, her interactions with other children, adults, and the world increase and are exhibited through her play.

127

The preschool years are the optimum time for the development of social attitudes and behaviors. Through repeated interactions and practice during the preschool years, the child exhibits an emerging sense of self-identity and self-esteem. During the preschool years, typical social and emotional development includes many skills and behaviors. The child learns that he is a boy or she is a girl and belongs to a particular family with a particular set of customs and habits. At this time, too, the child learns the skills of self-control: to follow rules and routines and to begin to express emotions in appropriate ways. In the child's small society, he learns the rudimentary skills of social behaviors such as an awareness of his own feelings and those of others, an understanding of and respect for differences, and the abilities to share, take responsibility, help others, and negotiate solutions to problems.

The Interdependence of Areas of Development

The security of a young child's emotional development forms the foundation of further learning. Growth—whether it is within the social, cognitive, or even physical realm—does not occur in isolation. The domains are interrelated. A crawling baby will look to the expression on her mother's face before attempting something difficult or scary. If the mother looks pleased, the child will proceed; if the mother looks worried, the child will stop. This is called "social referencing" (Klinnert et al., 1986). Children will explore much more vigorously if they feel they have a "safe base," a devoted caregiver to return to (Leiberman, 1993). Children who were classified as securely attached at 12 months were followed over time and showed advanced cognitive, social, and emotional development as they moved into school (Erikson and Pianta, 1989).

The Importance of Play

Play is the most important activity of early childhood. "As research and theory become more refined, children's play is increasingly seen not only as a normal part of development, but also as an instrument for development" (Garwood, 1985). Play integrates all domains of development. Almost any play vignette will demonstrate small or large muscle development, communication skills both verbal and nonverbal, cognitive skills, and social interaction of varied types. Play relates previous knowledge and experiences to the real world and extends the knowledge into more complex and sophisticated realms. Play also allows children opportunities to explore materials that promote risk-taking.

Play is important for all children. With increased exposure, children become more skilled at play. Play is considered to lead a child's development (Fromberg, 1987). When children are engaged in play, they are believed to be functioning close to their optimal level of development (Vygotsky, 1967). For children with disabilities it is therefore extremely important that child-centered classrooms provide ample opportunities for play.

Piaget identified three categories of play. Practice play is characterized by exploration and repetition. Through practice play, a child learns to master activities. In symbolic play, a child sees that an object can represent or symbolize another object. For example, during pretend play, a child may use an umbrella as a horse. Games with rules require complex communication and cooperative skills.

The child moves through several stages of play. The child integrates his understanding of himself, of those around him, and of his world by first observing, then playing in isolation, then alongside another child, then interacting with one or more children, and finally cooperatively with several children. Because the child with special needs is often less adept socially than his typically developing peers, the teacher must use strategies to increase his interactions through play.

Research on play characteristics indicates that there are differences between the quality and quantity of play skills of children with disabilities and those who do not have disabilities. Children with disabilities may have difficulty using symbolic thinking to support their play. They may continue to need real objects, such as a toy telephone, when their nondisabled peers have begun to substitute words, actions that represent talking on a telephone, or nonspecific objects, such as a wooden block, to represent a telephone.

Children with disabilities may experience delays in developing the social interaction skills required for play. They may lose interest in play too soon for the play partner. The sounds and sights of activities taking place nearby may divert their attention. They may "mouth" toys or engage in rough and tumble physical play rather than role play. A child's play may be chaotic or too low-key. Some children with disabilities engage in repetitive behaviors, such as rocking, spinning objects, or putting objects close to their faces. These behaviors may prevent the child from participating in meaningful play with new objects and from making social contact with others.

Because play is the primary means by which children grow and develop in every domain, acquiring play skills should be considered of great importance for children with disabilities. Careful examination of a child's play skills should be a part of the assessment of the child. Teachers will want to develop skill in facilitating play in natural and spontaneous ways, as the following anecdote demonstrates.

Helping Ali Learn to Play With Others
Ali's parents and teacher, Vlad, have set long-term goals and short-term objectives in the social and emotional domain to increase Ali's play skills. Ali's play is characterized by a restricted repertoire of play skills, reduced language skills, less sophisticated representational play than many of his peers, and the use of a limited selection of play materials. Ali enjoys sensory play. He would like to play with other children. He watches their play, plays alongside other children, and imitates their actions but has some difficulty establishing a role in their fantasy play.

Vlad has observed Ali's ability to imitate others. Vlad recognizes that imitation is a fundamental means by which children learn. He also recognizes that Ali is stuck at a play performance level that is frustrating for Ali, and so Vlad will facilitate, or model, behavior that Ali can imitate. Vlad also sees that he will need to be selective in his use of language so that he can help Ali develop a wider vocabulary for play themes and social communication. Vlad recalls that many times he has come to Ali's aid to settle a problem involving social interaction.

Although play is spontaneous for most children, adults who facilitate the development of play skills in children must plan the play themes they will introduce. Vlad decides on a play theme that will build on Ali's strength in sensory play skills. He sets up a restaurant in the dramatic play area and gathers candlesticks, a small tablecloth, and menus. Ali likes pizza, so Vlad cuts material into shapes to represent pizza toppings. Vlad cuts cardboard in circular shapes to represent the pizza dough and labels each item for Ali. Vlad goes with Ali into the new "pizza restaurant," sits at the little table, and announces that he is hungry. He picks up a menu and begins to look over the words. He motions to Ali to come over to the table and asks if he works at the pizza restaurant. Ali smiles. Vlad wants to know if the restaurant serves cheese pizza with green peppers. Ali continues to smile. Vlad asks the same question again. Ali quietly replies, "Yes." "Great!" responds Vlad. *"I'll take a small cheese pizza with green peppers, no pepperoni please."*

Vlad waits for Ali to begin making the pretend pizza, but Ali appears unsure of what to do. Vlad asks for a glass of water. Ali goes to the cupboard and brings Vlad an empty glass. Vlad pretends to drink the water, saying, *"My, that's tasty! How's my pizza coming? Is it in the oven?"* Ali returns to the cupboard and begins to put yellow and green pieces of material onto a cardboard circle. He carries this to the oven and places it inside. Vlad smiles and tells Ali, *"Make sure that oven's hot!"* Ali pretends to turn the knob to make the oven hot.

Ali is delighted with this play and wants to do it again right away. Vlad continues to play with Ali that day and a little each day for several days in succession. Over time, Ali "learns" the skills needed to engage in this kind of thematic play, assuming different roles and playing with other children. Vlad and the children invite their parents to come to the pizza restaurant. Ali serves his parents a small cheese pizza with green peppers. Everyone is delighted.

At the end of the three weeks, Vlad talks to the children about changing the dramatic play area again. Some of the children want to change it to a fire station. Soon that plan is agreed to and preparations are made to gather the props the children will need to play firefighters. Vlad tells the children that firefighters have a kitchen in their firehouse and they take turns cooking for each other. In this way there is a link for Ali from the restaurant theme to the new firefighter theme. He can continue to use the vocabulary words he has just learned and play the role of chef, server, and diner as he adds new roles that will be a part of the firefighter thematic unit.

The Teacher as Facilitator of Social and Emotional Development

Creating the Environment for Emotional Development

Children learn best when they feel secure and successful. It is the role of the teacher to create an emotional environment that fosters the feelings of security and success in the young child. Many factors contribute to creating an emotionally secure learning environment.

Emotional supportiveness

The qualities that compose an emotionally supportive environment include empathy, acceptance, authenticity, respect, and warmth. An empathetic teacher recognizes and understands another person's point of view. The teacher is able to tune in to the child's moods, mirror the child's feelings, and label the emotions with nonjudgmental statements. The quality of acceptance enables a teacher to value a child regardless of physical appearance, family background, ability, or behavior. Genuineness means that the teacher is truthful, as well as reasonable and encouraging. The respectful teacher believes that the child is capable of learning. When we say a teacher shows "warmth," we mean that she is friendly and responsive and makes children feel comfortable, supported, and valued (Kostelnik, 1997).

Acknowledgment of the child's emotions

There are no right and wrong emotions. All emotions are legitimate. The teacher must acknowledge those that the child exhibits and not deny them, force the child to confront them, or ignore them.

Putting feelings into words

Because children learn most comprehensively within the context of personal experience, they benefit when their emotions are named and described to them as they occur. By saying, *"Katherine, you look angry,"* the teacher relates the experience to the concept of anger and gives the child an emotional vocabulary.

Consistency

Trust is engendered within the child when he can predict and depend on steady adult emotional responses.

Fostering the Development of Social Skills

For the child to develop social skills, the teacher must provide an environment of acceptance and respect within the classroom. When a child feels respected and accepted, he is able to extend these feelings to other children. He must have many and varied opportunities to practice choice, independence, and negotiation skills in an environment that the teacher constantly monitors. Below are some of the strategies that foster the development of social skills:

131

Modeling – Children learn powerful lessons when they observe adults and other children treating others with kindness and truthfulness and using reason to solve problems. Modeling is most effective when a positive behavior is demonstrated to children in combination with words (Kostelnik, 1997). For instance, *"I am wiping the table so it will be clean for all of us. Here is a sponge for you. You can help too."*

Setting clear rules – Rules should be specific, simple, stated in positive terms, and include reasons. *"We will speak softly so that we can hear other children."* Children can help establish the rules for the classroom.

Setting logical and appropriate consequences for behavior – Positive consequences, such as a smile or words of encouragement, promote repeated behaviors; corrective consequences reduce them. All consequences should be appropriate to the age of the child and the activity. For example, if a child spills another child's milk, he should help clean it up and pour another cupful.

Providing an environment for play and choices – Activity centers with a variety of materials that are both familiar and new provide children with multiple opportunities for exploratory play. Teachers who offer children activity choices promote independent learning and decision making.

Keeping the group relatively small –A smaller group size gives children more opportunities to interact and build relationships with one another.

Providing ample space and materials –The classroom environment and materials should promote children's creative endeavors and foster social interactions among all the children in the classroom.

Providing activities that require cooperation- Encouraging activity center play helps children learn to enter groups, negotiate the possession of materials, resolve conflicts, and carry on conversations (Abraham, Morris, and Wald, 1993).

Using peers to model social skills - A nondisabled child can demonstrate a skill or activity for the child with special needs and encourage the child to imitate the interactions.

Reinforcing positive social behavior with genuine praise – The teacher has an important role in helping children discover when they are behaving in a socially appropriate manner. Praising the child's specific behavior when it is positive will help a child realize the benefit of his or her actions.

Understanding individual differences – Children demonstrate different temperaments, learning styles, levels of activity, and abilities. Teachers who are accepting of individual differences will both demonstrate and foster these types of inclusive attitudes in children.

Although play promotes growth within all domains of development, it is particularly powerful for fostering social competence. The teacher controls the factors that support the development of play skills. These factors include time, space, setting, and props.

Time
Children require adequate time to plan and carry out interactive play. They need time to explore the available materials, choose roles, work out any conflicts about materials and roles, and discover a common script with which they feel comfortable. Play sessions should be repeated with similar materials and playmates so that children can develop and refine their mutual script. Preschool children may require thirty or more minutes for a play session. The teacher should dedicate an hour or more each day to activities in which children can choose either to play or to engage in other experiences.

Space
The dramatic play, art, manipulatives, blocks, water, sand, play dough, and the reading corner are centers of children's ongoing play. Each must have well-defined and ample space for a number of children to play with the materials in that center. Well-defined spaces, rather than wide open ones, increase the occurrence of play. Play materials should be visible when the children enter the room.

Varied play settings
Theme-related props can be sorted into storage containers and kept nearby, ready for the children's changing interests. Plan for play experiences outdoors as well as indoors. Allow children to bring materials from other areas into dramatic play, such as play dough food, delivery trucks filled with beads, or paper hats made at the art table.

Props, materials, and experiences
Props, materials, and real experiences related to thematic play give children the fuel they need to create many different play themes. Props trigger children's memories and promote the addition of new knowledge. A full-length mirror should be a permanent prop in the classroom. Unbreakable hand mirrors can be available with the dress-up props. A wide variety of props that are rotated in and out of the classroom offer more play possibilities than a few props always at hand. Children gain experience in different types of play when their play materials change.

Some props and materials need to be realistic, such as a telephone. Unstructured materials, such as cardboard boxes, cardboard blocks, or material scraps, suggest limitless variety. Children can respond divergently and creatively to both types of materials. An adequate amount of play props is necessary to stimulate role identification without conflicts arising over a shortage of materials.

Encouraging Play
Teachers should consistently monitor children's play and be resourceful in managing play sessions. They may be called on to mediate a dispute or assist children who need help to solve problems. They monitor the children's developing interpersonal and

inter-relational skills. Teachers need to assess a child's developmental strengths and weaknesses to encourage the most appropriate play activities.

A child who lacks attending skills, imitation skills, or communication skills cannot be expected to share or take turns. Developing these abilities takes time and is taught deliberately through modeling and reinforcement (Cook, Tessier, and Klein, 1996). Once a teacher determines that the child is able to sustain play with a toy and has greater social interaction, she can provide guidance for free play.

Appropriate supervision promotes quality play. A brief suggestion at the right moment can extend play. To encourage more engaged play from a reluctant child, the teacher can briefly interact as a player alongside the child by crawling along the floor with the train saying *"Whoo - Whoo"* or becoming a baby who wants to be fed. The teacher first plays alongside the child to promote engagement and then gradually withdraws as the child demonstrates a willingness to play independently or with peers.

Children with severe physical, visual, hearing, or mental impairments benefit from a teacher physically guiding their activities until they are able to approximate the activity on their own. However, directing play when guidance is no longer needed takes away the spontaneous nature of play. Children who are seeking adult attention may want teachers to remain and direct the play, but it is more supportive to disengage gradually. When a teacher hovers too near a group of children who are playing, she may stifle their play. She needs to observe from outside the play area, but adjacent to it.

Children's play can become highly embedded with personal experiences. Teachers may observe the mildest child transformed into a group leader in the midst of play. Sometimes children reveal personal ideas while engaged in play "on the telephone." The class may become witnesses to language and behavior that may cause some members discomfort.

Judging when to intervene in such circumstances can be difficult. Teachers may need to quickly consider many competing aspects of behavior as well as the delicate trust relationship they have with a child. Is the child authentically revealing a personal play idea? How damaging are the child's actions? What might the teacher gain by continuing to observe the child rather than interrupting the child? If the teacher does decide to intervene, what form should the intervention take?

If the teacher moves closer to the play, the child may react to the teacher's presence and reduce his or her intensity. The teacher might want to validate the child's experience. *"You said 'Shut up' loud and clear. You must want us to know how you feel. Can you tell me about that?"* Providing support sends a nonthreatening message of trust. It separates the individual from the behavior and creates opportunities for highly personalized teaching and learning (Jones and Reynolds, 1992).

Promoting Pro-Social Behavior

Pro-social skills represent the positive aspirations of society. Aspects of pro-social behavior include helping, sharing, giving, cooperating, sympathizing, aiding, encouraging, sacrificing, rescuing, defending, reassuring, and comforting. Pro-social skills are fostered when children have the opportunity to help one another, are encouraged to come to the defense of another, or are permitted to take personal action that is beneficial to all.

Adults have a major impact on the degree to which children learn to be helpful and cooperative. In group settings, the atmosphere most likely to promote pro-social skills has the following characteristics:

- Participants anticipate that everyone will do his or her best to support one another.
- Both adults and children contribute to decision making.
- Communication is direct, clear, and mutual.
- Individual differences are respected.
- Expectations are reasonable.
- People like one another and feel a sense of belonging to the group.
- There is an emphasis on group as well as individual accomplishments. (Staub, 1978)

Strategies for promoting pro-social behavior in children include the following:

- *Take advantage of naturally occurring opportunities to label children's pro-social acts.* When children help care for a school pet, describe how important their actions are and explain that they are showing concern for the animal's well-being.
- *When children take turns, mention that that is a way of cooperating with one another.*
- *Highlight pro-social behavior without lecturing or moralizing about it.*
- *Create opportunities for children to cooperate as a group, and clearly label and describe the acts of cooperation as they occur.* Children can run errands together with a buddy and perform many routine tasks as a small group. Encourage children to come up with group projects to collaborate on.
- *Create opportunities for children to help one another.* When individual strengths are valued, they benefit all of us. One child may know how to complete a skill before others, such as zipping a coat, tying shoelaces, or using a hole punch. Once the child can demonstrate the skill, that child can begin to help others who need assistance. Children will soon learn to go directly to the skilled child for assistance. When a child asks a teacher for help, the teacher can also direct the child to find a peer who can help, such as Peter. When a classmate is upset and needs comforting, the group can be invited to help, if they would like. Anna, for example, is known as a good friend when someone needs comforting.
- *Demonstrate constructive ways of responding to other people's pro-social acts.* Whether you accept or decline an offer of assistance, you can still send the message, "I'm glad you offered!"

- *As a teaching staff, demonstrate a variety of pro-social behaviors—sharing, helping, cooperating, and collaborating.* Creating a spirit of community improves the quality of living for all.

Social and Emotional Development In the Child with Disabilities

Because the interaction between caregiver and child so intensely defines the social and emotional competence of the young child, the child with disabilities often is less mature socially and emotionally than his peers. Across disabilities, research demonstrates it is difficult to separate the direct effects a disabling condition has on social and emotional development from the effects of the abnormal responses of the caregivers to the child (Fallen and Umansky, 1985) in infancy and the early years of childhood, as seen below.

Children with Cognitive Differences -The mentally retarded child often has difficulties giving the cues to the caregiver that elicit nurturing and reinforce the attachment process. If the child is lethargic, does not fix on the caregiver's face, or does not react to being touched or held, as often occurs with retarded children, the attachment between caregiver and child may be weakened (Berger and Cunningham, 1981). Retarded children are not born with feelings of inferiority or inadequacy, but evidence points to their consistent isolation from normal peers (Fallen and Umansky, 1985).

Visual Impairments - Characteristics of the visually impaired child may have a critical impact on the caregiver, causing him or her to ignore the child's requests for attention or help (Imamura, 1965; Tait, 1972a), become overprotective (Sommers, 1944), and have feelings of guilt and denial (Cohen, 1964). The visually impaired child is less apt to explore a world that he or she cannot see (Tait, 1972). The cumulative effect of these factors interferes with the child's development of self-concept and with the initiation of contacts in the environment (Fraiberg, 1972).

Hearing Impairments - Children with hearing impairments experience a high degree of frustration in their ability to communicate with the world. The high incidence of temper tantrums and physical expression of feelings of hearing impaired children is attributed to their inability to express frustration verbally (Mindel and Vernon, 1971). The problem often intensifies as the child's contacts with peers and adults expand, causing damage to the child's self-concept and confidence.

Emotional Disorders - Children with personality and conduct disorders have difficulty establishing interpersonal relationships. The personality characteristics associated with these disorders range from inhibition and anxiety to aggressive and destructive behaviors and often cause ridicule or punitive behaviors from those who interact with them.

Physical Disabilities - Children develop a sense of trust in their own bodies through repeated and deliberate movements. When physical movement is inhibited, the child experiences repeated frustration (Cook, Tessier, and Klein, 1996).

If not developed in infancy, trust and autonomy are harder to develop at later ages (and will not develop at all in isolation). This slowed development places additional requirements on the teaching staff to provide the emotional reinforcement to compensate for earlier stages. Consequently, one of the goals of inclusive programs is to provide an emotionally supportive environment in which disabled children thrive, especially when their conditions have adversely affected their self-esteem and social interactions with others. Moreover, inclusion promotes the acceptance of the disabled by reducing the social stigma. Perhaps the most persuasive argument for including children with disabilities in typical classrooms is that they learn new social behaviors through imitating their nondisabled peers.

However, research shows that simply placing children with and without disabilities together does not necessarily result in the desired imitation. (Jenkins, Speltz, and Odom, 1985; McLean and Hanline, 1990). By the age of five some children have already learned a negative attitude toward children with disabilities (Johnson and Johnson, 1980). Children who have not learned negative attitudes are able to learn positive attitudes toward disabilities when a positive model is provided through adults' actions, words, nonverbal behaviors, and explanations (Kostelnik, Stein, Whiren, and Soderman, 1993).

Strategies for Children with Special Social Needs

The teacher must establish a classroom environment that promotes learning for children with varying temperaments. Regardless of the cause of the behavior, the teacher must develop a repertoire of strategies to use with children who show reluctance to participate or who demonstrate aggressiveness.

The reluctant child is slow to participate, timid, or afraid to participate. This child lacks the very behaviors that bring him or her into social contact with others. To facilitate social development, the teacher can use some of the strategies listed below:

- *Provide a safe place for these children to observe the activities of others.* Often these children learn a great deal from observing and may be fully engaged in activities through observation.
- *Create consistent, predictable routines.* An inhibited child will feel more secure knowing where materials are kept and when events will occur.
- *Facilitate participation.* The teacher may use a variety of strategies to encourage the participation of the reluctant child. The teacher may move a toy or material physically closer to the child. She may "buddy" a reserved child with a classmate to do a job or an activity. She may assign this child a responsibility for caring for the class pet; sometimes a reserved child will become more engaged with an animal than with another child. Nonverbal activities such as painting, dancing, or playing a musical instrument may provoke expression indirectly.

- *Use positive reinforcement.* A quiet smile, nod, or pat can be more effective than a loud statement in front of a large group. Do not coerce the reluctant child to participate, but provide him or her the individual attention to build the trust that the child needs before joining activities. Reward positive activities by providing specific praise—for example, *"Thank you for helping with snack. You did a good job."*
- *Focus on the effort, not the outcome.* For the child with disabilities, it is important to acknowledge the motivation and effort behind the activity rather than the end product. For example, a teacher might say, *"It is so helpful when you do that!"*

The <u>aggressive child</u> lacks self-control and presents special challenges to the classroom teacher. His or her behaviors may range from highly active to hostile. The aggressive child requires clear rules and strategies that promote control and inner responsibility. The teacher can also use the following strategies:

- *Limit noise and visual stimulation.* The classroom should have places for children to work away from excessive noise or other activities. Some hyperactive children are overly stimulated both visually and auditorily by their environments and need a calm, structured environment in order to pay attention. Other highly active children require additional stimulation or they will lose interest.
- *Provide clear direction.* Children must understand what is expected of them. The class schedules should be posted. Materials should be clearly marked and placed in a defined location. Some children prefer having an assigned seating place. Classroom rules must be known and understood. Aggressive behaviors must be dealt with immediately. Use a short "time-out" period to quiet overly stimulated behavior.
- *Create opportunities for children to master control over their actions.* When children begin to feel like responsible individuals, their need for negative behavior is diminished (Glasser, 1969).
- *Create an expected daily routine.* Children have an easier time transitioning from one activity to another when they have internalized their daily schedule. They understand the flow of the day and can prepare their actions accordingly.

Including a child with disabilities requires a positive attitude on the part of the teaching staff toward the long-range benefits of inclusion, a willingness to collaborate with other professionals and agencies supportive of the child's development, and a willingness to put in the extra effort to work with exceptional children, including learning about the disability itself, and following the classroom practices listed below (Dunlop, 1977).

- Include open discussion of differences among children.
- Create a positive focus on learning, with associated expectations for the attainment of realistic goals.
- Structure daily time to evaluate and plan for the progress of each child.
- Provide opportunities for children to act independently.
- Promote cooperative activities to encourage social growth in all children.
- Involve parents in classroom activities.

In the end, there is no set formula for successfully including children with special social and emotional needs in the classroom. Instead, teachers need to apply the skills and strategies that are the fundamentals of sound early childhood teaching to their inclusive classrooms. These include: learning about the child from the child's parents; providing opportunities for learning through doing and making choices; teaching to the individual strengths and needs of each child; observing, assessing, and planning for the individual learning needs of each child; and working cooperatively as a member of the teaching team.

Instructional Activities that Facilitate Social and Emotional Development

One of the most important roles of a teacher in supporting social and emotional development is that of modeling expected behavior. It must be done constantly and consistently. Respecting other children, cooperating, compromising, and expressing emotions are some behaviors that the teacher models to promote a community of friends in the classroom. The children will follow the teacher's example and respond to the climate and tone set by the teacher. Setting a good example is the key. The teacher needs to say aloud the steps of an action so that young children can process them. Children need to hear the thought processes that take place as the teacher is modeling a behavior.

Social and emotional skills are not to be taught only at certain times during the day. They should be taught and reinforced every minute of the day. Take advantage of any occurrence in the classroom to reinforce these skills and to teach a social curriculum.

Questioning techniques used by the teacher are an invaluable way to interact with children. If done in a developmentally appropriate manner, questioning can support a child as he or she weaves a way through cognitive thought processes. Questioning challenges a child to reach a new level of understanding and also can give a teacher the information she may need to assess a child's needs.

Promoting Self-Identity and Self-Esteem
Help children describe themselves, their families, and their cultural groups.
- Use boy and girl dolls for role playing.
- In the dramatic play center, allow children to role play themselves and other members of their families. It might be necessary to ask the children specific questions to encourage them to engage in such an activity: *"What do you do to get ready to come to school in the morning? What do you do to get ready for bed?"*
- Show different pictures of families for discussion: *"This is a mom. She is reading a book to her daughter. What are some things your mom does with you? This is a dad. He is washing the supper dishes. What do you see your dad do at home?"* Naming specific objects helps children learn items in their environment.
- Make individual or class books such as "All About Me" (favorite activities at school

and home, favorite foods or colors, friends, talents, etc.) and "My Family" (members of the family or activities that the family does for fun on the weekend, for dinner, for holidays, etc.).

Help children to demonstrate positive attitudes toward themselves and others.
- Draw self-portraits.
- Put paper body parts together.
- Create songs or games that focus on parts of the body and that encourage positive ideas about a child: *"What do you like about yourself?"*
- Bring in music to demonstrate a holiday tradition: *"Do you know this song? Is it the same or different from songs you sing in your family?"*
- To promote a smooth separation when the parent drops off the child, create a morning routine. The parent and child may read a book or draw a picture together each morning before the parent leaves. Sometimes the routine can be getting morning chores done together—hanging up a jacket, checking in for attendance, choosing an activity, and giving five kisses and a hug before the child continues independently.
- The child can draw a picture for the parent and dictate a letter to bring home at the end of the day.
- Set aside a specific amount of time for a parent to stay and let the child know the length of time. *"Your mom will stay with you for ten minutes before it is time for her to go."*
- Make sure the child knows the schedule and exactly when the parent will come to pick him or her up. Help the child create his or her own picture schedule that he or she can refer to during the day if necessary.
- Have the child bring something of comfort from home—a toy, a blanket—to keep with him or her or in his or her cubby. A child can keep a family photo in a pocket to look at during the day.
- Make sure the teacher is available for the transition between one comforting adult and another.
- Some children want to know they will have a friend at school—someone to sit next to, play with, etc. Have another child be a "special friend" to that child.
- Have the child cut out pictures or draw pictures of favorite things—activities, foods, colors, etc., and make a mobile or collage of the pictures.

Promote confidence in self.
- Have a box with strips of paper that can be used to create a growing paper chain. Each time a child learns a new skill or has a success in the classroom, write it on a strip and add it to the chain.
- To support a child's confidence as well as to reinforce skills and make practicing skills fun, change the materials or manipulatives to be used. If a child is learning to count by rote from one to five, have him or her choose the objects to be counted. Have snack tables set up in groups of five so that the child sets out five napkins, five cups, etc.; the learning is then meaningful and useful. If a child is identifying the numbers one to five, have snack places numbered for the child to find the correct place to sit by recognizing or matching a number. Have the child make a numbers

book to read to a friend or stuffed animal.
- At the end of the day, everyone can share one positive thing about the day with the group. For a child who is unable to do this alone, prompt with, *"Did you work at the art table? What did you do? You used lots of colors and covered an entire page with colors."*
- Have the child dictate a note to take home about an accomplishment—big or small.

Promote independence.
- Encourage the buddy system so that children will sometimes ask each other for help instead of asking an adult.
- Ensure that the classroom environment, expectations, and routines are understood by being consistent, putting labels on shelves to indicate where materials are stored, and having a daily schedule displayed in pictures.
- Make sure materials are accessible to the children by putting the most commonly used materials on lower shelves within easy reach.
- Give children jobs to do to maintain the classroom—water the plants, help with snack, be the leader, etc.
- If a child asks for help when it is not needed, your goal is to encourage the child to attempt the task or activity independently. *"I will watch you try to put the puzzle together. What piece will you try first? What can you do now?"* The next time the child asks for help, say, *"Please show me the puzzle when you are finished."* Encourage the child to draw on past experiences by saying, *"Remember when you did it before by yourself? I know you can do it—give it a try."*
- Post a list of the names of each class member at the different centers. As a child works in a center, he or she can check off his or her name on the list. That will help the child follow a plan of work for the day. It will also help a teacher keep a record of a child's activities and show a pattern of which activity centers he or she frequents.
- Allow for differences in the way children use materials or participate in activities. When children feel that they must follow a set example, they do not feel free to be independent. When they are working on their own, their creativity grows.

Encourage children to respect the rights of self and others.
- Provide verbal explanations along with modeling respectful behavior by saying, *"I am moving over to make room for Julie to sit with the group."*
- Play group games during morning meeting where everyone is included and no one gets "out."
- During morning meeting greeting, ask each child to say one positive thing about the friend sitting next to him or her.
- Create a class photo album.
- Create a class flag or banner.
- At the beginning of the year, play games so that the children learn each other's names.

Promoting Self-Control and Positive Interactions

Help children to follow rules and routines.

- Make sure the day's plans are written and displayed—using both words and pictures—so that each child can understand them.
- Create a picture flip book of the child during routine activities. Help the child sequence the pictures and encourage him or her to flip the page as it is time to move onto another part of the plan.
- Involve the children in creating the class rules and state the rules in a positive manner—for example, *"We take care of our classroom and materials."*
- Use role playing to show what happens when someone does not follow the rules.
- Have children sign their names to the list of class rules to show responsibility, understanding, and ownership.

Help children to expresses emotions in appropriate ways.

- Model appropriate expressions by providing words for the emotions. *"I am feeling sad because one of our books was ripped today during choice time."*
- Create a board game with pictures of different emotions. When a child lands on a picture, the child can choose one or more responses: (1) identify the emotion, (2) say what might have caused the emotion, (3) express what makes him or her feel that way.
- Use a puppet or stuffed animal to communicate with a child. Children often are more willing to talk to a toy when asked how they feel.
- Use a puppet or animal to model the appropriate expression of emotions. *"Osgood is happy today because Jenny read a book to him."*
- Make "emotion puppets" out of paper plates. Children can choose a puppet face to show how they feel when they are unable to express an emotion.
- The teacher can wear emotion tags during the day and express how she feels. A child can put on an emotion tag if he or she is unable to express a feeling. Then the teacher knows if there is a problem to be addressed.
- Play the guessing game "Whose Voice," in which one child hides and another child has to guess who is hiding by identifying the voice. Give specific directions about what kind of voice to use—happy, sad, afraid.
- Make books for an individual child or a class book about emotions.

Facilitate age-appropriate play.

- Provide play activities that are developmentally appropriate. Younger children may play alone or alongside another child without interaction. As children mature, they will be involved in activities with others and assign roles or tasks to each person (such as assigning roles in dramatic play).
- Provide activities and manipulatives that reflect the development or growth of a child—for example, Duplos to Legos; group dance to specific dance with a partner; or pull on dress-up clothes to clothes with buttons and zippers.

Promote cooperation in play and interactions with peers.
- Activities should allow for the developmental levels of the children. Younger children may not be ready to use language to communicate with others while older children should be expected to use words to express themselves.
- Activities for younger children should include enough "props" for play (one doll or fire chief hat for each person in dramatic play). As children mature, they are able to cooperate and share these props.
- If a child is playing alone and has difficulty joining a group, ask, *"Who would you like to play with today?"* Then bring that child to the other. *"John would like you to be his friend today. He would like to play your game with you. Please explain the game to him so he can join you."*
- When there is trouble over sharing toys, verbally reiterate the process of sharing. *"It is Bob's turn to use the truck, but when he is finished, he will let you have a turn."* Then you may have to remind Bob that his turn is ending so that he can pass the truck to someone else.
- When children have trouble taking turns with materials or as part of a game or play activity, verbally walk them through the process. Encourage two children to participate together (reading together instead of taking turns) or encourage them to bend the rules to fit their needs (*"You can have two moms in dramatic play today"*).

Promoting Social Behavior

Help children to show empathy.
- Assign the job of helper-for-a-day or appoint many helpers for different jobs in the classroom. One job can be helping a friend in need.
- Each time one friend helps another without teacher instruction, put a penny or a ball or a gumdrop in a jar. When the jar is full, the group receives a treat (candy, a new toy for the classroom, or learning a new game).

Encourage children to understand and respect differences.
- Organize cooperative games using partners.
- Use pictures of diverse people in all activities, posters, books, manipulatives, etc.
- Discuss what activities you do on a special occasion like a birthday, and ask the children what they do in their families. Also talk about commonplace routines like preparing for bedtime. By discussing differences, children begin to understand that each family has a unique culture.
- Create activities to discover likes and dislikes among the children. Make a graph to show favorite food, color, book, stuffed animal, etc.
- At the beginning of morning meeting, pass out colored paper pieces to everyone. *"If you are holding a red piece, stand up and switch places with someone else who has a red piece."* Go through all the colors you used. The children will end up sitting next to someone different to pass the greeting or to partner with for a game.
- Have children pick names from a box or choose the person sitting next to them. They need to say one positive thing about the other person. The focus should not be about appearance or clothing, but rather personality characteristics or talents.

143

- Verbalize your actions to the group. *"I will add a chair to this table so my friend Ellen can play this game with us."* Show the children that everyone in the class will be included in activities.

Help children learn to share.
- Set a timer so the child knows when his or her turn is over or is about to begin.
- Have several toy choices available.

Help children to assume responsibility.
- Use verbal encouragement when a child acts responsibly. *"Thank you for remembering to close the door so that we won't be cold."*
- Delay the clean-up activity, if necessary, to ensure that the child carries out his or her responsibility.
- Assign children to be the helpers for centers in the classroom.
- Role play different classroom situations. *"What happens if the toys are not put away and are left on the floor? What happens if the toys are not put back in the proper place? What happens when we don't put on the tops of the magic markers? What happens if you don't do the work asked of you?"*
- Verbalize your actions. *"I am putting our new book on the bookshelf so someone else can read it later. I am picking up these pieces of Lego so they won't be lost. I am setting up the science table so we can learn about magnets."*
- Make sure that there is a place for all materials and that children have a place for their own belongings.

Encourage children to use compromise and discussion to resolve problems.
- Explain your thoughts and actions aloud when resolving problems in the classroom.
- Ask questions to help a child discuss a problem. *"Why do you think he did that?" "What would be a better way to act?"*
- Help the child figure out a solution before a situation occurs again. *"What can you do the next time this happens?"*
- Refer a child back to the class rules and their consequences.
- Role play a situation that needs to be resolved. Sometimes it works well if the teacher plays the role of a child who reacts badly. By overreacting and overacting, the teacher helps the child to see how inappropriate a behavior can be.

CHAPTER EIGHT

FACILITATING LANGUAGE DEVELOPMENT

8. FACILITATING LANGUAGE DEVELOPMENT

Chapter Overview
- Language and Literacy Development in the Young Child
- Facilitating Language Development in the Classroom
- Language Development and Children with Disabilities
- Instructional Activities that Facilitate Language Competence

Language and Literacy Development in the Young Child

Understanding and using language is a human characteristic most of us take for granted. We use language to organize and communicate our thoughts as well as to converse with others. Language allows us to be social beings, to express ourselves, and it helps us to learn about the world. When children are delayed or impaired in their language acquisition, it places them at risk in our ever-changing world.

Equally important is the role language plays in providing a foundation for early literacy skills such as reading and writing. Receptive language refers to language that a child receives through listening or reading. Expressive language is what a child uses in his or her own speaking and writing. By observing each child's language, we will recognize the interdependence between the language a child absorbs and the language a child uses.

Language appears in several forms: oral language (listening and speaking), reading, and writing. All of these parts are integrated through an underlying language system. Experiences in listening (the input, or receptive, side of language) precede speaking (the output, or expressive, side of language) (Lerner, 1988). The ability to speak does not depend solely on an individual's ability to listen. The interrelationship of both listening and speaking provides reinforcement that shapes speaking behavior. For example, when nurtured by parents' conversations, children adapt their speaking patterns.

Though receptive language or listening is a skill that is expected to occur without special instruction, many children do not acquire functional listening skills by themselves. Receptive language involves creating meanings and organizing information according to relationships. Additionally, one evaluates the information, and selects whether or not to accept or reject the ideas. Listening is the foundation of all language growth, so the child with a deficit in listening skills has an impairment in all communication skills. Through research, however, we know that teachers can improve a child's listening ability by providing appropriate classroom activities and practice.

Expressive language or speaking begins at birth with the cry. Vocalization, such as babbling, occurs throughout the first nine months of life. During this babbling period, infants and toddlers enjoy making many different sounds. Children with language disorders may not naturally engage in babbling activities. Teachers and parents can help these children by promoting oral play activities.

147

At about nine months of age, children enter a new stage of speaking, called "jargon." They begin to imitate the rhythm and intonation patterns of those around them. Although children are making the sounds of their language system, they are not yet using words. Moving from single words to short two-word utterances, the child's social language development begins to take a more recognizable form. By three years of age, a child's vocabulary rapidly expands and the child is able to speak using complex sentences.

By observing children's language development, researchers have categorized stages that the child goes through in a relatively short time span, from birth to full acquisition of speech. Children with language impairments do not follow a normal developmental language pattern. Some have difficulty producing particular sounds; still others have difficulty remembering words and forming sentences. Teachers can help children build a speaking vocabulary by taking advantage of daily opportunities for conversations and by designing classroom activities that promote speaking skills.

Components of a Language System

Often, the terms *speech, language,* and *communication* are used interchangeably. For purposes of distinction, a definition will be provided for each of the terms.

> *Language* is an organized set of symbolic relationships used to communicate ideas and experiences using conventional verbal language, including pragmatics, semantics, and syntax.

> *Communication* is any attempt by a speaker to exchange information and ideas with another person. We can communicate verbally, nonverbally, pictorially, or through gestures, sign language, written language, or any number of representational systems.

> *Speech* is the auditory-articulatory code by which we represent oral language. Stuttering, articulation, and voice disorders such as hoarseness or harshness are a few of the disorders associated with speech. It is important to remember that even if a child is unable to speak, it does not mean that he or she cannot communicate.

Language systems have at least three basic components (Fairfax Country Public Schools, Developmental Language Instruction Curriculum, 1991):

* pragmatics (language intents and conversational devices)
* semantics (word and sentence meaning)
* syntax (word order and grammar).

Pragmatics deals with the purpose and use of language and is the underlying foundation of all communicative acts. Initiating, maintaining, and ending conversations are all a part of pragmatics. Conversational devices such as clarifying the topic being discussed, changing topics, and furthering discussions are skills children need to understand and use effectively to realize the full potential of language.

Another aspect of pragmatics involves the environmental context in which conversation occurs. How one speaks or communicates depends on the context the person is in when speaking, not the location of the conversation. Being aware of the effect of environmental factors on communication is an important component in the fluent use of language.

Semantics involves the meaning of the symbols that are used in language. Individual words have meaning. A series of words, when combined into a sentence, expresses a complete thought. Expanding a group of sentences can convey meaning in paragraphs, conversations, speeches, books, plays, etc.

It is possible for the same word to have a variety of meanings depending on its place in a sentence. For example, a teacher might ask, *"Did you water the flowers?"* or might say, *"The flowers need water."*

Syntax refers to the order in which words occur in language. It also has to do with grammar and morphology (plurality and tense markers). Syntax contains the "structure" through which semantics and pragmatics are communicated.

Facilitating Language Development in the Classroom

Although learning to use language and to communicate with others seems to be achieved effortlessly by most children, two conditions need to be present in order for communication to develop: interaction and information. Language learning occurs daily through the child's interactions with his or her teachers, other adults, and peers. Through active participation, a child is better able to become a more effective communicator. In fact, children gain information from their conversations with others. The information exchanged in conversations needs to be both relevant and appropriate to the child's language level. By taking a close look at communication in the classroom, a teacher can become aware of a child's need for interaction and information.

Creating a Language Responsive Classroom

Child-initiated communication is a primary goal for child-centered classrooms. Just as language skill develops functionally and responsively from children's interests, so should classroom language content be child-centered. Teachers should design the classroom setting and schedule to give children the maximum amount of time to initiate speech and language and to communicate in a variety of ways with each other and adults.

Experiences in classrooms for young children should be based on multiple, naturalistic opportunities for language learning (Goodman, 1986). Each of the basic functions of language – communication, expression, and reasoning – develop simultaneously in an interactive process. Facilitating communication skills is a process involving cognitive, social, and linguistic skills (Owens, 1988). Conversations are more likely to be initiated and prolonged when adults promote general learning (Linder, 1993).

Questions such as *"What color are your shoes?"* create ineffective interactions, since it is quite clear what color a child's shoes are. At the same time, awareness of a conditioned or conditional response is also necessary on the child's part. Teachers should encourage children to expand the language they typically use.

The phrasing of inquiries can have direct implications on the response given. When children are working (building, painting, engaging in woodworking, etc.), it is better to ask *"Would you like to tell me something about your work?"* than *"What is it?"* In the child's mind, the work may not have a label. However, the child may be quite interested in describing the work process and relating personal observations.

The Importance of Conversations

Teachers who use the following guidelines will be effective communicators in the classroom.

- *Be an effective listener.* The complex process of listening is a primary means for gaining accurate information and conveying interest in the messages communicated. Listening helps establish rapport with the speaker. When an adult demonstrates an understanding of what a child has said, the child will perceive the adult as supportive and trustworthy. Alternatively, a rapid and inaccurate response to a child's comments suggests little concern for the child's frame of reference, and even less for the child as a significant individual.

- *Be an active listener.* Show sincere interest in what the child is saying, even when the child is difficult to understand. Position yourself so that you are on the child's level, maintain eye contact, and provide supportive gestures such as nodding and showing anticipation with facial gestures (e.g., raising eyebrows, smiling slightly, turning an ear toward the child). Pause and allow time for the child to speak. As the child begins to speak, nod encouragement or offer a comment for the child – *"I'm rolling the dough." "I want to make a cookie."*

- *Speak clearly and expressively.* Use short sentences of three to four words. Frequently repeat key words that describe actions and objects, if necessary. Try to be playful and display an array of facial expressions intended to stimulate the child's interest and response. As children understand more and speak at greater length, increase the length and complexity of sentences, add vocabulary to theirs, and decrease repetition.

- *Use key vocabulary.* Key words are those that the child is particularly familiar with. Follow the conversational lead of the children, adding descriptive vocabulary and details. Describe actions and provide linkages by offering vocabulary or descriptive accounts when the child has difficulty recalling words.

- *Pause when speaking.* Rest and relax between sentences. Allow time for the child to speak. Silently count to five before speaking again.

- *Talk about the here and now.* Referring to the past or speculating about the future might confuse the child and bring a quick end to a conversation. Discuss experiences that the child is engaged in.

- *Be aware of children's communicative intent.* Watch for and encourage nonverbal communication – eye gaze, pointing, a shrug, a sound, a word. If the demand for verbal communication is too high, children may misbehave or withdraw. Show warmth and a positive regard; value each child's level of communication.

- *Limit your own talking, especially questions.* Pause often during conversations to encourage the child to initiate communication and take a turn. Reduce sentence length if warranted, but try not to sacrifice content. Some children need more content but may not be able to process or retain the content of lengthy sentences. Be genuine in your question-asking; avoid asking what is obvious to both you and the child. For a child who has difficulty expressing him- or herself, questions from the teacher may lead to "shutdown"; comments are more likely to promote conversation. For an expressive child, on the other hand, open-ended questions promote conversation.

- *Remember that answering questions is often difficult for young children.* Who, what, why, where, and when can be especially difficult for many children because they are not yet able to pose the appropriate response. Limit questioning to problem solving or open-ended speculation. Lots of questions in a series are not a conversation.

- *Consider the conversational skills in your classroom.* Do classmates listen to each other? Do children initiate conversations? Do they take turns? Are topics maintained over a few minutes or from the beginning to the end of a play session? Are topics maintained from one day to another or throughout the year? Are children asking questions? Are responses given? Are responses given to requests for clarification? Can children propose or change a topic?

Classroom Accommodations that Facilitate Language Comprehension and Expression

The following suggestions will assist a teacher in developing children's ability to comprehend language and build their communication skills:

- *Describe actions.* Few teaching strategies engage learners more than a teacher describing the actions of a learner – *"I see you have stacked a tall tower." "You are using the bike pedals today." "You rolled the dough."* In other words, name the action as well as the

151

object. Narrate what is taking place. Repeat key concepts, such as the conditions or effects of the actions. For example: *"You are rolling the play dough."* Encourage the child to fill in the word that completes the sentence: *"When you roll your hands back and forth, you make a . . . ."*

- *Model appropriate syntax while validating the message.* Ali says, *"This baby sleepy."* Vlad says, *"Yes, this baby is sleepy."* Ali asks, *"Where Tina?"* Vlad responds, *"Hmm, where is Tina?"* or Ali says, *"It is raining?"* Vlad replies, *"Let's ask Martin, 'Is it raining?'"*

- *Encourage verbal role playing and nonverbal negotiations.* Dialogue during pretend play is especially crucial in the child's acquisition of language skills. Comments such as *"Go to sleep, baby"* and *"Father, go quiet the baby!"* may be overheard during solitary or interactive peer play. A child may initially talk in the form of a monologue while playing. Conducting conversations during pretend play with peers can be a difficult task, one which may need teacher support, particularly if a child is experiencing sensory motor and/or speech and language delays.

As children increase their cooperative play, there will be conflicts over, for example, who wants to play which role or who had a certain prop first. If the children have the skills to handle the verbal negotiations, the teacher should maintain an observer's role and allow them to attempt to resolve their own conflict. If a child makes no effort to use words, the teacher can ask questions and suggest possible approaches.

- *Encourage children to be in a leading role.* When playing alone with a child, a teacher should let the child lead the play so that the child experiences what it is like to lead the verbal interaction. If the skill level is parallel play, repeat the child's actions and sounds. Play animatedly with an object or a toy and occasionally comment on the object or action. In other words, the teacher becomes the passive participant for a time to permit the child the opportunity to develop the viewpoint of a leading role.

- *Be alert to environmental barriers to communication.* To decrease background noise during listening activities, close doors or windows. Seat the child with special needs in a place where he or she can see visual cues. Point to cue cards or song cards during music. Have the child sit near the front of the group during story time.

- *Use open-ended questions.* Open-ended questions permit more than a single word answer. They promote conversation and encourage the speaker's point of view. An example of an open-ended question is *"What were you thinking about at the end of the story?"* Young children typically learn to process questions in the following sequence: what, whom, where, why, and when.

- *View the functions of language as a means of finding out why children use language.* Language is used to communicate about ourselves, to find out something that we want to know, to respond to others, and to negotiate social transactions. Consider what a child's gestures, vocalizations, and verbalizations imply. The possibilities may include seeking attention; requesting an object, an action, or information; protesting; commenting on an object; greeting someone else; or answering and acknowledging another's speech.

- *Be available to children.* Teachers promote meaningful interactions in many ways: by listening to children with care, respect, and affection; by asking them questions and answering their questions; and by engaging in conversations at their eye level.

- *Use specific techniques to facilitate communication.*

  Expansion – when adults expand a child's response by restating the child's idea in longer phrases and sentences.

  Parallel talk—when an adult talks about what a child is doing as he or she is doing it. Parallel talk helps children select and produce vocabulary, develop usage skills, and learn styles of speaking for specific activities or settings.

  Prompting—prompting often involves saying a single sound or word to help a child remember what to do or say. Prompts should be reduced gradually until they can be eliminated. Methods of prompting include the following:
    - visual signs or gestures that demonstrate a word
    - providing information concerning the function, purpose, or use of a word
    - suggesting a category or a group member of the word
    - offering a context clue—a sentence or phrase in which the word commonly occurs, but omitting the word
    - giving information (descriptive words) about the target word, such as color, parts, and size
    - offering a "forced choice," such as, *"Would you like to use the rolling pin or the cookie press?"*

Promoting Communication During Group Discussions and Meetings

Teachers should actively involve children during group times by offering a variety of activities or a familiar sequence of activities that children will be able to anticipate during group times. Monitor the activities you are asking the children to follow. Periodically check to be sure that activities are appropriate to their expanding language skill levels.

In addition, teachers should do the following:
- *When planning for group meetings or circle times, be aware that group size has an important impact on individual participation during group discussions.* If the program goal for circle time is to allow for language development, then the smaller the group size, the more opportunity for language expression. Several small groups rather than one large group might better meet overall program goals.

153

- *Select an appropriate time to have circle time.* In many classrooms, circle time is during the morning before children are restless, tired, and hungry.

- *The pacing of activities during a circle or meeting time is crucial. Balance active and passive activities; energetic activities should follow listening activities.* Of course, the more actively involved that children are in the activity, the more learning will occur. Teachers cannot assume that when children are sitting and listening that learning is occurring.

- *Be physically proximate when delivering important information during a group meeting, story time, or presentation.* Stand, kneel, or sit near a child when giving directions. Let children know with a song, visual cues, or motion that you are asking them to pay attention to you.

- *Maintain eye contact with children who are comfortable with this communication style.* For the child who has difficulty maintaining eye contact, look to the side, but suggest that the child watch you as you talk.

- *Use a clear but quiet voice.* Pace your delivery and increase or decrease the rate of delivery for the needs of those listening. Use children's names while you speak.

- *Ask children for clarification; have them restate their understanding of your message so that you can confirm whether the children are familiar with all the terms used.* Provide quiet moments between breaks in your message. Make your message brief and concise. When you are finished, tell them that you have finished.

- *Give directions in small units.* Choose specific directions carefully and limit directions given at group meetings. Wait for demonstration of understanding and then proceed. You may need to repeat directions quietly again to a specific child after you have given them to the group. You might ask the child to repeat and explain the directions to you.

- *Allow children to use ideas and information introduced by their peers in order to communicate their own ideas.* Some children respond best if they have the first turn. Others have more success if they watch and listen to their peers first – for example, Tina says, *"A fly is a bug."* Don says, *"A spider is a bug."* The teacher says, *"Molly, tell me another name of a bug."*

- *Demonstrate and encourage respectful speaking manners; do not allow children to interrupt or speak or finish words for others.* Deal directly and fairly with the children. State the desired outcome in a positive manner—for example, *"Let's listen until Molly is all finished talking."*

- *Restate children's comments and questions.* Remark on the significance of a comment, to be sure everyone has heard a remark or to show respect for effort made. Be respectful and accurate. When transcribing children's ideas onto a chart during a group meeting, be sure to restate the comment for clarification from the speaker. Ask brief questions for clarification or encourage the child to expand his or her comment. Successful meetings produce meaningful conversations between all participants – children and adults. Children's length of response during group activities should approximate their conversational length of response in play situations.

- *Provide visual aids to help maintain the interest of the group and to provide clarity.* Use charts, flannel boards, song cards, or cue cards with pictures of children, children's names, objects, and routine events for music, playground, and room activities. If the class is going to have a meeting to talk and share ideas and information about the incubating duck eggs, ask the children to bring in books or drawings about eggs or ducks, perhaps a clay model of a duck nest, or any other items relevant to the meeting.

- *Sharing familiar objects or experiences can be valuable language experiences for children.* Sharing involves speaking to a group; the goal of group sharing is to present information in a clear and organized manner. If objects are shared, care must be given not just to the toys that are shown but to the meaningful experiences associated with them. To prevent boredom during sharing time, a small group of children can be scheduled to share their items each day. If all children in the class share during one sitting, children will lose interest and all learning will be lost.

Promoting Early Literacy Activities

In every classroom, certain activities should occur that support early literacy development. We know that children's literacy experiences will vary prior to formal schooling; our teaching methods and approaches need to be flexible and inclusive to account for this wide variance. Through research, educators know that good literacy instruction builds on what children already know and expands their knowledge and skills. Therefore, it is necessary for teachers to instruct children in the specific skills of literacy and to enhance their ongoing growth in thinking and reasoning. Below, we list the components needed for literacy development in the classroom (Neuman, 1998).

A print-rich classroom
Teachers must carefully plan the physical setting for literacy learning. Early childhood classrooms should contain a writing area, library corner, book-making table, and listening center. Materials such as paper (lined and unlined), pencils, pens, crayons, and markers can be contained within the literacy center and placed in other areas of the classroom. Children will be stimulated to use these items when there are interesting things to read and write about. Signs and labels around the room, books placed everywhere, play centers, bulletin boards with written messages—all of these materials invite children to explore literacy; they send the message that literacy is an important part of the children's day.

Each daily schedule should contain time for children to explore their print-rich environment. Whether children are writing letters in the writing center or using the dramatic play center to act out a favorite scene from a book, they are nourishing their interests in becoming literate long before they are formally reading and writing.

Integrated language experiences and explorations
Teachers in an effective literacy program respect each child's early efforts in reading, writing, spelling, and speaking (Coughlin et al., 1997). As a result of that respect, children become comfortable using their emerging skills to investigate their world and make discoveries. Planning activities for in-depth studies on real topics is interesting to children. Children ask meaningful questions when they are engaged in a study that is worth their attention.

Integrated learning activities give each child the opportunity to use language when cooperating with other children of varying skills and abilities. Activities such as planting a garden or painting a mural to illustrate a book encourage children to learn from one another and practice their emerging literacy skills together. One child may be highly verbal, while another might be more adept at writing words to go along with the mural.

Reading and responding
Introducing children to a wide variety of literature each day is a vital early childhood activity. Children need to hear fiction, nonfiction, poetry, and biographies read aloud to them daily. The books should reflect not only a range of listening and reading levels but also the ages and interests of the children within the classroom. Books expose children to rich language and extend their vocabularies.

Use a variety of methods to extend and reinforce the content of books read aloud. Finger plays, music, and singing are fun for children and build on the story. Retelling a story using pictures or puppets, illustrating a story, or engaging in small and large group discussions about a book are strategies that enhance children's comprehension and enthusiasm. Though simplistic, rereading old favorites is important because the repetition helps children come to know the regularity of language and the permanence of letter symbols.

Encourage children to investigate books independently. Independent reading allows children to practice looking at books, turning pages, and examining print. It also prepares them for reading independently in higher grades and promotes reading habits that build a foundation for lifelong learning. Books that are appropriate for emergent readers have a familiar subject matter, a simple language pattern, many high-frequency words, illustrations that correspond to the text on the page, and about ten lines of text per page. Enlarged print is also helpful.

Skills and strategies
Teachers can teach skills and strategies within the context of a story. Through daily literacy activities, many children learn to distinguish between letters, sounds, and words,

and begin reading and writing naturally. Nevertheless, most children require direct instruction. Whether they are beginning or fluent readers, children need modeling, coaching, praise, and practice with reading strategies.

The terms reading skills and reading strategies are sometimes confused. Skills are routine behaviors, such as recognizing sight words. Some skills are automatic and others are not. For example, a child who uses his or her knowledge of letters or sounds to decode an unfamiliar word is practicing skills. Strategies are plans that a reader puts in place to accomplish a goal, such as predicting what a story will be about. Reading strategies are flexible, planned, and conscious. Young readers have some reading skills in place before they can effectively use their strategies.

Language Development and Children with Disabilities

Slowed language development extends across a wide range of disabilities, some of which are presented below.

Hearing Impairments—Hearing loss, whether mild or profound, can have a significant impact on both speech and language development. Children with mild hearing losses do not hear all speech sounds with equal clarity. In the case of more profound hearing impairments, children usually use sign language as their method of communicating. While children with hearing loss can be taught to speak and understand language, the task requires special language intervention and instruction. The longer the hearing loss goes on undetected and untreated, the more likely it will be a serious problem.

Visual Impairments—Much attention has been devoted to the development of communication skills in children with visual impairments. It is important that teachers work collaboratively with specialists in visual disabilities, including orientation and mobility specialists, to ensure that optimal adaptations are made (Cook, Tessier, and Klein, 1996).

Cognitive Disabilities—With some children, speech and language may be delayed due to cognitive disabilities. Providing these children with a language-nurturing environment that supports and extends their current language capabilities is necessary. Those children who have mild and moderate cognitive disabilities are said to be able to acquire speech and language in the expected developmental sequences, yet at a slower pace. Children who have cognitive impairments may need to have special attention paid to their pragmatic language skills, such as time to practice interacting and conversing with others.

Autism—Two identifying characteristics of children with autism are their difficulties with social skills and atypical language development. Because of their problems with attachment and social interaction, instructional areas to emphasize in the classroom are conversing with others and expressing themselves and their needs.

Lack of Stimulation—Appropriate stimulation enhances language development and promotes communication skills. Conversely, lack of stimulation can contribute to a language delay and hinder communication ability. Parents and teachers can build time each day to teach communication skills. Activities such as cooking or gardening can provide excellent opportunities to strengthen speech and language learning.

Emotional Disabilities—Children with emotional disabilities may have many different forms of language delays or disorders, ranging from deviant language development to refusal to converse with others. In addressing these problems, parents and teachers need to first provide a caring learning environment that sets reasonable behavioral limits and boundaries.

Learning Disabilities—Children with learning disabilities can have a variety of language-based problems. Some of the complexities in language learning manifest themselves in poor listening skills, word retrieval problems, distractibility, and hypo- or hyperactivity. Many young children with learning disabilities need extra attention in order to master the basics of oral language. They also may require language instruction in the semantic and syntactic areas of language.

Instructional Activities that Facilitate Language Competence

Listening skills, communicating with language both verbally and nonverbally, and pre-writing, writing, and reading skills should not be thought of as isolated skills and taught separately. They are interdependent. The most important factor in developing language skills is to give children many opportunities to practice. Children need constant and consistent practice and repetition to develop their language and communication skills. Any activity or task used to support these skills should be used many times in many different situations and on many different levels. A teacher's questioning techniques are essential to help the child progress to a higher level of ability and understanding.

Promoting Receptive Language

Encourage children to listen with understanding.

- Make sure that the meaning or intention of a child's nonverbal language has been explained and understood. Do this by verbalizing your interpretation of the meaning.
- Create a game where the children use nonverbal language to try to convey meaning to others—for example, use pantomime: *"Let's pretend we are sweeping the floor."*
- To make sure that instructions have been understood, ask a child to repeat the instruction or to fill in the pertinent information: *"I just said that we are going to . . . . What are we going to do?"*
- During a story, stop at different points to summarize and review what has already been read.

- Use questioning techniques as you go through a story to make sure a child is following the concept or story.
- Read and reread favorite stories so that a child's comprehension can be further developed. Read a poem or nursery rhyme and ask the children to close their eyes and try to make the poem into pictures in their minds. After the reading, ask them to open their eyes and draw the images that they imagined.

Help children to respond appropriately to verbal information.
- For any child who has difficulty in following directions, begin with only one part of the directions, such as, *"Give me the blue ball,"* or *"Put the book on the bookshelf."* Then add one more step to the directions. Have the child repeat the directions.
- Sing the directions and make motions that coincide with the words, if possible.
- Ask the child to give the directions to someone else.
- When a child asks a question that is not appropriate or related to the topic, ask him or her if it is appropriate. *"We are looking at pictures of farm animals. Is your question about the moon related to this?"* Sometimes the child's question is related in that child's mind even when the connection is not obvious to the teacher. Other times, however, the question is not appropriate, and you can take this opportunity to explain and remind the child of the best time to share news or thoughts or ask these other questions.
- Give three-to-five-step directions for making something. Have all the materials ready and ask the child to follow the directions step by step.
- Sit with the child and a picture book. First talk about the items on the page and what they are called. You can name the item and ask the child to find it, or you can point to an item and ask the child to name it.
- With a single child or a small group, play the *"Simon Says"* game. Here are the rules: Give the children commands, one at a time. The children need to listen carefully and carry out the command only if it is preceded by the words "Simon says." For example, *"Simon says touch your foot"* means that the children should do so. After three or four other commands preceded by Simon Says, the teacher gives a command such as *"Clap your hands."* OOPS! It was not preceded by the magic words, so the children should have done nothing. Do not eliminate children who make mistakes—it is just a fun learning game.

Help children to recognize familiar verbal text.
- Make sure to give enough explanation, practice, or repetition for nonverbal signals. Provide extra time for some children to review the text of a song or poem so they feel comfortable with it.
- Have children fill in the last word of each line or the rhyming word in a song or poem.
- Create a rhythm with your hands or voice.
- Have children listen to nursery rhymes, poems, finger plays, and songs or stories that contain rhymes (*cat* and *hat*), alliteration (*large lazy lions lounging*), or nonsense sequences (*fee fi fo fum*). It is important to share the joy of reading selections in which

playing with language has a major role. Animate your reading, and the children will follow your lead.

- Highlight word play in a selection by drawing the child's attention to the words within phrases and the sounds within words. For example, the teacher might ask, *"Did you hear all the words that rhymed?"*
- At morning meeting, write a simple message leaving out beginning sounds in known sight words. For example, "Good morning _oys and _irls." The teacher can also leave out whole words, leaving a _____blank in the sentence.
- Establish a word wall in the classroom so that "sight words" on cards are added when they are used in a morning message or in a book.

Promoting Expressive Language

Help children to speak in a manner that is clear to listeners.

- Tape record a child singing or telling a story. By listening to the tape, the teacher can more easily identify sounds or words that present a problem to that child.
- Select silly poems or tongue twisters that focus on specific sounds.
- If a child uses a sentence with the incorrect sound or verb, repeat the sentence correctly.
- Use flannel board figures while telling a story. Deliberately create inconsistencies between what is said and what is placed on the board. Have the students listen to correct the mistakes.
- Place pictures of toys or other objects in a small box. Have four to five letter cards representing the beginning sound of the items in front of the child. Ask the child to select an item from the box and then select the card that represents that item's beginning sound.
- Focus on initial consonant sounds. Say three words, two of which have the same initial consonant. Ask the child to identify the word that begins with a different sound—for example, car, dog, cat.

Promote the use of language to communicate ideas and feelings.

- Converse with children often and on an individual basis to give them practice communicating their ideas and feelings. *"Tell me about this photo of your family."*
- Ask the children to draw a picture and then use words to communicate their ideas about the picture.
- Use questioning to help children share information and organize their ideas and thoughts.
- Create a class list of ideas or class stories about experiences so everyone can contribute at least one thought.
- Create scenarios in the dramatic play center for children to experiment with or practice communication skills. The teacher can join in the play by being herself or another character. Children can react to situations, change their responses, repeat responses, or direct the response in a certain way. This activity gives children a safe time to experiment with communication.

- Ask open-ended questions to encourage conversations. *"How did you feel during the thunderstorm last night?"*
- Have conversations with children during mealtimes and throughout the day.
- Using a small collection of puppets, ask the child to have the puppet act out routines of daily living such as brushing teeth, combing hair, and putting on shoes. Ask the child to let the puppet use words to describe what is happening.
- Using a "feely bag," ask a child to put his or her hand into the bag, feel an object, and describe it using two attributes—for example, *"This is something hard and round"* to describe an acorn.

Have children experiment with words and sounds.
- Use songs and poems often.
- Begin a rhyme and let the child finish it. Animals are an easy starting place for rhymes. *"We'll catch a fox and put him in a _____."*
- Put actions to rhymes. *"If you're wearing red, then shake your head."*
- Put the body in motion. *"When you hear a word that starts with the sound 'B,' sit down; if you hear another word that starts with 'B,' stand up."*
- Repeat words and sounds so that children can become more familiar with differences and similarities between them. Also, allow opportunities for children to experiment with words and sounds when they feel comfortable doing so.
- Arrange a collection of magnetic letters in alphabetical order. Then, tell the children that you are going to say a word. Their job is to find the letter that makes the first sound in the word and the letter that makes the last sound in the word. The teacher can ask the children to think of some words beginning with the same sound.

Have children tell a story or other text in sequence.
- Read stories and poems and sing songs. After several repetitions, stop and let the child finish them.
- Use a flannel board and ask the child to retell a familiar story.
- Use creative dramatics to act out a familiar story.
- Use the questioning process. *"Then what did the wolf say?"*
- If the child is not yet able to retell a story, let the child practice naming various objects. Next, encourage the child to talk in phrases or sentences about the objects.
- Sit with a child and look over a wordless picture book or sequence of picture cards. Look at the pictures, naming some of the items, and then go back to the beginning and ask the child to tell a story about what is happening.

Help children to understand perceptual concepts.
- Have tangible objects to match descriptive words.
- Pick two words (e.g., *rough, smooth*) and a box of objects. The child can sort them according to the texture. You can add new words (and objects) as understanding progresses.
- Put actions to words. *"Can you be as quiet as a mouse? Make yourself small like an ant."*
- Make an observation chart. Show the children some sand and elicit responses about

what they see (*white, smooth, it moves*, etc.). Then show something else, such as sugar or paint. Collect observation responses. Take the children through the process of comparing the two materials and finding a common characteristic.

Promoting Pre-Reading and Literacy Skills

Help children learn to concentrate on spoken text.
- Read a story individually with a child. Ask questions, discuss the story, and ask the child to predict what will happen next.
- Use family volunteers for more one-on-one reading activities.
- Read to the children or play a story tape during rest time.
- Use puppets, flannel board pieces, or other props to motivate and encourage participation.
- Have a standard list of questions for children to respond to after hearing the story. *"What was your favorite part? Did you expect that ending? How did the character feel when _____ happened? How did the story make you feel? Why?"* Add more challenging questions as the children become better equipped to answer them.
- Share books with children several times a day, including big books, poems with enlarged print, and predictable and rhythmical text. These books and poems usually have a pattern, refrain, or sequence and encourage children to repeat the predictable elements.
- Reread favorite stories, poems, and nonfiction books.
- Well-illustrated books and poems sometimes work best for holding children's attention. For poems written on chart paper, teacher drawings can be as effective as published material.
- Create related response activities to the stories using a variety of materials and manipulatives.

Show children how to tell a story following the pictures in a book.
- Have pictures of a situation for a child to put into sequence. To begin with, there should only be three or four pictures—for example, the sequence for getting dressed in the morning: (1) getting out of bed, (2) choosing clothes, (3) changing clothes, (4) getting completely dressed. Ask the child to explain the sequence.
- Have flannel board pieces of a familiar story or photocopied pages of the story and ask the child to put the pictures in sequence before telling the story.
- Allow opportunities to make predictions about a story. *"What do you think will happen next?"*
- Have a child retell or draw a story, or write a different ending to a story to create a new story.
- Tell or write a group story with a small group of children. *"Once upon a time there was a purple mouse. One day he came out of this mouse hole and saw _____."* Then the next person adds a sentence or thought.

Promote independence in activities related to literature.
- Choose the library center for the child and say, *"I will meet you in the library center to*

read to you."
- Show the children that you read often for information and for fun.
- Allow opportunities to look at books independently and with a partner.
- Have materials available for children to create books on their own time and not only at your direction.
- Encourage children to draw pictures to make a book; then they can dictate the words.
- At sharing time or reading time, let children share or read their books with the class.
- If a child is having trouble recreating or relating literature themes, you can participate in dramatic play activities so that you can lead or direct an activity when necessary. Through questioning, you can draw out information from the child and guide him or her through a related activity.
- Encourage individuality by providing a variety of materials for dramatics, writing, and drawing.

Help children to recognize the association between spoken and written words.
- Use classroom labels or point them out when speaking with the children.
- Make labels a part of everyday routines. Create new labels with the help of the children as the year progresses.
- Encourage children to make their own labels. For example, the children can make signs to use in the block center (*airport, zoo, parking*). Have an envelope or space for the signs to be saved and reused another time.
- The children's names should be everywhere. Names can be placed on snack tables or on an attendance chart for children to find when they arrive at school. Names should be written on every paper, artwork, and note sent home.
- Provide many opportunities for storytelling. Supply materials (art supplies, puppets, etc.) to help with storytelling.
- Use the tape recorder for dictation.
- Have a listening center where the child follows a story on tape while looking at the pictures and words. Have each family make a story tape for the listening center.
- When reading books and poems with enlarged print, point to the words as you are reading to model reading behaviors.
- Provide opportunities for children to draw and print letters using a variety of materials (crayon, markers, paint, etc.).
- If the child just likes to draw, ask the child to describe his or her work and then, with the child's permission, write his or her words down on paper. Read back to the child what has been written.
- From a dictated class story, big book, or poem, write sentences on paper. Give a sentence to each child and have the child stand up when his or her sentence is read.
- Cut up a sentence strip into words and have the child assemble the words in order to reproduce the sentence. You may want to have a model available so that the child can place the words right on top of the matching sentence strip.

Promoting Prewriting Language and Literacy Skills

Encourage an interest in using writing for a purpose.
- Provide many daily opportunities for children to draw and write.
- When children pretend to write, ask what they have written. At first, they may say nothing, but with encouragement and time, children will begin to put meaning into their scribbles.
- Encourage children to write about their pictures or to write a note home. As they read their words to you, write them on a separate sheet of paper. With time, children will begin to be aware of the correct letters and words.
- Children can make signs or labels for the classroom or to use in their play and work activities.
- Have manipulative letters available for children to use or to copy (block letters, magnetic letters, sponge letters, stamp letters, template letters, etc.).
- Make these skills a tactile experience. Use play dough to make the letters of a child's name. Place paper over sandpaper letters and rub to make letters appear. Trace letters in sand.
- Allow many opportunities for practice and repetition.
- Make a class alphabet book where each child makes a letter page.
- Model writing a thank-you letter to a parent for helping in the classroom, a shopping list, or a journal entry.
- Help children to develop a willingness to approximate spelling while writing—for example, *"How do we spell cat? What is the first sound you hear? That's right, a 'c' sound. So let's write c. Now what is the next sound you hear in the word 'cat'. That's great, a 't' sound. Let's write an 'a' before that 't'. Now we have the word 'cat'."*
- You can extend the preceding lesson by asking the children to think of words they know that rhyme with *cat—fat, pat, rat, mat, bat.*

Help children to use letters and similar shapes to create words or simple ideas.
- Have a pocket or envelope of words that children have access to. They can choose a word to copy and make a sign or write a note.
- Use manipulative letters.
- Write notes, reminders, and lists for yourself and the class; verbalize aloud as you are writing.
- Create a literacy-rich environment where print is in every center of the classroom. All text should be at the children's eye-level and be enlarged so that the children can easily see it.
- Help children learn to segment spoken words into individual sounds and blend the sounds into whole words. Model this process on paper in front of small groups of children.
- Search for rhyming words and beginning sounds in big books or class-dictated stories. Make a very small frame out of paper for the child to use when searching for the words and sounds.

CHAPTER NINE

ENCOURAGING THE DEVELOPMENT OF COGNITIVE SKILLS

9. ENCOURAGING THE DEVELOPMENT OF COGNITIVE SKILLS

Chapter Overview
- Cognitive Development in the Young Child
- Facilitating Cognitive Development in the Classroom
- Cognitive Development and Children with Disabilities
- Instructional Activities that Promote the Development of Cognitive Skills

Cognitive Development in the Young Child

Most young children come to school filled with wonder and an interest in exploring their world. From their explorations, they manipulate materials and information, engage in thinking, and generate new ideas. As they investigate their environments, they learn about their world and become enthusiastic about their new discoveries. In studying cognition, we are most interested in finding out how children learn rather than with the actual body of information that children know (Essa, 1992). Essentially, educators search for how children acquire, organize, and apply knowledge (Copple, DeLisi, and Sigle, 1982).

Many children with special needs have cognitive impairments that interfere with the development of conceptual and reasoning skills necessary for the mastery of academic skills. A teacher can recognize these challenges and provide support necessary for the achievement of important cognitive skills, such as developing the ability to think and use problem-solving strategies.

What Is Cognitive Development?

The field of cognitive development of young children examines how children develop their thinking abilities. Although we are only at the beginning of understanding how this takes place, we do know that young children create their own knowledge (Beaty, 1994). Using their senses and mental tools, children interact with their environment to make meaning of it. By interacting with their environment, children create mental images, collect information about a variety of objects, and make associations and relationships based on the information they acquire.

In general, all children need a multitude of multisensory, hands-on experiences. Environments that foster children's cognitive growth provide opportunities for: rich language stimulation, exploration of learning materials, appropriate tasks that fit their levels, positive modeling by teachers, and a structure sufficient to ensure safety and security. Such quality environments encourage the development of thinking skills.

Time that is spent on active looking and listening furthers the child's capacity to consider the viewpoints of others. During a group cooking activity, for example, the teacher draws everyone's attention to the process at hand. Everyone observes the forces of change on ingredients, the effects of the mixing of solutions, and the impact of temperature change. Anyone can offer ideas in this neutral setting. Ideas are considered for their own merit. Thinking becomes part of the fun of being together in this activity. Time spent on thinking together becomes the outcome of the activity, not merely the baking of bread.

Attention, Perception, and Memory

Three basic processes related to information processing are important to the development of cognition: attention, perception, and memory (Cook, Tessier, and Klein, 1996).

Attention is basic to many cognitive tasks. Attention in the form of concentration requires that the child learn to master two contradictory skills: (1) the ability to focus on the aspects of the environment that are relevant and have the greatest value to the task at hand and (2) the ability to ignore a multitude of irrelevant stimuli. The development of selective attention begins at birth and continues to be refined throughout the early childhood years. The child who attempts to attend to too many irrelevant stimuli is distracted (Cook, Tessier, and Klein, 1996). Attention disorders may be spotted by teachers when they notice children displaying the following behavioral characteristics: impulsivity, distractibility, and/or over-activity.

Perception is the process of interpreting what is received by the five senses. Perceptual abilities are dependent on the sensory systems of touch, taste, proprioception (the reception of stimuli), smell, hearing, and vision. The perceptual system usually develops in utero and enables a newborn to begin processing information at birth. Information must be stored in the nervous system for perception to occur.

Individuals differ in the way they perceive information. Some individuals will gain more information through the visual modality, while others may gain more information through the auditory system. While many teachers tend to teach predominantly by talking—and expecting verbal responses from children—young children are best served when they get a combination of cues: physical, visual, and verbal. The key is for teachers to match their teaching methods to the developmental needs of the children in their class. Children who have difficulty acquiring accurate information from their environment need teachers who are flexible with their teaching methods.

Memory is the process by which information that is received through attention and perception is stored in the central nervous system (Cook, Tessier, and Klein, 1996). Memory can be broken into three component parts:
1. *Incoming sensation* is perceived briefly (about one second).
2. If attended to, it will be placed in *short-term memory,* which can store information for ten to fifteen seconds.
3. Depending on a number of factors, some information will be placed in *long-term memory,* where it can be stored indefinitely.

Young children need repeated experiences of the same event before it can be stored in long-term memory. As children grow in their experiential background, information goes into their short-term memory and is stored in long-term memory.

The ability to learn is highly associated with memory. The most common kinds of memory include: long-term, short-term, sequential, auditory, visual, rote, recognition, and recall (Cook, Terrier, and Klein, 1996).

Attention, perception, and memory are interdependent processes. If a child cannot attend, he will be unable to perceive the information and store it in his long-term memory. This same child will have difficulty making interpretations and forming relationships among ideas if he does not have it stored in memory.

Facilitating Cognitive Development in the Classroom

Concept development is fundamental to the development of academic skills. In the early years, children formulate the basic skills that precede concept development—those of classification and seriation. Classroom expectations move from the concrete to the abstract, from the simple to the complex, and from the here and now to the remote in time and space (Hohmann, Banet, and Weikart, 1979).

Classification: Analyzing Pertinent Features

Teachers help children gain experience with classification in many constructive, hands-on ways. To classify, a child has to note similarities and differences among objects. Classification involves two simultaneous processes: sorting (separating objects) and grouping (joining objects) (Essa, 1992).

Sorting activities should be considered along a continuum. Children's initial experience with classification and sorting might include one relevant feature: *"Let's put all the beads in the bucket."* As children's sorting skills develop, teachers give them more opportunities to think up their own features to recognize and group. Multiple criteria, varying conditions, and multiple uses of certain materials provide challenges to children as they learn to classify sets of materials.

Encouraging children to establish their own criteria for the classification of materials presents teachers with a "window of opportunity." Simply doing the activity is not enough; the teacher should clarify what the children have intuitively perceived by asking questions—for example, *"Why are cows, cows and horses, horses?"* What are the children's frames of reference? How do they perceive the relevant features? What organization do they bring to the task? The teacher will observe a child's behavior during classification tasks to better understand the child's perceptual base.

When children attend to relevant features, they begin to discover "rules" or the use of a constant feature to guide their sorting. The understanding of "rules" is the basis of concept formation. A young child who has functional awareness of rules is attending to an abstract notion long before the time when all academic learning will be based on such conditions.

Young children sort and group items naturally, and the learning environment should provide a rich variety of objects and experiences that can be used for such activities (Essa, 1992). The following list includes features to consider when designing classification activities:

- attributes—visual and tactile features, such as shape, color, size, and texture
- function—what something is used for
- composition—what something is made of
- source—where something is from
- intangibles—any number of divergent features particular to the child's experience.

Seriation: Ordering Based on a Rule

Seriation, or the ordering of materials, events, or ideas based on a rule, is the second major feature of concept development in the early childhood years. Children need time and multiple experiences to absorb this concept. Seriation is fundamental to language development, organizational skills, social skills, analysis of cause and effect, and all concept development. Teachers should provide and support multiple multisensory conditions in which children can discover and learn to rely on the "rules" of seriation. Spoons, cups, nuts, and bolts are examples of items that children can order in the classroom.

Ways Teachers Can Help Children Develop Attention

Frustration on the part of the child and the adult can be avoided when the adult helps the child to develop a longer attention span. Teachers can help to sustain children's involvement by selecting materials and equipment that match the children's developing capabilities. Puzzles have concrete beginnings and endings, but their difficulty level may be conducive to limited involvement. A child's inattentiveness to a particular puzzle may have more to do with the difficulty of the puzzle than with any difficulties the child has in maintaining focused attention.

To help children develop attention, teachers can do the following:
- Set up environments that do not create too much irrelevant stimuli.
- Offer tasks that match the child's abilities.
- Break tasks into manageable steps.
- Provide clear directions.
- Use vocabulary at an appropriate level.
- Support task work with a balanced sensory environment that pays attention to auditory, visual, and tactile stimuli.

When teachers provide routines and structure that are familiar to children and support their developmental capacities, they help children have productive contact with learning materials. Learning tasks should be visually concrete and redundant (to emphasize a point); they should also have clear beginnings and endings and should be functionally realistic in terms of the personal life of the child.

Perceptual and memory skills provide lasting meaning to the perceiver. One child may perceive more accurately through the visual channel, while another may gather information more efficiently through the auditory channel. Perceptions differ based on what is stored and on the strength of the perceptual modality. Perceptual modalities can develop unevenly, and so teachers need to match teaching input to developmental needs. Matching input to maximize output will contribute greatly to the progress of children with perceptual differences.

By structuring the environment to match the learning characteristics of children, teachers optimize learning opportunities. They can provide the following forms of structure:

- a routine location that may reduce distraction and assist task orientation
- concrete materials that support the concept being studied
- lots of tactile and visual information with limited spoken interpretation
- frequent breaks between motor activities, or the use of activities that require frequent motor responses from the child
- isolation of the concept being taught
- breaking the task into specific steps so that the child has created a visual product upon completing each step.

Teachers can also arrange materials to support the child's learning by:

- limiting materials to only those needed to complete the task
- setting out materials needed initially and allowing the child to start an activity without having to wait and possibly lose interest
- making sure the child can see and reach all materials
- putting materials in containers to avoid distracting spills
- providing visual cues, such as picture cards, picture checklists, and matching cards to help the child develop the means to organize.

Ways to Nurture Problem-Solving Skills

Solving problems creates within the child new structures or mental pathways. These mental relationships are unique for each child. With thoughtful planning, teachers set the stage for problem-solving to occur in the classroom and allow young children to experiment and evaluate what they are doing.

Certain conditions are necessary for problem-solving to occur:

Freedom from fear of failure. This is the most essential condition for learning new things. The freedom to take risks and having the courage to take risks are separate features of this condition and may need to be evaluated in a child to understand that child's disposition toward learning.

Opportunities to experience cause and effect through inquiry and experimentation. Listen to children's questions and watch their behavior to determine their level of inquiry. Act on what you observe, providing safe conditions and plenty of materials with which to experiment.

Encouragement and reinforcement. Cognitive learning is disrupted if children fear punishment or if multiple opportunities of learning are overlooked. Prompting and supporting curiosity and experimentation can produce problem-solving.

There are specific steps in the problem-solving process that are universally endorsed:

- recognition of the problem—saying, *"We have a problem. What shall we do?"*
- analysis of contributing factors—bringing the pertinent variables to the child's attention
- thinking of possible solutions—brainstorming and providing creative thinking time and opportunities for divergent thinking
- choice of optimal solutions—discussing optimal solutions (this process mixes language, vocabulary, and cognitive skills)
- evaluation of feedback to determine results—reviewing whether the goal has been met or whether it is necessary to go back to the drawing board.

Problem-solving supports the development of flexibility and independence. Rewarding problem-solving behavior causes it to flourish. There are, however, certain adult behaviors that can negatively affect the development of problem-solving skills. These include:

- having critical attitudes and finding fault—for example, by laughing at children's suggestions, reacting negatively to them, or not allowing them to be considered
- not allowing the problem-solving process to flow into the interpersonal realm so that alternative solutions, not necessarily the teacher's, can evolve
- forcing the "democratic process" or adult constraints on children's creative process— for example, by insisting that everyone has a turn, forcing premature closure, or imposing "right" answers.

Specific Skill Mediation
Just as teachers choose the appropriate skill level for a child's participation, they must also determine the appropriate level of teacher intervention or mediation to facilitate that participation. Teachers play a pivotal role in supporting children's involvement in activities. They plan activities for the general group and then guide each individual to reach his or her maximum potential within the overall curriculum.

Methods of mediating learning experiences include the following:
- Modeling—offering a demonstration.
- Individualizing—matching the task to the child.

- Using specific feedback—*"Anna, you used both hands."*
- Providing self-correcting materials—a completed puzzle.
- Using nonverbal and verbal cueing—personalized messages or signs.
- Expectations—the food is passed when a request is made.
- Humor—providing occasional surprises.
- Asking questions—*"Would you like to show me?"*
- Redirecting—boundless energy can be directed toward pounding the play dough.
- Manual guidance—holding a hand or steadying a balancing body.
- Contingency scheduling—less desirable activities are followed by more desirable ones (e.g., clean-up is followed by snack).

Additional specific mediation techniques include the following:

- *Equivalent practice*—used to prevent the boredom that can arise from repeatedly doing the same activity. The teacher provides equivalent practice by offering a variety of materials and activities that are designed to develop the same skill. To be equivalent, the task must be at the same level of difficulty and provide the same practice.

- *Expansion*—when adults expand a child's statement by rephrasing the child's idea in longer phrases or sentences—for example, Ali says, *"Ball."* Vlad says, *"Yes, you have a purple ball."*

- *Fading*—the gradual step-by-step removal of prompts. Physical prompts can be removed first, then physical gestures and cues, and finally spoken cues.

- *Parallel talk*—when an adult talks about what a child is doing as it is happening; parallel talk helps children to select and produce appropriate words for a specific activity and setting.

- *Prompting*—using cues and partial cues to build desired behavior. *Verbal prompting* often involves saying a single sound or word to help a child remember what to do or say. *Physical prompting* (physical assistance or touch) can be used to initiate a motor or self-help skill. Prompts should be reduced gradually until they can be eliminated.

- *Rapport*—when an adult establishes a harmonious relationship with children and develops a climate or atmosphere in which children feel comfortable to perform as well as they possibly can.

- *Reinforcer*—an event or a consequence that increases the likelihood of a behavior being repeated. May be concrete or social: a sticker, an extra turn at a favorite activity, or a visit to the bunny pen.

- *Reverse chaining*—when an adult begins teaching the last step of a task and works backwards. Particularly useful with self-help skills.

- *Shaping*—a technique of behavior modification in which behaviors that are successive approximations of the target behavior are reinforced until target behavior is acquired.

- *Successive approximation*—the process of gradually increasing expectations for a child to display behaviors that are more like the desired target behavior; used for shaping behaviors not previously part of a child's behavior pattern.

- *Task analysis*—when the teacher breaks down a difficult task into smaller steps that lead to accomplishing the difficult task.

Cognitive Development and Children with Disabilities

It is difficult and in some cases impossible to identify young children as having cognitive delays or disorders since they have not had the benefit of formal schooling. Some children, however, display significant cognitive delays and impairments across a wide range of disabling conditions. Listed below is a brief explanation of some of the disabilities:

Cognitive Disabilities: Early in life, children with cognitive disabilities display difficulty with the cognitive skills discussed earlier in this chapter. These cognitive deficits can be caused by many factors, including genetic disorders (e.g., Down syndrome); prenatal insult to the fetus from toxic substances (e.g., alcohol) or viral infections (e.g., rubella); perinatal complications (e.g., anoxia); and postnatal influences such as head injury, asphyxia (e.g., near-drowning), and poisoning (e.g., lead poisoning) (Cook, Tessier, and Klein, 1996). Although these factors do not always cause profound cognitive disorders, sometimes the result is significant. A child who is mentally retarded usually demonstrates cognitive deficits in the areas of attention and memory, which affects his or her performance as compared with that of normally developing peers.

Visual Impairments: Children who are visually impaired from birth may develop complex cognitive skills if they are taught to make maximal use of action learning (Piaget and Inhelder, 1969; Rapin, 1979). Since children with visual impairments do not acquire the same perceptions from their environments as sighted children, cognitive delays can occur. This is because the child is unable to use vision to integrate auditory and tactile cues to maintain contact with his or her environment (Fallen and Umansky, 1985). When children with visual impairments are given careful attention and guided opportunities to use other senses to explore the environment, their impairments need not limit the development of abstract thinking processes.

Hearing Impairments: Children with hearing impairments are more often identified as having language delays and disorders rather than cognitive impairments. In fact, there is research that indicates that children with hearing impairments can follow a normal course of cognitive development. What is critical is that these children have experiences that help them build another symbolic system in the absence of a linguistic symbol system.

Physical Impairments: A child who is unable to move and manipulate her surroundings is greatly hindered in recognizing her influence on her environment. Children with central nervous system damage, as in cerebral palsy and spina bifida, and children with chronic illnesses and orthopedic problems may perceive their universe in a different way than normal children because of the limitations or uniqueness in how they interact with their surroundings (Fallen and Umansky, 1985). Though it is estimated that over half of these children demonstrate a cognitive deficit of varying degrees, sometimes they may be identified incorrectly due to severe language problems. Depending on the severity of the physical limitation, they may display difficulty with tasks requiring visual, auditory, and perceptual skills. Because reading and writing development is dependent on visual-perceptual skills, these tasks may be difficult for children to acquire.

Autism: Children with autism pose an interesting puzzle of perceptual and conceptual skill development. They have difficulty controlling sensory input and, as a consequence, may show hyperresponsiveness or hyporesponsiveness to stimuli (Fallen and Umansky, 1985). Though these children appear to receive information through their senses, they demonstrate less ability to visually and auditorily attend. One of the problems seen is the way they treat different objects in stereotypical ways.

Instructional Activities that Promote the Development of Cognitive Skills

Initial activities to support cognitive development should relate to fostering self-esteem and confidence in children. How children feel about themselves and their abilities is directly related to the level of risk that they are willing to take in approaching activities. Children who feel worthwhile, accepted, and confident in their abilities will participate more readily, more fully, and with more willingness to challenge themselves and make mistakes. Teachers should use open-ended questions to guide children through the cognitive process.

Promoting Motivation and Problem-Solving

Offer ways to observe and explore.

- Allow time for observation and exploration of materials. Use questioning if the child needs support to feel comfortable to explore. *"What do you think will happen when you pull the yellow lever on the dump truck? Why? "* Let the child respond. *"Now you try it and see what happens."* Regardless of whether the child's answer was correct or not, the child is going through a cognitive process.
- Limit the materials to make choices easier and to extend the exploration for a fuller understanding of the materials or concepts. Change the choices to allow new discoveries. Add more materials as children ask for them or as you feel they are ready to intensify the challenge.

- Make a list with the child of all the ways to play with a new material or toy. Create a challenge to make the list as long as possible. Keep the questioning open-ended so the ideas are limitless.
- Guide the children in using activity centers and classroom materials. Take children in small groups or individually to each center and manipulative activity and generate rules and explore possibilities for center and materials use. Provide the children with a period of active exploration in a center or with a particular manipulative. Bring them back together and ask them what they did. This process promotes a child's ability to make good choices and contributes to a safer learning environment.

Promote curiosity and the desire to solve problems.
- Include activities to foster self-esteem and self-confidence so children will be ready to attempt and participate in tasks.
- Use simple activities in which cause and effect are immediate and easy to see. The activities should allow the children to manipulate the materials. Using eye droppers to mix colored water, ask:
    "What happens when you mix the red and the blue water?"
    "What happens when you mix red with another color?"
    "What will happen to the sand when you pour a bucket of water into it?"
- Use some of the same materials in different activity centers so children can experience materials in different settings with different expectations.
- Give a child a specific material (like play dough) and ask the child to change that material in some way. Play dough can be squeezed, pulled, cut, rolled, etc. *"How did you change the play dough? What did you do to it? What happened to it?"* Verbalize the process for them. *"When you squeezed the play dough, you made prints in it and changed the shape."*
- Identify a space in the room where children can leave an activity (puzzles, artwork, Lego creations) for safe-keeping and return to it later. Allow time during the day (or week) for children to return to past activities. For example, if a child makes a boat out of Legos one day, he or she may decide to look at a book about boats or make a boat at home with an older sibling. In a few days that child may return to the boat and change it into a cargo ship, an indication of growth in thinking and ability.
- Give new information, challenges, or materials to enhance a past activity.
- Make sure problem-solving activities are appropriate for each child. If an activity seems too frustrating (too challenging), find an activity at an easier level and let the child work up to the more challenging activity.
- Create a partnership in solving problems. *"You put in one piece of the puzzle and then I will put in a piece."* Have children act as partners for each other.
- Remember to ask children, *"How did you come up with that conclusion?" "Did anybody solve the problem differently?"*
- Act out a story or situation, such as setting out dishes for lunch.
- Have children use only designated blocks to build a bridge. *"Make the tallest tower you can with only these small blocks." "Now with only large blocks."*
- Have teachers model a problem, such as when two children want to play with the same toy.

- Use concrete objects, drawings, or other visuals to clarify problems or solutions.
- Create verbal story problems that are of interest to the children and within their experience—for example, *"If I had three apples and gave one to you, how many apples would I have left?"*

Foster constructive thinking.

- Motivate children to use their own experiences in their work in activity centers. Create a doctor's office in dramatic play. Make a post office with math manipulatives.
- Give a child manipulatives of different sizes and some play people to create a family. Label or identify the pieces for the child, if necessary. *"Here is the dad, the mom, and their children—a boy and a girl."* *"Look at the animals. Do you think they are the same in any way?"* Talking children through a cognitive process gives them practice with their thinking skills.
- Make sure questions are asked in an open-ended manner to foster divergent thinking. When a child finds a solution to a problem, encourage the child to go back and find a different way to solve it. Show the child that finding a solution is not the end of an activity.

Help children to make predictions and plans.

- As children choose centers to work in, visit each center and have the children express their plans for their work. Remember to revisit the centers to be able to see what really happened.
- Talk about the "next time" a child works in a center or participates in an activity.
- Express your predictions and plans for experiences in the classroom.
- When a child is expressing ideas for work, ask what he or she might need. *"You told me you want to make a crown; what will you need to make it?"* Paper and decorations. *"And how will you attach the ends?"* Oh—I will need tape.
- Use the questioning process to help children plan and predict outcomes of their work—for example: *"What would happen if we used shorter string to attach the pieces of our mobiles?"*
- Have children guess about what they will learn in the experiment and then check on whether the guesses were correct.

Promoting Logical and Mathematical Thinking

Have children classify according to attributes.

- Sorting activities help children recognize likenesses and differences between objects, describe an object's attributes, and make comparisons. Collect a wide variety of objects to sort, such as buttons, nuts, corks, rocks, leaves, keys, and blocks.
- In a small group, ask a child to think of a sorting rule for the buttons. According to that rule, have the rest of the children sort the buttons. Repeat the activity asking the other children to choose a different sorting rule.
- Have children work in pairs or small groups to sort containers. First, have them investigate the containers. Then discuss how they could be sorted, decide on one rule, and sort!

- A more challenging task is to put unlike materials together for children to classify by color, size, etc.—blocks, crayons, cars, Legos.
- Use the opposite strategy of the one above. Put groups of like items together—all reds, all large—and have the child reclassify according to functional group. As a group of items is put together, talk about their function (e.g., red cars are transportation vehicles and circles are shapes).

Have children arrange things in a series.
- Order objects according to weight, size, color, etc. Keep the collections or items small at first.
- Arrange Cuisinnaire rods incorrectly and have the child find the mistake and place the rods in the correct order. Then ask the child to provide a rule.
- Verbalize and demonstrate the process. *"I am looking for the shortest rod."* Hold two rods next to each other. *"This one is the shortest because it is smaller. The other one is taller."*
- Leave a space in a set of arranged items. The child chooses the appropriate item to add to the arrangement when offered a choice of two items.
- After a child has arranged items in the correct order, give the child one more thing to add to the series.

Have children reproduce patterns in different ways.
- Have children create patterns with you. Use objects, actions, and words—for example, clap knees, hands, knees, hands (or) red block, blue, red, blue (or) say hot, hot, cold, hot, hot, cold.
- Create a pattern (ABA or ABBA, etc.) and have the child copy it. Then have the child look at the pattern and keep the pattern going.
- Provide opportunities to use manipulatives or art supplies (bottle caps, keys, buttons, stones, corks, small sticks, etc.), so that children can create their own patterns.
- Have children create patterns with color blocks (like unifix cubes). Then give them colored paper squares and have them copy the pattern by gluing the squares onto a strip of paper.
- Use colored macaroni to create pattern jewelry.
- Make a pattern book.
- Encourage children to talk about the pattern they see. Talking about patterns will get children used to analyzing them.

Have children reconstruct and recall a sequence of events.
- Use pictorial clues to help children remember the sequence of an event or a day.
- Draw or write (or have children do it) the steps of an event on separate pieces of paper so they can be arranged or rearranged.
- Sing songs that use sequences of events ("Going on a Bear Hunt," "She'll Be Coming Round the Mountain," etc.), so that children will learn to rely on their memories.
- To tell a creative story from a set of pictures, a child may need to begin with only two pictures. *The boy woke up on a sunny morning. Then he got dressed so he could play out-*

side. Then you can add pictures one at a time.

- Use pictures from a familiar story and ask the child to put them in the order of the story.
- Ask the children to draw pictures of three things they do in the morning on separate pieces of paper. Have them paste the pictures in order on a larger piece of paper.
- Design an easy cooking activity and discuss the sequence of steps. Draw a picture of each step on a card to assist the child in recalling the sequence.
- Take three photos of a child performing a task—for example, a child setting up a table for lunch, a child eating lunch, and a child cleaning the table after lunch. Have the child sequence the photos in order from left to right.

Help children understand quantitative relationships.
- Use practice and repetition to reinforce the understanding of quantitative relationships. Supply a variety of materials for children to count. Count aloud every day and have the children do the same. Count the number of children in each center, the number of children at a snack table, the number of napkins or cups needed for snack, the number of pieces of a toy, etc.
- Move a child's finger from one object to another as he or she counts one number at a time.
- Have children pass out five napkins for snack to the five people at their table. As they hand out each napkin, they say one number.
- Play games ("Duck, Duck, Goose") where the child says one word for each person.
- Have the child use motions to show comparative words. *"Can you make your body small? Bigger? Biggest?"*
- Have a number line on the wall accessible to students and use it.
- Make counting errors and see if the child responds.
- Line up ten students, each in front of a chair. Together count four children at the end of the row and have them sit down. *"How many children are sitting? Let's count and find out how many in all."* Repeat this activity using other numbers.

Help children to show awareness of and use geometric shapes correctly.
- Use practice and repetition to reinforce the children's understanding of shapes. Identify and use shapes in all daily activities. Find objects in the classroom that can be identified as certain shapes.
- Have lots of circles cut out that are different sizes and have the child create a picture using only circles.
- Have shape templates available for children to trace shapes to use in their work.
- Create shapes in the block area. Children use the blocks to create squares, rectangles, and triangles.
- Outline various shapes of blocks with masking tape on the floor and have the children place blocks on the tape.
- Take a walk inside or outside the school and look for circles, squares, and triangles.
- Use clay, dough, finger painting, scissor-cutting, and tracing templates to emphasize shapes.

- Explore shapes with a geoboard and rubber bands.

Help children to understand basic spatial relationships.
- Have the child act out position words and verbalize the actions. *"Put your hands on top of your head. Put your hands behind your back. Sit next to Carolyn."*
- Make dog puppets and a doghouse. *"Put your dog in the doghouse. Put your dog under the doghouse. Put your dog anywhere. Where is your dog?"*

Develop awareness of time concepts.
- Have the daily schedule posted in the classroom in pictures and words so that children know what events will happen that day (such as music or a visitor).
- Make reviewing the class schedule a part of daily group activities.
- When incorporating the calendar each day in group activities, review what day yesterday was, what today is, and what tomorrow will be. Discuss what activities happened yesterday and what will happen tomorrow.
- Talk about the activities that take place during the different times of the day or night. The children can draw pictures of what they do at these different times. Cut a half-circle in yellow on which the child can draw a daytime activity and a half-circle in blue to draw a nighttime picture. Put the two pieces together and write the child's ideas on each picture.
- Have the children line up according to your instructions. *"Pam will line up first. Jenny will be next. Kate will line up after Jenny. Cassie will be last."*

Developing Knowledge and Information
Help children to acquire general knowledge.
- Practice and repeat the knowledge that children have gained.
- Practice naming colors and objects and expressing ideas.
- Repeat vocabulary words that name objects.
- As a child tries to tell information, he or she needs to repeat it more than once to say it correctly or to convey meaning—for example, *"An apple grows from leaves. Leaves grow apples after they fall off. Apples grow on the same part of the tree where the leaves grew."*
- Relate colors to what the child is wearing to school that day.
- Designate each day of the week a special color so Monday is RED DAY and Tuesday is ORANGE DAY, etc. Create activities at each center to focus on that one color.
- Use different objects in the room as props for storytelling or role playing.
- Arrange to visit different places in the community—grocery store, library, post office, bank, restaurant, etc. Or, have someone from each place visit the classroom and talk about his or her role in the community.
- Again, have visitors come to the classroom and talk about their careers. This is a great opportunity to have parents and other family members participate in the classroom.
- Change the dramatic play center or other activity centers in the classroom to simulate careers that interest children.
- Set up a store in the dramatic play center. One student can act as the customer while

the other is the store clerk. The customer can only purchase items by naming them. The store clerk can collect the items and then name them as he or she gives the customer the order.

- Take pictures of a child's house, school, family, etc. to stimulate conversation.

Help children to seek information from various sources.
- Provide a variety of books (both fiction and nonfiction, picture books and text books) that can give children information.
- When you need information, verbalize the actions and processes that you go through to find what you need. *"What is the problem? What is my plan to solve it? Am I using my plan?"*
- Make lists of what children know about a topic and lists of what they would like to know about a topic. Show them the different ways that this information could be found (by using picture books, by asking people, by exploring nature, etc.).
- Use the questioning process. Try not to give information to a child. Instead, help the child to ask specific questions; lead the child in the right direction.
- Ask the child to brainstorm with a person or persons who could help find an answer.

CHAPTER
TEN

HELPING CHILDREN DEVELOP PHYSICAL SKILLS

10. HELPING CHILDREN DEVELOP PHYSICAL SKILLS

Chapter Overview
- Physical Development in the Young Child
- Facilitating Physical Development in the Classroom
- Physical Development and Children with Physical Disabilities
- Instructional Activities that Promote Physical Growth and Development

Physical Development in the Young Child

Movement is the way young children learn about their bodies. Crawling, skipping, running, throwing, and grasping are activities that require balance and coordination. Discoveries regarding their bodies in space happen naturally when children's motor skills develop along a normal developmental sequence.

For many children with motor problems or delays, movement experiences are often limited. Additional instruction, therapeutic intervention such as physical therapy or occupational therapy, and encouragement are essential to minimize the disability and maximize children's potential in all aspects of development (Cook, Tessier, and Klein, 1996).

What Is Physical Development?

When we think of physical development in young children, we usually think of two general areas of motor development: gross or large motor skills, and fine or small motor skills.

Gross motor development involves movements of a child's arms, legs, body trunk, and neck. Nonlocomotor (or stability), manipulative (reaching, grasping, and releasing), and locomotor skills (creeping, crawling, and eventually walking) are specific areas of gross motor development that occur soon after birth.

Small motor development for manual control involves a child's hands and fingers. Fine motor skills such as copying, stringing beads, and pasting require the eyes to direct the hands (Beaty, 1994). To perform these activities, a child must develop his or her perceptual-motor, visual-motor, sensorimotor, ocular-motor, or eye-hand coordination.

Environmental factors such as amount of sleep and exercise, quality of medical care, and adequacy of nutrition may influence the rate and ultimate degree of physical and, thus, motor development (Cook, Tessier, and Klein, 1996). However, the combination of both environmental and genetic factors appears to determine a child's potential for motor skill development.

Facilitating Physical Development in the Classroom

The development of sensory awareness, a sense of balance, and control of large and small muscles is each a fundamental milestone during the early years. Often, children with disabilities require specialized support to master those milestones. Teachers in inclusive programs will want to present all children with sensory-rich learning experiences and activities that support overall physical development and integrated motor skill.

Supporting the Development of Sensory Integration

Young children are exposed to sights, sounds, textures, smells, and tastes every day. As they grow and mature, they become competent sensory processors. They develop discriminating tastes, preferences for smells and textures, and expansive vocabularies for describing the sights and sounds of their worlds.

Some young children with disabilities may have specific impairments that limit their ability to process sensory input. Other children may develop patterns of behavior that limit the amount of sensory input that they will tolerate. These conditions have tremendous implications for learning. Teachers will want to help some children become more aware of sensory input and help other children to tolerate and integrate sensory perceptions so that the children can increase their ability to learn from their environment.

When planning activities and accommodations for young children, the teacher should keep in mind two additional sensory systems that the human brain uses to process sensory information. *Vestibular receptors* help the brain process sensory information about body movement and head position. *Kinesthetic receptors* help the young child to be aware of muscle movements and adjustments that will become increasingly automatic as the child grows and develops.

Activities that provide a sensory-rich diet for young children include the following:
- Whole-body activities that encourage swinging, hanging upside-down, and spinning. Let children accept movement experiences that are comfortable for them. Never pressure a child into accepting a movement experience. If a child avoids whole-body activities, suggest that he or she participate on a limited level, such as for one minute, or with a helping hand.
- Carrying heavy toys, such as hollow blocks or weighted balls, which provide sensory input to tendons, muscles, and joints.
- Tactilely stimulating toys and activities, such as sand play, clay, finger paint, waterplay, mud play, crayon rubbings, and a wide variety of art activities.
- Cooking activities, which provide multiple sensory experiences: smelling, tasting, and manipulating the cooking tools.
- "Feely boxes," which isolate and accentuate tactile perceptions and encourage children to develop the vocabulary necessary for labeling touch sensations. Boxes may contain feathers, brushes, fabrics of different textures, sandpaper, and other items that provide touch stimulation.

Snack and mealtimes are particularly good times to encourage sensory exploration. Children can identify their favorite foods and learn to describe the taste sensations they like and dislike.

Helping Children Balance and Coordinate Large Muscle Movements

A young child must first develop strength and stability in the neck, trunk, arms, and legs to become accomplished at many of the fine motor skills necessary for independent life and success in school. Young children need to be able to exercise for many years in safe environments that are free from obstacles and full of encouragement. Ease and balance in coordinated big muscle movements develop gradually during toddlerhood and the preschool years.

Differences in motor development may originate early in prenatal development. Neuromuscular dysfunction originating in the central nervous system, specifically in cerebral palsy, is the most common physically disabling condition among young children. Cerebral palsy is a continuum of motor dysfunction due to insult to the brain, ranging from mild clumsiness to an impairment so severe that coordinated movement is impossible.

Teachers need to be cautioned against having low expectations for children with central nervous system dysfunction. Such dysfunction is not an accurate predictor of cognitive potential and academic performance, and many individuals with appropriate support for their physical needs excel in school.

Deviations in muscle development that may require consideration in individual planning include the following:
- *Muscle tone*—the degree of tension present in a muscle at rest. "Hypotonicity" refers to low muscle tension or "floppy" muscles. Children with hypotonicity may be less active and may become more easily fatigued by normal physical activities than their typically developing peers. "Hypertonicity" refers to an excess of muscle tension (muscles becoming tight and rigid) that results in muscles working against each other. Fluctuating muscle tone may also occur in individuals. For example, when a child is resting, he or she may experience low tone, but an attempt at voluntary movement may set off heightened muscle tone, resulting in an uncoordinated movement pattern.
- *Muscle control*—muscle tremors that interfere with voluntary movements. Fine motor activities will be more difficult to carry out when muscle control problems exist. Posture and involuntary facial movements may also be adversely affected by compromised muscle control.
- *Muscle strength*—may be permanently affected due to degenerative muscle disease, paralysis of muscles related to spinal cord damage, or contagious diseases, such as polio.

Team assessment is highly important in order to develop appropriate goals and objectives for children with motor delays or dysfunction. Specialists who can assist in the assessment of motor abilities include pediatricians, physical therapists, occupational therapists, and orthopedists. From assessment information, the team can develop an appropriate program for an individual.

Therapeutic intervention to support motor functioning may include: stimulation of normal developmental growth sequences, creating of an environment that is conducive to motor skill development, and rehabilitative techniques designed to prevent or minimize the possible effects of motor inactivity. Inactivity over prolonged periods of time can cause serious damage to the growing child's muscles and bones.

Specialists will develop specific approaches to each individual's treatment. Often, parents and teachers can implement some therapy techniques at home and school, following demonstration by a specialist. When parents and teachers understand the rationale for therapeutic procedures, they can promote the child's motor objectives and support the child's daily program.

Adaptive equipment for children with motor difficulties is designed to maximize an individual's ability to function independently.

- A prosthetic is an artificial device designed to function as a limb.
- Braces, or orthopedic devices, are aids for mobility and stability, such as ankle and wrist molds, leg and arm braces, and molds placed inside shoes.
- Mobility devices are walkers, wheelchairs, or positioning aids.
- Technological aids, such as telephone text writers, calculators, and message boards, support an individual's ability to perform functional, educational, or vocational tasks.

All these devices enhance the development of independence. The choice of adaptive equipment for a child should be done in consultation with a specialist and the child's parents. Adaptive equipment may be available to a child through the family's medical insurance or through a rehabilitative community service organization. School programs may purchase adaptive equipment, especially technology-related devices, or a specialist or other skillful person may make equipment for a child. Teachers in inclusive classrooms will want to become familiar with the use of adaptive equipment in order to support a child's ability to interact more effectively in the class.

Promoting Coordinated Use of the Eyes and Hands

Fine motor skills involve smaller muscle systems, primarily those of the eyes and hands. Manual control involves finger and hand strength, flexibility, and dexterity. Coordination of the hands and eyes relies on visual-perceptual skill. While hand dominance, or the establishment of hand preference for fine motor tasks, is not often achieved until age six, teachers of young children will want to support the development of hand skills during the preschool years.

Adapted materials for fine motor tasks are an important consideration in program planning. Velcro straps, strips, and bands can be fashioned to increase a child's ability to hold a crayon, paintbrush, or large knob attached to a puzzle piece. Electrical switches, sometimes called touch pads, attached to mechanical toys allow a child to participate in directing the actions of toys. These devices may also be used for learning activities. Linking fine motor exercises to daily activities encourages independence and functionality.

Physical Development and Children with Disabilities

Children with special needs display a wide range of motor skills and abilities. Some children demonstrate normal motor development, while others show extremes in motor variability, depending on the disability and the individual child. Listed below are some descriptions of common attributes found in children with disabilities.

Cerebral Palsy: There is much variability in the disorders of cerebral palsy. One child can have minimal muscular disorder, while another child can lack all muscle control. Cerebral palsy can involve one limb, both legs, or diplegia (primary involvement in both legs, and slight affliction in the arms), hemiplegia (arm and leg on same side are afflicted), triphegia (three limbs affected), and quadriplegia (involvement of all four limbs) (Fallen and Umansky, 1985). Though cerebral palsy is not progressive, it can affect children's physical growth in later years. Children with cerebral palsy may also be affected by mental retardation and visual and hearing impairments.

Mental Retardation: In general, children with mental retardation are less capable of performing precise motor tasks than normally developing peers. In many cases, children with mental retardation can become better able to carry out motor tasks as they get older. Though delayed maturation may be the cause of impaired motor movements, lack of opportunities to engage in exercise and other movements may hinder their development.

Learning Disabilities: Children with learning disabilities often have deficits in their motor skills. Some characteristics that are frequently observed in these children are: lack of coordination, awkward gross and fine motor skills (e.g., using scissors, catching a ball), and lack of awareness of their body in space. These deficits may be caused by an impairment in motor mechanisms and/or a perceptual-motor problem. These problems are compounded when the child has not had proper experiences to develop his or her motor skills.

Visual Impairments: In many cases, children with visual impairments do not develop an accurate body image, which may be due in part to their lack of environmental exploration and restricted movement. Research tells us that the motor performance of blind children is inferior to partially sighted children and the performance of partially sighted children inferior to normally developing children (Fallen and Umansky, 1985).

Emotional Disabilities: Children with emotional disabilities may display motor problems. A child who is withdrawn or aggressive may not have had enough practice and experience to reinforce his or her developing motor skills.

Instructional Activities that Promote Physical Growth and Development

The physical development of young children has an impact on other areas of development. Without physical strength to support the body properly, a child may be unable to participate appropriately in activities that require sitting in a chair or even sitting on the floor. Without physical strength in the hands and fingers, a child may be unable to use manipulatives easily or to participate in art activities. Physical development allows children to be ready for academic skills that are beginning to evolve. The physical development of young children requires time to build strength and coordination and is enhanced through repetition of activities.

Promoting Gross Motor Skills

Help build physical strength.

- Use lighter objects to carry, lift, or throw, and gradually increase the weight and difficulty.
- Use music for dancing and creative movement to help develop children's flexibility. Stretching techniques can help children use the full range of motion in their arms. This action is necessary for throwing a ball.
- Always allow a "safety net" (it could be your hand to hold onto) when children are balancing and a soft place for them to tumble onto.
- Plan a nature walk on uneven terrain. Children will need a range of motor skills to negotiate the terrain.
- Have children toss a ring or bean bag into a box.
- Turn on music and give children the freedom to choose to hop or jump in place or to hop or jump forward.
- Children may practice jumping over a variety of items such as a block, box, stick, book, or rope.

Promote moving with coordination and balance.

- Start with simple skills that lead progressively to more complex skills. Rolling a ball to a destination may be the final goal, but begin with rolling a ball on the ground for any distance at all.
- Music and games are always an enjoyable way to reinforce and practice coordination skills: pretend to be different animals or machines; make an obstacle course; play "hot potato"; learn dances (limbo, square dance, disco).
- Help children build running coordination and strength by asking them to run to a destination and back to the starting place. Give all children their own individual turns—this will eliminate competition.
- Play music fast and slow and allow children to run in place in time with the tempo of the music.
- Establish a course and ask children to walk forward, backward, sideways, etc.
- Place a ladder flat on the ground. Have a child walk between each of the rungs, alternating feet and shifting his or her body weight. Tires will work as well.

Promoting Fine Motor Skills

Provide ways to develop control.

- To help in determining hand preference (which should be obvious by age three or four) look for:

     which hand a child uses to pick up or grab an object

     which ear a child uses when playing with the telephone.

- Help a child cross the mid-line of his or her body by having the child connect a dot diagonally from one corner to another or touch the left toes with the right hand.

- A child needs finger strength in order to grip a pencil correctly. Provide many activities to develop this:

     tear newspaper or scrap paper (not pull apart, but tear)

     tear colored paper and use the pieces to make a mosaic

     play with play dough and clay

     string beads or use sewing cards

     easel paint, finger-paint, and draw

     make constructions with blocks and Legos

     play with sand in a deep sandbox or at the sand table.

- Have a child use alternating hands to stack blocks or small manipulatives, with one color on the left and a different color on the right.

- Place five to ten coins on a table. Ask the child to pick up and hold as many as he can in his hand without dropping them.

- Ask a child who is holding coins in her hand to drop them one at a time into a container.

- Place a circular object, such as a jar lid, in a child's fingertips. Have the child slowly move his or her fingertips around the lid, making it rotate.

- To help a student establish an appropriate pencil grip, have the child write on the chalkboard with small pieces of chalk

- Have a child use shortened pencils. A shorter pencil or crayon is usually easier for small hands.

Provide ways to develop coordinated movements.

- Provide many manipulatives with small pieces (like Legos, puzzles).

- Make sure dramatic play clothes have varying kinds of clasps (buttons, zippers, snaps) on doll clothing and dress-up clothing. Encourage children to fasten the buttons for each other. Give them time to do it themselves.

- Encourage the children to dress themselves and ask for help only when needed.

- Provide free time at the art table!

- Have children pour water from one container to another at the water table.

- Teach children how to set the table and have them set up lunch and snack.

- Make available a variety of patterns or objects (basic geometric shapes and animals) for children to trace.

- With teacher supervision, encourage children to develop small motor strength and coordination using small hammers and large headed nails. To ensure safety, limit the number of children hammering, and require that all children wear safety goggles.

CHAPTER
ELEVEN

FINDING THE
SUPPORT YOU WILL
NEED

11. FINDING THE SUPPORT YOU WILL NEED

Chapter Overview
- Effective Helpers: Paraprofessionals and Volunteers
- Professionals and Specialists Who Can Help
- A Definition of Disability
- A Brief Overview of Significant Disabling Conditions
- A Brief Overview of Health Conditions that May Contribute to a Child's Special Learning Needs

Parents, teachers, and school administrators know that including children with disabilities in regular education programs for the first time is an enormous task. Even the very best intentions require time, attention, planning, training, and support from others in related fields of professional work. There are many ways of developing the support you will need to include children with disabilities in your program.

General information about early childhood special education, specific disabling conditions, and inclusion can be gathered from many agencies, organizations, and professional societies. The mission of these groups is to inform the general public about the many positive ways that individuals with disabilities contribute to society. Many groups offer support to families raising a child with disabilities. Some organizations help parents and teachers develop networks of caring and helping individuals. Other organizations raise funds for needed research to treat disabling conditions and to develop preventative measures for the future.

Effective Helpers: Paraprofessionals and Volunteers
Paraprofessionals are those who assist teachers and students and thereby extend the capacity and effectiveness of inclusive programs. Training for paraprofessionals includes learning about emergency care and first aid, about child development and learning, and about the individual children in an early childhood inclusive program. Paraprofessionals are employed by programs and receive payment for their services. Their wages are lower than what trained professionals receive.

Volunteers with training provide a broad range of assistance to programs for young children, but they receive no salary or payment for their services. Volunteers may provide direct classroom support, supplementary services, or additional, enriching experiences, such as sharing special talents or skills.

Including paraprofessionals in inclusive programs often provides the right amount of additional adult support. It is important to design and define jobs, even for volunteers, so that everyone involved can make effective use of each other's time and skills. The activities and tasks that the paraprofessional will be responsible for should be identified.

195

Basic descriptions of a program, such as the program's goals, should be presented to potential employees, so that the conditions under which their work is to be performed will be clear.

Orientation of paraprofessionals and volunteers is an important practice. When program administrators and paraprofessionals and volunteers discuss common goals, establish basic relationships, and discuss specific key issues, it is likely that the parapro-fessionals and volunteers will be placed in the right job and that they will be satisfied with their roles in the program.

Paraprofessionals benefit from constructive feedback and should be recognized and rewarded for their time and service. Formal recognition is valuable, as are spontaneous, natural expressions of gratitude and thanks.

Professionals and Specialists Who Can Help

One of the most effective ways of developing needed support is to enlist the help of spe-cialists from related professional fields. They can work with you in meeting the educa-tional needs of individual children and may also be available to provide training to teachers and parents. Specialists include audiologists, early childhood special educators, occupational therapists, physical therapists, school psychologists, speech and language pathologists, and other specialists.

Audiologists

Clinical audiologists are health-care professionals whose specialty is the evaluation of hearing. When a hearing loss is found in an individual, audiologists help to restore normal or optimal states of hearing. Audiologists study the hearing sciences and hold advanced degrees in the field. They conduct hearing examinations, test for middle ear disease, conduct hearing rehabilitation, and fit hearing aids.

The services of an audiologist include:
- Identifying hearing loss.
- Identifying the range, nature, and degree of hearing loss.
- Recommending further medical or other professional attention when necessary.
- Providing activities designed to increase a person's ability to communicate, such as therapy for expanding communication competence, auditory training, training in speech reading or lip-reading, and ongoing hearing evaluations to individuals whose hearing is at risk for fluctuation or change.
- Creating and administering community programs for the prevention of hearing loss.
- Counseling and guidance of students, parents, and teachers regarding hearing loss.
- Determining an individual's need for group and/or individual amplification, selecting and fitting an appropriate aid, and evaluating the effectiveness of amplifi-cation on an ongoing basis.

196

Early Childhood Special Educators

Early childhood special educators do the following:

- Promote young children's growth and development in the areas of social and emotional, physical and adaptive, communication, and cognitive skills.
- Enhance the young child's emerging self-concept by helping the child achieve independence and self-control. Early childhood special educators make use of many instructional methods in order to maximize an individual child's learning potential. Often early childhood educators use assistive or adaptive materials or equipment to help a child master new skills.
- Work closely with the families of young children with special needs to coordinate educational intervention with families' needs and abilities.

Early childhood educators provide services to young children with disabilities in many different ways. They:

- Plan and implement inclusive programs in collaboration with other community providers, such as child care providers, preschool teachers, audiologists, speech and language therapists, social workers, psychologists, and medical care providers.
- Develop relationships with family members based on respect for the family as the primary means of support to the young child with disabilities. In preschools, child care centers, and other community settings, early childhood special educators emphasize the importance of developing successful partnerships with families.
- Share helpful information about the needs of young children with disabilities and their families with others who are active in developing programs for these children.
- Highlight the unique geographic, linguistic, and culturally diverse needs of children, families, providers, and communities. Early childhood special educators assist in successfully bringing together a wide variety of children in educational programs.
- Develop individualized, child-centered educational plans for children with disabilities. These plans are designed to take advantage of local community resources and to make use of educational resources that exist in areas where children reside. Where educational opportunities need developing, early childhood special educators are trained to create and administer community programs that meet the needs of diverse young learners.
- Develop curriculum plans and instructional objectives, in collaboration with other specialists, that emphasize meeting the different educational needs of young children with special needs.

Occupational Therapists

Occupational therapy is a profession that assists individuals with different abilities to be more functional in their daily living skills. With young children, occupational therapy focuses on the functional aspects of school life. Occupational therapists (OTs) provide support in developing:

- Ease of mobility and strengthening of a child's capacity to make smooth transitions from one physical skill to the next, such as when transitioning from sitting on the

197

floor to standing or from standing to mounting and pedaling a tricycle.

- Handling classroom materials, such as climbing equipment, scooters and tricycles, paintbrushes, and scissors, with age-appropriate levels of skill.
- Self-help skills, such as becoming independent in caring for oneself at school, eating independently in a school cafeteria, moving through school hallways, hanging up one's coat and hat, stowing personal items in a cubby or locker, and locating and using classroom materials and tools.
- Handwriting skills or help in developing other means of producing writing when use of the hands is not an appropriate method for a child. An occupational therapist may recommend the use of alternative devices, such as assistive technology, voice-activated devices, computerized touch controls, switches, and/or eye- and gaze-activated devices. Occupational therapists provide training in the use of such alternative devices.
- Competence in routine school tasks (for older children), such as organizing materials for desk work, taking notes, and completing assignments in a timely manner.

In addition, because they recognize that social competence is vital to success in school and in later life, occupational therapists often support students in developing the skills necessary for successful social relationships with classmates and teachers.

Occupational therapy involves the therapeutic use of work, self-care, and play activities to increase independent function, enhance development, and prevent, through early intervention, initial or further impairment or loss of function. Occupational therapy includes adaptation of desired daily life tasks, or "occupations," in the school environment to achieve maximum independence and to enhance an individual's quality of life.

An occupational therapist is a health-care professional who uses functional activities and play as a means of preventing, reducing, or overcoming physical, social, and emotional disabilities in individuals. Occupational therapists help children with disabilities benefit from their educational programs. They focus on the young child's performance in the areas of:
- hand skills
- eating skills
- self-care skills
- social skills
- play skills.

Occupational therapists also:
- Provide assessment and evaluation of an individual's strengths and areas needing support.
- Collaborate with the families of young children with disabilities, teachers, and other specialists engaged in helping a specific child.
- Provide recommendations on environmental and material adaptations.
- Develop strategies and activities to enhance an individual's performance.

198

- Provide student-specific interventions or therapy.

Occupational therapists evaluate and treat individuals with:
- cognitive impairments
- developmental or learning disabilities
- physical disabilities
- sensory integration dysfunction.

The role of an occupational therapist in the treatment of young children also includes:
- Designing, making, and applying orthopedic devices—that is, devices designed to treat deformities, diseases, and injuries of the bones, joints, and muscles.
- Training children, their families, and their teachers in the use and maintenance of orthopedic or prosthetic devices.
- Designing, developing, and adapting assistive technology devices and training individuals in their use.

Physical Therapists

A physical therapist (PT) is a health-care professional who evaluates and treats individuals with problems resulting from disabling conditions, injury, or disease. A physical therapist assesses joint motion, muscle strength and endurance, function of the heart and lungs, and performance of activities required in daily living. Treatment includes therapeutic exercise and training in activities of daily living.

Physical therapists focus on the skills a child may need to perform specific physical skills such as sitting, crawling, standing, walking, climbing, and running. They develop therapeutic activities to enhance a child's ability to become independently mobile. PTs also assist individuals in avoiding the development of undesirable movement patterns, such as sitting positions that contribute to spinal curvature. PTs help individuals develop muscle strength and range of motion in joints that contribute to ease of movement.

Physical therapy and occupational therapy are closely related fields. Some children have both physical and occupational therapy when they are young. The PT and the OT might use similar techniques and therapies in treating the same child. However, the PT and the OT are focusing on two distinct capacities. The PT is concerned with how the individual is moving. The OT focuses on how effective the individual's movements are in meeting his or her need to function successfully.

For example, when assisting a three-year-old child with physical delays, a PT would support the child's ability to use muscles and joints to bear his or her own weight, to stand on one foot momentarily, and to maintain balance while stepping off on one or the other foot. The OT would make use of the child's mastery of each of the preceding skills to help the child go up and down stairs independently.

School Psychologists

A school psychologist, also referred to as an educational psychologist, is a provider of health and psycho-educational services in a school. A school psychologist is trained to deal with a wide range of issues that children, parents, teachers, and school administrators face, including health issues, academic challenges, and behavioral adjustment.

Psychologists are often called upon to provide support to children in social skills training and to help families function successfully in raising their child with disabilities. Psychologists also help children, families, and teachers to cope with events and issues that develop in families and communities, such as the emotional consequences of war, famine, family displacement, divorce, and the effects of abuse and neglect.

School psychologists are experts in evaluation and assessment. They may provide individual and group counseling services and social skills training. They use research to promote educational planning, use data collection to evaluate programs, and provide parent and staff training on topics of specific interest or need. The school psychologist often uses a problem-solving framework to advocate not only for individual children within the school setting, but also for children throughout the wider community.

The school psychologist may be called on to give advice based on expert assessment and observation of a child's strengths and areas needing specialized support. School psychologists use a range of techniques to put together a picture of an individual child's strengths and challenges. They also identify important factors affecting a child's ability to learn and manage behavior.

Speech and Language Pathologists

A speech and language pathologist (SLP) is trained to assess, train, and correct speech, language, and communication disorders in children and adults. An SLP works on these difficult areas by developing a treatment plan based on an individual's strengths and pre-existing skills and determining what needs to be accomplished as treatment outcomes.

For children, speech and language therapy may involve:
- Developing language—the process of understanding and using words, phrases, and sentences that represent ideas about the world that are meaningful to others.
- Improving articulation or phonology—the speech sound system of language.
- Strengthening oral motor skills—the underlying physical skills necessary for speech: regulation of breathing, swallowing, and developing muscle strength in the tongue, lips, and mouth.
- Improving fluency—the ability to speak easily, smoothly, and expressively.

SLPs develop treatment plan objectives, or therapy goals, that are discussed with families, teachers, and other specialists working with the individual child. Therapy goals are modified based on the progress the child makes over time.

200

SLPs also make decisions related to whether a child needs an augmentative and/or alternative communication system in order to communicate effectively. An augmentative and alternative communication system is a total integrated network of techniques, aids, strategies, and skills an individual uses either to add to or to replace inadequate speaking ability. The system could include any combination of the following aids: sign language, use of gesture, facial communication, eye pointing, graphic symbol systems (picture symbols), adaptive switches, electronic touch pads, joysticks, light beams, or sensors.

The SLP designs an appropriate system and trains the child to use it in order to communicate his or her wants and needs. The SLP also works with the child's family and teachers to support the use of the system on a daily basis.

Other Specialists
Neurologists—Medical doctors who can screen, diagnose, and treat disorders of the brain and central nervous system.

Nutritionists—Medical care professionals trained to evaluate eating habits. Nutritionists counsel families and schools about normal and therapeutic nutrition plans. They may develop special feeding techniques, as in the case of a child with cleft palate.

Ophthalmologists—Medical doctors who screen, diagnose, and treat diseases, injuries, or birth defects that limit vision.

Opticians—Medical care professionals who assist in fitting children with glasses and frames and/or contact lenses prescribed by an ophthalmologist or optometrist.

Optometrists—Doctors trained to examine a child's vision to determine the presence of visual problems and eye diseases or to evaluate a child's visual skill and development.

Orthopedists—Medical doctors who screen, diagnose, or treat diseases or injuries to muscles, joints, and bones.

Otolaryngologists—Medical doctors who screen, diagnose, and treat disorders of the ear, nose, and throat.

Psychiatrists—Medical doctors who screen, diagnose, and treat psychological, emotional, or developmental problems that relate to mental health. They may prescribe medication or provide individual, group, or family treatment or counseling.

Social Workers—Professionals trained in counseling families who are experiencing difficulties in meeting their family responsibilities. Social workers often help families to make use of community services.

A Definition of a Disability

The term *individual with a disability* refers to a person who receives the diagnosis from a professional and:

- has a physical or mental impairment that substantially limits one or more major life activities; major life activities are defined as walking, seeing, hearing, speaking, breathing, caring for oneself, performing manual tasks, learning, and working
- has a history of such an impairment
- is regarded as having such an impairment.

Physical or mental impairment means:

- Any psychological disorder or condition, cosmetic disfigurement, or anatomical loss affecting one or more of the body systems: neurological; musculoskeletal; special sense organs; respiratory, including speech organs; cardiovascular; reproductive; digestive; urinary; hemic (blood) and lymphatic; skin; and endocrine.
- Any mental or psychological disorder, such as mental retardation, organic brain syndrome, emotional or mental illness, or specific learning disability.

A Brief Overview of Significant Disabling Conditions

Autism and Pervasive Developmental Disorder

Definition

Autism and pervasive developmental disorder not otherwise specified (PDD-NOS) are developmental disabilities that share many of the same characteristics. Usually evident by age three, autism and PDD-NOS are neurological disorders that affect a child's ability to communicate, understand language, play, and relate to others.

A diagnosis of autism is made when an individual displays eight of sixteen symptoms listed across three major areas: social interaction, communication, and repertoire of activities and interests. When a child displays similar behaviors but with fewer than eight of the sixteen symptoms, professionals may make a diagnosis of PDD-NOS.

Readers should be aware that revisions in the diagnoses of autism and PDD-NOS are being considered by international mental health organizations. These changes may not permeate the field for quite some time.

Characteristics

The causes of autism and PDD-NOS are unknown. Currently, researchers are investigating areas such as neurological damage and biochemical imbalance in the brain. These disorders are not caused by psychological factors.

Some or all of the following characteristics may be observed in mild to severe forms of the disorder:

202

- communication problems: using or understanding language
- difficulty in relating to people, objects, and events
- unusual play with toys and other objects
- difficulty with changes in routine or familiar surroundings
- repetitive body movements or behavior patterns.

Children with autism or PDD-NOS vary widely in abilities, intelligence, and behaviors. Some children do not speak; others have limited language that often includes repeated phrases or conversations. Individuals with more advanced language skills tend to use a small range of topics. Individuals with autism or PDD-NOS may have difficulty tolerating loud noises, lights, and the texture of certain food and fabrics.

Educational Implications
Autism and PDD-NOS are developmental disabilities that adversely affect a child's educational performance. Early diagnosis and appropriate educational programs are very important to children with autism or PDD-NOS. The treatment and educational needs are essentially the same for both diagnoses.

Individualized educational plans for students with autism or PDD-NOS focus on improving communication, social, cognitive, behavioral, and daily living skills. Behavior and communication problems often interfere with learning. When a child's ability to learn new skills is limited by the child's autistic behaviors, teachers and parents should seek the assistance of a knowledgeable professional in the field of autism. Individuals who are associated with The Autism Society of America and other advocacy groups can meet with families and assist them in developing behavior and learning plans that can be carried out at home and at school.

The classroom environment should be structured so that the daily program is consistent and predictable. Students with autism or PDD-NOS learn better and are less confused when information is presented visually as well as verbally. Interaction with typically developing peers is important because those students provide models of appropriate language, social, and behavioral skills. To overcome frequent problems in generalizing skills learned at school, it is very important for the teacher to develop plans with parents, so that learning activities, experiences, and approaches can be carried over into the home and community.

Children with autism have successfully been included in regular education classrooms. In every case, there have been two fundamental reasons for this success. First, the school, in collaboration with the student's family, designed an individualized plan to meet the student's unique needs. Second, the programs provided additional adult support services for the child with autism. When these two conditions have been met, children with autism have made progress toward achieving their individual goals.

Deafness, Deaf-Blindness, and Hearing Impairment

Definition

Deafness—A hearing impairment that is so severe that a child is impaired in processing linguistic information through hearing, with or without amplification. Deafness is viewed as a condition that prevents an individual from receiving sound in all or most of its forms.

Deaf-Blindness—Concomitant hearing and visual impairments, the combination of which causes severe communication and other developmental and educational problems.

Hearing Impairment—An impairment in hearing, whether permanent or fluctuating, that adversely affects a child's educational performance. A child with a hearing impairment can generally respond to some auditory stimuli, including speech.

Characteristics

Sound is measured by its loudness or intensity in units called decibels (dB) and its frequency or pitch in units called hertz (Hz). Impairments in hearing can occur in either or both areas, and may exist in only one ear or in both ears. Hearing loss is generally described as slight, mild, moderate, severe, or profound, depending on how well a person can hear the intensities or frequencies most greatly associated with speech. Generally, only children who require sound to register at least 71 to 90 decibels are considered deaf for the purposes of educational placement.

There are four types of hearing loss. Diseases or obstructions in the outer or middle ear or the conductive pathways for sound to reach the inner ear cause *conductive hearing losses.* Conductive hearing losses usually affect all frequencies of hearing evenly and do not result in severe losses. A person with a conductive hearing loss usually is able to use a hearing aid well or can be helped medically or surgically.

Sensorineural hearing losses result from damage to the delicate sensory hair cells of the inner ear or the nerves that supply it. These hearing losses can range from mild to profound. They often affect the person's ability to hear certain frequencies differently than other people do. Thus, even with amplification to increase the sound level, a person with a sensorineural hearing loss may perceive distorted sounds, sometimes making the successful use of a hearing aid impossible.

A *mixed hearing loss* refers to a combination of conductive and sensorineural loss and means that a problem occurs in both the outer and the inner ear. A *central hearing loss* results from damage or impairment to the nerves or nuclei of the central nervous system, either in the pathways to the brain or in the brain itself.

Educational Implications

Hearing loss or deafness does not affect a person's intellectual capacity or ability to learn. However, children who are either hearing impaired or deaf generally require some form of specialized education services in order to receive an adequate education.

Such services may include:
- regular speech, language, and auditory training from a specialist
- amplification systems
- services of an interpreter for those students who use manual communication
- favorable placement in group seating to facilitate speech reading and reading of captioned films and videos
- assistance of a note taker, who records spoken content for a student with a hearing loss, so the student can fully attend to the instruction
- instruction for the classroom teacher and classmates in the alternative communication method, such as sign language, that is used by the student with the hearing impairment
- counseling.

Children who are hearing impaired will find it much more difficult than children who have normal hearing to learn vocabulary, grammar, word order, idiomatic expressions, and other aspects of verbal communication. For children who are deaf or have a severe hearing loss, early, consistent, and conscious use of visible communication modes, such as sign language, fingerspelling, Cued Speech, and/or amplification and aural/oral training, can help reduce this language delay.

By age four or five, most children who are deaf are enrolled in school on a full-day basis and engage in intensive work on communication and language development. It is important for teachers and audiologists to work together to teach the child to use his or her residual hearing to the maximum extent possible, even if the preferred means of communication is manual. Since the great majority of deaf children (over 96 percent) are born to hearing parents, programs should provide instruction for parents on the impact of deafness upon the family.

Individuals with hearing loss may use oral or manual means of communication or a combination of the two methods. Oral communication includes speech and speech reading and the use of residual hearing. Manual communication involves signs and fingerspelling. Total communication, as a method of instruction, is a combination of the oral method plus signs and fingerspelling.

Individuals with a hearing loss, including those who are deaf, have many helpful devices available to them. Text telephones, known as TTs, TTYs, or TDDs, enable persons to type phone messages over the telephone network. The Telecommunications Relay Service (TRS) makes it possible for TT users to communicate with virtually anyone via a telephone.

Specific intervention strategies helpful to those with hearing impairments include the following:

- Seat the individual up close for good visibility of the speaker, the activity, or the other children.
- Determine the best speaking distance for the student with the hearing impairment.
- Provide the child with experiences that make use of his or her residual hearing.
- Speak at a normal speed and volume without exaggerating lip movements.
- Avoid speaking with your back to the student or with a bright light behind you. Don't inadvertently cover your mouth when speaking. Mustaches and beards interfere with visibility of lip movements. Lipstick may enhance visibility.
- Use normal vocabulary and sentence structure. Be prepared to repeat, rephrase, point out, or demonstrate if the child does not understand.
- When seeking the student's attention, be certain to use his or her name. Teach the child to attend to your face. Avoid providing pertinent information until you have the student's focused attention.
- Use visual and tactile learning aids to supplement curriculum. Model desired behavior, or encourage peer modeling whenever possible.
- Learn to replace the hearing aid battery.
- Encourage the student with a hearing impairment to speak in group activities by allowing time for the child to start and finish speaking.

Adaptations made for children with speech and language delays will also be effective for hearing-impaired children.

Developmental Delay

Definition

Developmental delay is defined as a condition that represents a significant delay in one or more of the domains of development for a child below age eight. It does not refer to a condition in which the child is slightly or momentarily lagging in development. The presence of developmental delay is an indication that the process of development is significantly affected and that, without special intervention, it is likely that educational performance at elementary school age will be affected.

Characteristics

A determination that a child is experiencing a developmental delay is made when an appropriate assessment measure or other procedure reveals the presence of a delay in one or more of the following areas:

- physical development and self-care skills
- cognitive ability
- communication skills
- social and emotional development
- perceptual skills, including making good use of vision, hearing, touch, balance, and movement sensations.

A delay in development in any one of these areas may require special education and therapeutic services to promote increased development, learning, and skills acquisition.

The manifestation of specific learning disabilities in very young children is not well understood or easily identified. The concept of developmental delay allows educators and parents to identify young children for early intervention who otherwise might have gone unserved due to the difficulties inherent in applying the other traditional categories of disabling conditions to the population of young children.

Educational Implications
The delivery of appropriate services should be based on a child's existing strengths and areas of need, rather than on a categorical disability label. Given that the term *developmental delay* implies a continuum of developmental status, services are more likely to be delivered in inclusive settings than in segregated settings that are made up solely of children from a particular disability category.

The period of childhood development typically characterized as early childhood is birth through age eight. The developmental status of children during this period is best characterized by a broad range of behaviors across developmental domains and is more accurately described by developmental metrics than by those that have a more educational or academic focus.

The use of the developmental delay category during the full span of early childhood years facilitates a broader, whole-child perspective for intervention. The overriding focus should remain on the child's needs and identification of services to meet those needs in developmentally appropriate ways. The use of a multisetting, multimeasure, and multi-informant model is appropriate for the assessment and identification of developmental delay in young children. In the implementation of this model, which embraces a child-centered developmental perspective within a family-centered approach, team members may be guided in their evaluations by information gained through the administration of norm-referenced, criterion-referenced, and judgment-based assessments.

Multiple sources, such as parents, other family members, caregivers, and early care and education providers, may also be helpful in providing information concerning the abilities of the child in different settings, such as home and school. In using this model, educators make appropriate decisions guided by informed clinical opinion as well as the child's performance on standard measures of achievement. Assessment strategies should be selected and administered by a multidisciplinary team, including the child's parents, and should be based on observations of the child performing routine activities in typical and natural environments.

Mental Retardation

Definition

Individuals with mental retardation are those who develop at a below-average level of functioning and experience difficulty in learning and social adjustment. The technical definition for mental retardation includes:

- significantly below-average general intellectual functioning;
- concurrently existing deficits in adaptive behavior that are manifested during the developmental period and that adversely affect a child's educational performance, including adjustment to everyday life, communication, social, academic, vocational, and independent living skills; and,
- impaired general intellectual functioning as measured by intelligence tests, with individuals with mental retardation usually scoring 70 or below on such tests.

Mental retardation is not a disease, nor should it be confused with mental illness. Children with mental retardation become adults; they do not remain "eternal" children. They do learn, but slowly, and with difficulty.

The greatest numbers of children with mental retardation have chromosome abnormalities. Other biological factors include, but are not limited to:

- asphyxia or lack of oxygen during the birth process
- blood incompatibilities between the mother and fetus
- maternal infections during pregnancy, such as rubella or herpes
- the effects of certain drugs linked to problems in fetal development.

Characteristics

Many authorities agree that individuals with mental retardation develop in the same way as individuals without mental retardation, but at a slower rate. Other authorities suggest that persons with mental retardation have difficulties in particular areas of basic thinking and learning such as attention, perception, and/or memory. Depending on the extent of the impairment—mild, moderate, severe, or profound—individuals with mental retardation will display a wide range of individual variation in academic, social, and vocational skills.

Educational Implications

Persons with mental retardation have the capacity to learn, develop, and grow. The great majority of these citizens can become productive and full participants in society. Appropriate educational services that begin in infancy and continue throughout the developmental period and beyond will enable children with mental retardation to develop to their fullest potential.

As with all education, modifying instruction to meet individual needs is the starting point for successful learning. Throughout their child's education, parents should be an integral part of the planning and teaching team.

In teaching individuals with mental retardation, it is important to:
- Use concrete materials that are interesting, age-appropriate, and relevant to the student.
- Present information and instruction in small, sequential steps and review each step frequently.
- Provide prompt and consistent feedback.
- Teach children, whenever possible, in the same school they would attend if they did not have mental retardation.
- Teach tasks or skills that students will use frequently in such a way that students can apply the tasks or skills in settings outside of school.
- Remember that tasks that many people learn without instruction may need to be structured, or broken down into small steps or segments, with each step being carefully taught.

Children and adults with mental retardation need the same basic services that all people need for normal development. These include education, vocational preparation, health services, and recreational opportunities. In addition, many individuals with mental retardation need specialized services for special needs. Such services include diagnostic and evaluation services and early intervention, beginning with infant stimulation programs, and educational services that continue throughout preschool and elementary and secondary school. Educational programs should include age-appropriate activities and functional academics. Care should be given to planning for the transition from school to work through training, making use of any opportunities for independent living, and developing opportunities for competitive employment to the maximum extent possible.

Down Syndrome

Definition
Down syndrome is the most common and readily identifiable chromosomal condition associated with mental retardation. It is caused by a chromosomal abnormality: for some unexplained reason, an accident in cell development results in 47 instead of 46 chromosomes. This extra chromosome changes the orderly development of the body and brain. In most cases, the diagnosis of Down syndrome is made according to the results from a chromosome test administered shortly after birth.

Characteristics
There are over 50 clinical signs of Down syndrome, but it is rare to find all or even most of the characteristics in one person. Some common characteristics include:
- poor muscle tone, or loose muscles lacking strength
- slanting eyes with folds of skin at the inner corners, called epicanthal eyelids
- hyperflexibility or an excessive ability to extend joints
- short, broad hands with a single crease across the palm on one or both hands
- broad feet with short toes
- flat bridge of the nose

- short, low-set ears
- short neck and a small head
- small oral cavity
- short, high-pitched cries in infancy.

Individuals born with Down syndrome are usually smaller than their nondisabled peers, and their physical, as well as intellectual development, is slower.

Besides having a distinct physical appearance, children with Down syndrome frequently have specific health-related problems. A lowered resistance to infection makes these children more prone to respiratory problems. Visual problems such as crossed eyes and far- or near-sightedness are more frequently found in children with Down syndrome, as are mild to moderate hearing loss and speech and language difficulties.

Approximately one-third of babies born with Down syndrome have heart defects, most of which are now successfully corrected with surgery. Some individuals are born with gastrointestinal tract problems that can also be surgically corrected.

Some individuals with Down syndrome also may have a condition known as atlantoaxial instability, a misalignment of the top vertebrae of the neck. This condition makes these individuals more prone to injury if they participate in activities that overextend or flex the neck. Parents of children with Down syndrome generally have their children examined by a physician to determine whether the child should be restricted from sports and activities that place stress on the neck. Although this misalignment is a potentially serious condition, proper diagnosis can help prevent serious injury.

Children with Down syndrome may have a tendency to become overweight as they grow older. Besides having negative social implications, this weight gain threatens the individual's health and longevity. A supervised diet and exercise program may help reduce this problem.

Educational Implications
Shortly after a diagnosis of Down syndrome is confirmed, parents should be encouraged to enroll their child in an infant development or early intervention program. These programs offer parents special instruction in teaching their child language, cognitive, self-help, and social skills and specific exercises for gross and fine motor development. Research has shown that stimulation during early developmental stages improves the child's chances of developing to his or her fullest potential. Continuing education, positive public attitudes, and a stimulating home environment have also been found to promote the child's overall development.

Just as in the normal population, there is a wide variation in mental abilities, behavior, and developmental progress in individuals with Down syndrome. Their level of retardation may range from mild to severe, with the majority functioning in the mild to

210

moderate range. Due to these individual differences, it is impossible to predict future achievements of children with Down syndrome.

Because of the range of ability in children with Down syndrome, it is important that families and all members of the school's educational team place as few limitations as possible on potential capabilities. It may be effective to emphasize concrete concepts rather than abstract ideas. Teaching tasks in a step-by-step manner with frequent reinforcement and consistent feedback has been proven successful. Improved public acceptance of persons with disabilities, along with increased opportunities for adults with disabilities to live and work independently in the community, have expanded families' and society's goals for individuals with Down syndrome. Independent living centers, group-shared and -supervised apartments, and support services have proven to be important lifelong resources for persons with Down syndrome.

Orthopedic Impairment

Definition
A severe orthopedic, or skeletal, impairment is one that adversely affects a child's educational performance.

Characteristics
The term includes impairments caused by congenital anomalies, such as clubfoot or the absence of one or more limbs. It also includes impairments caused by diseases such as poliomyelitis, bone abnormalities, or osteo-arthritis. Orthopedic impairments may have other causes, such as cerebral palsy, amputations, fractures, or severe burns that cause contracture (abnormal shortening of the muscles or tendons), often resulting in distortion of a joint, the place where two bones come together.

Educational Implications
It is important for educators to familiarize themselves with the particulars of an individual's orthopedic impairment. A written history should be available that includes the length of time the individual has been impaired, the causes and conditions of the impairment, and activities recommended by the child's physician or therapists.

It is useful for educators to understand the level of adjustment the individual has made. Focus should be directed to the adjustments that a child is continuing to accomplish. The greater the number of joints that are missing, the more challenging is the adjustment for the individual. The level of adjustment is related to the age at which impairment occurred: the earlier the loss, the more likely that the child will make successful adjustment.

Prosthetic devices are often used to aid an individual with an orthopedic impairment. How well these fit, how functional they are, the child's attitude toward them, and how easily the child can manage them are all factors that will require attention.

Classroom adaptations for individuals with orthopedic impairments may include:

- Developing activities that increase the acquisition of self-help skills and that support social success.
- Adapting the position of a toy or the height at which something can be used—for example, raising or lowering a table, easel, sink, or coat hook.
- Creating games and activities that engage other children along with the child with an orthopedic impairment, rather than isolating the child.
- Removing any existing barriers that would reduce an individual's access to outdoor and indoor activity times.
- Incorporating all types of media in school activities, so that the child is exposed to a rich sensory diet.

Proper handling and positioning of the child is extremely important. The child needs to feel comfortable and well balanced to be able to concentrate. A prone position over a bolster will allow the child to make visual contact with the environment. A side-lying position may assist the child in making hand, arm, and leg movements. A child will need to be changed every twenty to thirty minutes.

Teachers will need to become proficient in the use of the child's equipment: wheelchairs, crutches, braces, artificial limbs, and other mechanical aids. It is also important that teachers do not underestimate a child's capabilities, but at the same time remain realistic.

Other Health Impairments

Definition
Other health impairments are present when an individual has limited strength, vitality, or alertness—due to chronic or acute health problems such as a heart condition, tuberculosis, rheumatic fever, arthritis, asthma, sickle cell anemia, hemophilia, epilepsy, lead poisoning, leukemia, attention deficit disorder/attention deficit hyperactivity disorder, or diabetes—that adversely affect a child's educational performance.

Characteristics
An individual with a chronic, or acute, health problem may, for example, experience recurrent and persistent pain, swelling, stiffness of joints, and difficulty in breathing and may have overall growth deficiencies and general behavioral challenges resulting from those characteristics. Individuals with health impairments may have specific, individual requirements due to their medical conditions. They may have increased thirst and appetite; from time to time they may become listless or easily fatigued; they may need to urinate frequently; or they may become dizzy and/or sleepy. Each individual's physical and behavioral characterizes vary and will require individualized program accommodations.

Educational Implications
In collaboration with the child's family and physician, educators should familiarize

themselves with the particulars of the child's health impairment. A written history should be available that includes the length of time the individual has had the health impairment, the causes and conditions of the impairment, and any recommended activities from the child's physician or therapists.

Procedures for the administration of medicine at school should be established for each individual in regard to his or her specific condition or health impairment. If appropriate, the child should wear a medic alert bracelet identifying the child's medical condition.

Children with health impairments are more prone to common illnesses, such as colds, ear infections, or diarrhea. Children with chronic health needs usually miss more school, spend more time convalescing at home, and are hospitalized more frequently than are children with most other handicapping conditions. Repeated separation and trauma can create emotional and physical stress.

Great responsibility is placed on parents who must continually monitor their child's health and facilitate their child's access to necessary health care. In addition, some chronic health impairments are potentially life-threatening. Educators must, then, be sensitive and supportive to those families, when appropriate, while continuing to honor the child's rights of access to an education.

Serious Emotional Disturbance

Definition

A serious emotional disturbance is a condition that exhibits one or more of the following characteristics, over a long period of time and to a marked degree, and that adversely affects a child's educational performance:
- an inability to learn that cannot be explained by intellectual, sensory, or health factors
- an inability to build or maintain satisfactory interpersonal relationships with peers and adults
- inappropriate types of behavior or feelings under normal circumstances
- a general pervasive mood of unhappiness or depression
- a tendency to develop physical symptoms or fears associated with personal or school problems.

Characteristics

The causes of emotional disturbance have not been adequately determined. Although various factors such as heredity, brain disorder, diet, stress, and family functioning have been suggested as possible causes, research has not shown any of these factors to be the direct cause of serious emotional disturbance and accompanying behavior problems.

Some of the characteristics and behaviors seen in children who have emotional disturbances include:
- hyperactivity, including a variable, often short attention span, and impulsivity

- aggression toward others and/or self-injurious behavior
- withdrawal or retreat from social interactions
- excessive fears and anxieties
- immaturities, as seen in inappropriate crying, frequent temper tantrums, and poor coping skills
- learning difficulties that cause significant discrepancies in school performance.

Children with the most serious emotional disturbances may display some of these same behaviors at various times during their development. When children have serious emotional disturbances and these behaviors continue over long periods of time, the presence of the behaviors may signal the child's inability to cope with the demands of his or her environment and/or the individuals in it.

Educational Implications
Educational programs for individuals with a serious emotional disturbance should emphasize mastering cognitive skills, developing social skills, and increasing self-awareness, self-esteem, and self-control.

Behavior modification is one of the most widely used approaches to support functional learning in children with a serious emotional disturbance. However, there are many techniques that may also prove successful. Some of these may be used in combination with behavior modification. Psychological and/or counseling services are important to consider as a related service to children with serious emotional disturbance. Qualified social workers, psychologists, guidance counselors, or other qualified personnel may provide these services.

Children should be provided services based on individual needs, and all persons who are involved with these children should be aware of the care they are receiving from other service providers. It is important to coordinate all services between home, school, and the therapeutic community with open communication.

Parent support groups are also important. Families of children with serious emotional disturbance may need help in understanding their children's condition and in learning how to work effectively with their children. Help is available from psychiatrists, psychologists, or other mental health professionals.

There is growing recognition that families of children with serious emotional disturbance, as well as their children, need support, respite care, intensive case management services, and, where available, multi-agency treatment plans. Many communities are working toward developing and providing broader community-based therapeutic services. As the number of agencies and organizations actively involved in establishing and providing support services in communities increases, families and teachers will have more opportunities to promote inclusion for individuals with serious emotional disturbance.

Severe and/or Multiple Disability

Definition

Individuals with severe disabilities are those who traditionally have been labeled as having severe to profound mental retardation. These individuals require ongoing, extensive support in more than one major life activity in order to participate in integrated community settings and enjoy the quality of life available to people with fewer or no disabilities. They frequently have additional disabilities, including movement difficulties, sensory losses, and behavior problems.

Characteristics

Children and youth with severe or multiple disabilities may exhibit a wide range of characteristics, depending on the communication and severity of disabilities and the person's age. Some of these characteristics may include:
- limited speech or ability to communicate
- difficulty in basic physical mobility
- tendency to forget skills through disuse
- associated severe behavior problems
- trouble generalizing skills from one situation to another
- a need for support in major life activities, such as caring for oneself, performing manual tasks, learning, and working.

Medical Implications

A variety of medical problems may accompany severe disabilities. Examples include seizures, sensory loss, hydrocephalus, and scoliosis. These conditions should be considered when establishing school services. A multidisciplinary team consisting of the student's parents, educational specialists, and appropriate medical specialists should work together to plan and coordinate the necessary medical services.

Educational Implications

Early intervention programs for infants and toddlers, preschool programs, and continuing educational programs with appropriate support services are important to children with severe disabilities and their families. Educators, physical therapists, occupational therapists, and speech and language pathologists are all members of the treatment team, along with others, as needed for each individual. Assistive technology, such as computers and augmentative communication devices and techniques, may provide valuable instructional assistance in educational programs for students with severe and/or multiple disabilities.

To address the considerable needs of individuals with severe and/or multiple disabilities effectively, educational programs need to incorporate a variety of components, including language development, social skill development, and functional skill development, including self-help skills. Related services are of great importance and the appropriate therapists need to work closely with classroom teachers and parents. Related services are best offered during the natural routine of the school and the community, rather than by removing the student from the class or community for isolated therapy.

Classroom arrangements must take into consideration students' needs for medications, special diets, or special equipment, such as mobility devices. Adaptive aids and equipment enable students to increase their range of functioning. The use of computers, augmentative/alternative communication systems, communication boards, head sticks, and adaptive switches are some of the technological advances that enable students with severe disabilities to participate more fully in integrated settings.

Integration, or inclusion with nondisabled peers, is another important component of the educational setting. Research is showing that attending the same school and participating in the same activities as their nondisabled peers is crucial to the development of social skills and friendships for children and youth with severe disabilities.

Children with severe disabilities traditionally have been educated in center-based, segregated schools. Increasingly, however, many neighborhood schools are effectively and successfully educating children with severe disabilities within the regular classroom, making sure that appropriate support services and curriculum modifications are available. Inclusion can benefit not only those with disabilities but also their nondisabled peers and the professionals who work with them.

Schools address the needs of students with severe and/or multiple disabilities in several ways, generally using a team approach. *Modifications to the regular curriculum* require collaboration on the part of the special educator, the regular educator, and other specialists involved in the student's program. *Community-based instruction* is also an important characteristic of educational programming, particularly as students grow older and spend more time in the community. *School-to-work transition planning* and *working toward job placement* in integrated, competitive settings are important to students' success and their long-term quality of life.

Specific Learning Disability

Definition
A learning disability is a disorder in one or more of the basic psychological processes involved in understanding or in using spoken or written language. It may manifest itself in an imperfect ability to listen, think, speak, read, write, or spell or do mathematical calculations.

The definition of learning disabilities includes conditions such as perceptual disabilities, brain injury, minimal brain dysfunction, dyslexia, and developmental aphasia. Learning disabilities do not include learning problems that are primarily the result of visual or hearing impairments, motor disabilities, mental retardation, or environmental, cultural, or economic disadvantage.

216

Having a single term to describe this category of children with disabilities reduces some of the confusion, but there are many conflicting theories about what causes learning disabilities and how many there are. The label *learning disabilities* is a comprehensive term. It is used to describe a syndrome, not a specific child with specific problems.

The definition of learning disabilities helps educators to classify children but not to teach them. Parents and teachers need to concentrate on the individual child. They need to observe both how and how well the child performs, to assess strengths and weaknesses, and develop ways to help each child learn. It is important to remember that there is a high degree of interrelationship and overlapping among the areas of learning. Therefore, children with learning disabilities may exhibit a combination of characteristics. These problems may mildly, moderately, or severely impair the learning process.

Characteristics
Learning disabilities are characterized by a significant gap between the child's achievement in some areas, and his or her overall intelligence.

Students who have learning disabilities may exhibit a wide range of traits, including problems with reading comprehension, spoken language, writing, or reasoning ability. Hyperactivity, inattention, and perceptual coordination problems may also be associated with learning disabilities.

Other symptoms that may be present include uneven and unpredictable test performance, perceptual impairments, motor disorders, and behaviors such as impulsiveness, low tolerance for frustration, and problems in handling day-to-day social interactions and situations.

Learning disabilities may occur in the following academic areas:
*   spoken language
*   delays, disorders, or discrepancies in listening and speaking
*   written language
*   difficulties with reading, writing, and spelling
*   mathematics
*   difficulty in performing arithmetic functions or in comprehending basic mathematical concepts
*   reasoning
*   difficulty in organizing and integrating thoughts
*   organization skills
*   difficulty in organizing all facets of learning.

Educational Implications
Because learning disabilities are manifested in a variety of behavioral patterns, the individualized education plan (IEP) must be designed carefully. (See Chapter Four for how to construct an IEP.) A team approach is important for educating the child with a

learning disability, beginning with the assessment process and continuing through the development of the IEP. Close collaboration among all teachers and others will facilitate the overall development of a child with learning disabilities.

Teachers report that the following strategies have been effective with students who have learning disabilities:
- Capitalize on the student's strengths.
- Provide high structure and clear expectations.
- Use short sentences and a simple vocabulary.
- Provide opportunities for success in a supportive atmosphere to help build self-esteem.
- Allow flexibility in classroom procedures, such as allowing the use of tape recorders for note taking and test taking when students have trouble with written language.
- Make use of self-correcting materials, which provide immediate feedback without embarrassment.
- Use computers for drill and practice and teaching word processing.
- Provide positive reinforcement of appropriate social skills.
- Recognize that students with learning disabilities can greatly benefit from the gift of time to grow and mature.

Speech and Language Impairment

Definition

Speech and language impairment refers to challenges in communication and related areas such as oral motor function. These delays and disorders range from simple sound substitutions to the inability to understand or use language or use the oral-motor mechanism for functional speech and feeding. Some causes of speech and language disorders include hearing loss, neurological disorders, brain injury, mental retardation, drug abuse, physical impairments such as cleft lip and cleft palate, and vocal abuse or misuse. Frequently, however, the cause is unknown. Language disorders may be related to other disabilities such as autism, developmental delay, cerebral palsy, or a specific learning disability.

Characteristics

A child's communication is considered delayed when the child is noticeably behind other, same-aged children in the acquisition of speech and/or language skills. Sometimes a child will have greater *receptive* understanding of communication than he or she has *expressive*, or speaking, skill. But that is not always the case.

Speech disorders refer to difficulties producing speech sounds or problems with voice quality. They may be characterized by an interruption in the flow or rhythm of speech, such as stuttering, which is also referred to as dysfluency. Speech disorders may include problems with the way sounds are formed (called articulation or phonological disorders), or an individual may have difficulties modulating the pitch, volume, or quality of his or her voice. There may be a combination of several problems.

218

Children with speech disorders have trouble using some speech sounds, which can also be a symptom of a delay. A child may say "see" when the child means "ski," or a child may have trouble using sounds such as /l/ or /r/. Listeners may have trouble understanding the young child with a speech disorder. Young children with voice disorders may have great difficulty recognizing, or localizing, the problem without therapeutic assistance.

A language disorder is an impairment in the ability to understand and/or use words in context, both verbally and nonverbally. Some characteristics of language disorders include improper use of words and their meanings, inability to express ideas, inappropriate grammatical patterns, reduced vocabulary, and/or an inability to follow directions. One or a combination of these characteristics may occur in children who are affected by language learning disabilities or developmental language delay. Children may hear or see a word but may not be able to understand its meaning. They may have trouble getting others to understand what they are trying to communicate, based on the linguistic elements of their expressive language.

Educational Implications
Because all communication disorders have the potential to isolate individuals from their social and educational surroundings, it is essential to locate and deliver appropriate, timely intervention. While many speech and language patterns can be called "baby talk" and are part of a young child's normal development., they can become problems if they are not outgrown as expected. In this way an initial delay in speech and language or an initial speech pattern can become a disorder that can cause difficulties in learning. Because of the way the brain develops, it is easier to learn language and communication skills before the age of five. When children have muscular disorders, hearing problems, or developmental delays, their acquisition of speech, language, and related skills is often affected.

Speech and language therapists assist children who have communication disorders in various ways. They provide individual therapy for the child, consult with the child's teacher about the most effective ways to facilitate the child's communication in the classroom, and work closely with the family to develop goals and techniques for effective therapy in school, at home, and in the community. Technology can help children whose physical conditions make communication difficult. Electronic communication systems allow nonspeaking individuals and individuals with severe physical disabilities to engage in the give-and-take of shared thought.

Communication skills are at the heart of the educational experience. Vocabulary and concept growth continue throughout the years children are in school. Reading and writing are taught and, as students get older, the understanding and use of language become more complex. Speech and/or language therapy may continue throughout a child's school years either in the form of direct therapy or on a consultant basis. The speech and language therapist may assist teachers and counselors in establishing communication goals related to play experiences and suggest strategies that are effective for the important goal of establishing reciprocal communication.

Communication has many components. All communication goals should serve to increase the way young children learn about the world around them, use knowledge and skills, and interact with community members, family, and friends.

Traumatic Brain Injury

Definition

Traumatic brain injury (TBI) is defined as an acquired injury to the brain caused by external physical force, resulting in total or partial functional disability or psychosocial impairment, or both, that adversely affects a child's educational performance. The term applies to open and closed head injuries resulting in impairments in one or more areas, such as: cognition; language; memory; attention; reasoning; abstract thinking; judgment; problem-solving; sensory, perceptual, and motor abilities; psychosocial behavior; physical functions; information processing; and speech. The term does not apply to brain injuries that are congenital or degenerative, or brain injuries induced by birth trauma.

Characteristics

TBI has been referred to as "the silent epidemic," because many children have no visible impairments from a head injury. Symptoms can vary greatly, depending on the extent and location of the brain injury. However, impairments in one or more areas, such as cognitive functioning, physical abilities, communication, or social/behavioral disruption, are common. These impairments may be either temporary or permanent in nature and may cause partial or total functional disability as well as psychosocial maladjustment.

Children who sustain TBI may experience a complex array of problems, including the following:

- Physical impairments: speech, vision, hearing and other sensory impairments; headaches; lack of fine motor coordination; muscle spasms; paresis or paralysis of one or both sides of the body; seizure disorders; and balance and gait impairments.
- Cognitive impairments: short- and long-term memory deficits; slowness of thinking; limited attention span; impairments of perception, concentration, communication, and reading and writing skills; and impairments of the ability to plan and sequence actions and to make reasonable decisions or judgments.
- Psychosocial, behavioral, or emotional impairments: fatigue; mood swings; denial; self-centeredness; anxiety; depression; lowered self-esteem; sexual dysfunction; restlessness; lack of motivation; inability to self-monitor; difficulty with emotional control; inability to cope; agitation; excessive laughing or crying; and difficulty relating to others.

220

Any or all of the above impairments may occur to different degrees. The nature of the injury and its attendant problems can range from mild to severe, and the course of recovery is very difficult to predict for any given student. It is important to note that, with early and ongoing therapeutic intervention, the severity of these symptoms may decrease, but in varying degrees.

Educational Implications

Despite its high incidence, many medical and educational professionals are unaware of the consequences of childhood head injury. Students with TBI are often inappropriately thought of as having learning disabilities, emotional disturbance, or mental retardation. As a result, the needed educational and related services may not be provided within education programs. The designation of TBI signals that schools should provide children with neuropsychological, speech and language, educational, and other evaluations necessary to provide information needed for the development of an appropriate individualized education plan.

While the majority of children with TBI return to school, their educational and emotional needs are likely to be very different from the way they were prior to their injury. Although children with TBI may seem to function much like children born with other disabling conditions, it is important to recognize that the sudden onset of a severe disability resulting from trauma is very different. Children with brain injuries can often remember how they were before the trauma, which can result in a constellation of emotional and psychosocial problems not usually present in children with congenital disabilities. Further, the trauma affects family, friends, and professionals who recall what the child was like prior to injury and who have difficulty in shifting and adjusting goals and expectations.

Therefore, careful planning for school re-entry, including establishing linkages between a hospital or rehabilitation center and the educational team, is extremely important in meeting the needs of the child. It will be important to determine whether the child needs to relearn material previously known. Supervision may be needed—for example, when the child goes from the classroom to the restroom—as the child may have difficulty with spatial orientation. Teachers should also be aware that, because the child's short-term memory may be impaired, what appears to have been learned may be forgotten later in the day.

To work constructively with students with TBI, educators may need to:
- Provide repetition and consistency.
- Demonstrate new tasks, state instructions, and provide examples to illustrate ideas and concepts.
- Avoid figurative language.
- Reinforce lengthening periods of attention to appropriate tasks.
- Probe skill acquisition frequently and provide repeated practice.
- Teach compensatory strategies for increasing memory.

- Be prepared for students' reduced stamina and increased fatigue and provide rest breaks as needed.
- Keep the environment as distraction-free as possible.

Initially, it may be important for teachers to gauge whether the child can follow one-step instructions well before challenging the child with a sequence of two or more directions. Often attention is focused on the child's disabilities after the injury, which reduces self-esteem; therefore, it is important to build opportunities for success to maximize the child's strengths.

Visual Impairment and Blindness

Definition

Visual impairment is the consequence of a functional loss of vision, rather than the eye disorder itself. Eye disorders, which can lead to visual impairments, can include retinal degeneration, albinism, cataracts, glaucoma, muscular problems that result in visual disturbances, corneal disorders, diabetic retinopathy, congenital disorders, and infection.

The terms *partially sighted, low vision, legal blindness* and *total blindness* are used in the educational context to describe students with visual impairments. They are defined as follows:

Partially sighted—indicates some type of visual problem that may result in a need for special education, education adaptations, or assistive devices. In some cases a child may simply move closer to the board or hold books closer to his or her eyes.

Low vision—refers to vision loss that cannot be corrected with conventional glasses, medication, or surgery. Vision may be affected by a loss of clarity (visual acuity) or a loss of peripheral or side vision (visual field). People with low vision generally have a visual acuity worse than 20/60. Typically, people with low vision have a large amount of useable vision for text, etc. They often use aids or devices such as magnifiers, telescopic devices, or electronic magnification devices. In some cases, people with low vision do not read print (standard or large print), but use Braille, as this gives them better fluency and reading efficiency.

Legal blindness—indicates that the best corrected distance visual acuity is 20/200 or worse in the better eye, or the horizontal visual field is less than 20 degrees across the better eye. A child is considered legally blind if he or she can, at best, see with correction at 20 feet what ordinarily can be seen at 200 feet. A person whose vision is 20/200 needs to be 10 times closer or have things magnified 10 times as the person whose vision is 20/20.

Total blindness—indicates no sight.

Characteristics
There are a number of causes of visual impairment in children. These include: a deficiency of vitamin A, wounds, infections, juvenile diabetes, complications associated with premature birth, birth defects, disorders of the retina, tumors, meningitis, and retinitis pigmentosa, a hereditary disorder that at first adversely affects night vision and later involves a degeneration of the retina's neurons.

The effect of visual problems on a child's development depends on the severity, type of loss, age at which the condition appears, and overall functioning level of the child. Many children who have multiple disabilities may also have visual impairments.

A young child who is blind has little reason to explore interesting objects in the environment and, thus, may miss opportunities to have experiences and to learn. This lack of exploration may continue until learning becomes motivating and/or until intervention begins.

A child may be unable to imitate social behavior or understand nonverbal cues because he cannot see his parents or peers. Visual handicaps can create obstacles to a growing child's independence.

Educational Implications
Children with visual impairments should be assessed early to benefit from early intervention programs. Technology in the form of computers and low-vision optical and video aids enable many children with visual impairments to participate in regular class activities. Large-print materials, books on tape, and Braille books are available.

Students with visual impairments may benefit from the additional help of special equipment and modifications in the regular curriculum focusing on listening skills, communication, orientation and mobility, vocation/career options, and daily living skills. Students with low vision or those who are legally blind may need help in using their residual vision more efficiently and in working with special aids and materials. Students who have visual impairments combined with other types of disabilities have a greater need for an interdisciplinary approach and may require greater emphasis on self-care and daily living skills.

For some children with visual impairments, peripheral vision may be best. Therefore, do not assume that a child's head turned to one side means inattention. Orient the child to the classroom layout and materials location. Provide a new orientation whenever changes are made to the environment. Different floor coverings or labels can identify areas of the classroom with objects or textures to denote the activities that will take place in the area.

Be aware that children with visual impairments rely heavily or their other senses. The general noise level of the classroom and school must be considered. Encourage independence both by your actions and in the way the environment is arranged. Do not change the environment without first telling the child. Giving a child a cubby at the end of a row may make it easier to locate. Include bright, shiny, and lighted objects of various sizes, shapes, and textures for visual stimulation.

Encourage other children to identify themselves and their activities to the child with a visual impairment as the child approaches an activity center or play area. Be alert for opportunities to physically prompt or describe nearby actions. When teaching new self-help skills, work from behind the child—or do a hand-over-hand model—and then gradually reduce the help given.
Before beginning a new activity, simply state what is going to happen. For a child with partial sight, black borders or a color contrast on the edges of paper will help the child know the boundaries of the drawing paper.

A Brief Overview of Health Conditions that May Contribute to a Child's Special Learning Needs

Various health conditions may contribute to a child's need for specialized educational support, accommodations, or modifications to the educational program.

Allergy and Asthma

Definition
Allergy—An allergy is an abnormal reaction to a certain substance called an allergen. Allergies can be severe or mild. The tendency to be allergic is frequently inherited. An individual can develop allergic symptoms at any time. An infant or young child may not yet be diagnosed when the child begins school.

Asthma—Asthma is a chronic disease in which airflow in and out of the lungs may be blocked by muscle squeezing and excess mucus. Children with asthma may respond to factors in the environment, called triggers, which do not affect nonasthmatics. In response to a trigger, an asthmatic's airway may become narrowed and inflamed, resulting in wheezing and/or coughing symptoms. Childhood asthma differs from adult asthma in that infants and small children may not show the usual signs of asthma. Instead, asthma in children may appear as rapid respiration, noisy breathing, retraction of the chest area, and chest congestion.

Characteristics
Allergic responses to environmental allergens, such as dust, indoor pets, and poor air quality, also cause asthma to worsen. Allergies can remain unrecognized because of the mistaken idea that children cannot develop allergies until they are several years old.

Physical and behavioral characteristics of an allergic response include:
- Skin reactions, such as red blotches, hives, and eczema.
- Respiratory reactions, such as runny, itchy, red, swollen eyes; dark circles under the

eyes; a stuffy and/or runny nose; ears that itch or feel clogged; mouth breathing; sneezing; drooling; snoring; wheezing; and frequent coughing.

- Digestive reactions, such as symptoms of nausea and/or vomiting, stomach cramps, constipation, or diarrhea.
- Overall reactions, such as unexplained fevers, excessive sweating, a general feeling of illness, weight fluctuations, headaches, irritability, shortness of temper, frequent crying, and a poor appetite.

Parents and teachers may notice that a child may have less stamina during active play than other children. A child may try to limit physical activities to prevent coughing or wheezing. Other subtle signs of asthma, such as chest tightness, may be overlooked, especially if a young child does not have the ability to identify, or alert an adult to, the signs of asthma or an allergic reaction. Recurrent or constant coughing spells may be the only common observable symptom of asthma in young children.

Educational Implications
Because the school is the child's home away from home, it is one of the most important environments to safeguard for children. School personnel must make a conscientious effort to understand childhood asthma and allergy, and take appropriate measures to meet the needs of children with those conditions. Parents should inform school personnel of their child's history and current condition and explain the treatment protocol they follow for their child.

Children with childhood asthma and allergy have an increased level of absenteeism because of disease symptoms or because of visits to the doctor. Teachers will occasionally send a child home because they think the child is exhibiting symptoms of a contagious infection. Teachers who are well informed about the symptoms of asthma and allergy will lessen that problem. In some cases, extra tutoring will be needed for the child with asthma or allergies. As long as daily activities can be carried out, parents and teachers should promote regular school attendance.

Teachers and parents should work together to create a regular routine for taking medications. If children do need to take medication at school, procedures for doing so should be established, as should a safe, quiet environment for receiving treatments.

Classrooms may contain allergens and irritants, such as pets, dusty carpeting, chalkboards, and mold. Proper classroom ventilation is essential, especially when children are working with powder paints, pets, and science projects that produce certain fumes. Sometimes, to avoid the allergen or irritant, a child will need to change classrooms.

Some children with nasal symptoms of allergy may develop associated ear problems that interfere with their hearing. Teachers may observe symptoms of hearing loss, including inattentiveness, trouble following directions, behavior changes, and deterioration of learning performance.

Children with asthma and allergies may have a sensitivity or severe allergy to food or food preservatives. On certain occasions, the school may need to provide alternative foods, or the child may bring food substitutions from home.

Teachers should be aware that asthma medications may alter a child's ability to perform or behave appropriately. Side effects from medication, which include headaches, hand tremors, stomachaches, and lethargy, can affect a child's ability to learn. Many of the necessary medications may affect the child's concentration level and may alter fine motor coordination and, later, handwriting legibility.

Participating in physical education sometimes creates problems for the allergic or asthmatic child. Certain environmental conditions, such as cold, dry air, wind, smog, increased levels of allergens, and the presence of a viral upper-respiratory illness, may cause more asthma symptoms if a child exercises. It is important for educators to maintain an exercise program for all children, but they must also try to prevent or reduce exercise-induced asthma or allergic responses. Schools can help young children with asthma or allergies to participate in physical education and sports and to develop self-awareness of personal limitations and healthy habits of disease management.

Attention Deficit/Hyperactivity Disorder

Definition

Attention deficit/hyperactivity disorder (ADHD) is a neurobiological disorder. Typically children with ADHD have developmentally inappropriate behavior, including poor attention skills, impulsivity, and hyperactivity. These characteristics arise in early childhood, typically before age seven, are chronic, and last at least six months. Children with ADHD may also experience problems in the areas of social skills and self-esteem.

Even though the exact cause of ADHD remains unknown, it is known that ADHD is a neurobiologically based disorder. Scientific evidence suggests that ADHD is genetically transmitted and, in many children, results from a chemical imbalance or deficiency in certain neurotransmitters, which are chemicals that help the brain regulate behavior.

Characteristics

ADHD is diagnosed according to certain characteristics. Children with ADHD are often described as having short attention spans and as being distractible. They may have difficulty with one or all parts of the attention process. They may have difficulty focusing their attention (or selecting something to which to pay attention), sustaining focus, or paying attention for as long as is needed. They may shift their focus away to something else before it is productive to do so.

Some symptoms of *inattention* include:
- Often failing to give close attention to details, making careless mistakes in schoolwork or activities.
- Often having difficulty sustaining appropriate levels of attention in tasks or play activities.

- Often appearing inattentive when spoken to directly.
- Often having difficulty following through on spoken instructions or failing to finish schoolwork, chores, or duties (when the inattention is not due to oppositional behavior or failure to understand instructions).
- Often having difficulty organizing tasks and activities.
- Often avoiding, demonstrating a dislike for, or showing reluctance to engage in tasks that require sustained mental effort.
- Often losing things necessary for tasks or activities, such as toys, school assignments, pencils, books, or tools.
- Often being distracted by extraneous stimuli.

Some symptoms of *hyperactivity* include:
- Often fidgeting with hands or feet or squirming in seat.
- Often leaving seat in classroom or in other situations in which remaining seated is expected.
- Often running about or climbing excessively in situations in which this is inappropriate.
- Often having difficulty quietly playing or engaging in leisure activities.
- Often being "on the go" or acting as if "driven by a motor."
- Often talking excessively.

Impulsiveness with ADHD appears when children act before thinking. Symptoms of *impulsivity* include:
- Often blurting out answers before questions have been completed.
- Often having difficulty waiting a turn.
- Often interrupting during conversations or play or intruding on others.

From time to time all children will be inattentive, impulsive, and overly active. In the case of ADHD, these behaviors are the rule, not the exception.

Educational Implications
Planning for educational needs begins with an accurate diagnosis. Children who show indications of having ADHD must be appropriately diagnosed by a knowledgeable, well-trained clinician, usually a pediatrician, child psychologist, or pediatric neurologist. Treatment plans include behavioral and educational interventions and sometimes medication.

Many children with ADHD experience difficulty in school, where paying attention and impulse and motor controls are virtual requirements for success. Children with ADHD tend to overreact to changes in their environment. Whether at home or in school, children with ADHD respond best in a structured, predictable environment. When rules and expectations are clear and consistent, and consequences are set forth ahead of time and delivered immediately, the child develops a reliable reference point for experience. By establishing structure and routines, parents and teachers can cultivate an environment that encourages the child to control behavior and thereby succeed in learning.

Adaptations that may be helpful in managing a child with ADHD include the following:
- Posting daily schedules and assignments.
- Calling attention to schedule changes.
- Setting specific times for specific tasks.
- Designing an alternative, quiet workspace for use when needed.
- Providing regularly scheduled and frequent breaks.
- Using computerized learning activities.
- Teaching organization and study skills.
- Supplementing verbal instructions with visual or written instructions.
- Minimizing the amount of detailed, spoken directions.

Cerebral Palsy

Definition

Cerebral palsy is a condition caused by damage to the brain that usually occurs before, during, or shortly following birth. "Cerebral" refers to the brain and "palsy" to a disorder of movement or posture. It is neither progressive nor communicable. It is also not "curable" in the accepted sense, although education, therapy, and applied technology can help persons with cerebral palsy to lead productive lives. It is not a disease and should never be referred to as such. It can range from mild to severe muscular involvement.

The causes of cerebral palsy include illness during pregnancy, premature delivery, or lack of oxygen supply to the baby; it may also occur early in life as a result of an accident, lead poisoning, viral infection, child abuse, or other factors. Chief among the causes is an insufficient amount of oxygen or poor flow of blood reaching the fetal or newborn brain. That can be caused by premature separation of the placenta, an awkward birth position, labor that goes on too long or is too abrupt, or interference with the umbilical cord.

Other causes may be associated with premature birth, RH or A-B-O blood type incompatibility between parents, infection of the mother with German measles or other viral diseases in early pregnancy, and microorganisms that attack the newborn's central nervous system. Lack of good prenatal care may also be a factor. A less common type is acquired cerebral palsy; head injury is the most frequent cause, usually the result of motor vehicle accidents, falls, or child abuse.

Characteristics

There are three main types of cerebral palsy:

Spastic—stiff and difficult muscular movement.

Athetoid—involuntary and uncontrolled muscular movement.

Ataxic—disturbed sense of balance and depth perception.

There may be a combination of these types for any one individual. Other types do occur, although infrequently.

Cerebral palsy is characterized by an inability to control motor function completely. Depending on which part of the brain has been damaged and the degree of involvement of the central nervous system, one or more of the following may occur:
- muscle spasms
- tonal problems that result in too loose or too tight muscles when the body is at rest
- involuntary movements of the muscles and joints
- disturbances in gait and mobility
- seizures
- abnormal sensations and perceptions, such as an inability to perceive pain or a heightened sense of touch
- impairment of sight, hearing, and/or speech
- mental retardation.

Developmental, Educational, and Employment Implications
Early identification of cerebral palsy can lessen developmental problems and lead to appropriate intervention when it helps the most. Early intervention programs that are family-centered—that is, those in which professionals and families work together with the child in specific activities—offer substantial needed support to individuals with cerebral palsy and their families. Educators, physical and occupational therapists, social workers, speech and language therapists, psychologists, and physicians can assist families by providing information and education.

Activities for children with cerebral palsy may include:
- speech and language therapy
- occupational therapy
- physical therapy
- medical intervention
- family support services
- early education
- assistive technology.

As a child gets older and begins formal schooling, the intensity of services will vary from individual to individual. Persons with cerebral palsy are usually able to attain a substantial degree of independence but, in some cases, may need considerable assistance. Services for the school-aged child may include continuing therapy, regular or special education, counseling, technical support, community integration and recreation opportunities, and, possibly, personal attendants.

A supportive family is often the key factor to the well-being of a person with cerebral palsy. People extensively affected by cerebral palsy can still be highly functional and independent. A significant number of students with cerebral palsy are enrolled in colleges and universities.

Important advances have taken place since the mid-1980s that have had a great effect on the long-term well-being of children born with cerebral palsy. Advanced technologies, including computers and engineering devices, have been applied to the needs of persons with cerebral palsy. Technological innovations have been developed in the areas of speech and communication and self-care and have been applied to living arrangements and work sites. The future may bring even more significant applications.

Another important development has been the increased ability of persons with disabilities, including those who have cerebral palsy and other severe disabilities, to live independently in the community. Adults with cerebral palsy are now living, with or without assistance, in their own apartments or townhouses. Independent living centers have also proven to be important resources for persons with such disabilities.

Cleft Lip with or without Cleft Palate

Definition
Cleft lip with or without cleft palate is among the most common of birth defects. The cause is unknown, but may be influenced by genetic or chemical agents introduced during gestation that cause malformations in the developing embryo. A cleft lip can occur with or without a cleft palate. Cleft lip affects about one in 1,000 babies. The majority of affected infants are males.

Characteristics
A cleft lip is marked by the separation of the two sides of the lip and possibly the upper gum as well. It appears as a split in the upper lip and gum. Cleft lip ranges from mild (a slight notch in the lip) to severe (a separation extending up to the nose). It may occur on one or both sides of the lip.

A cleft palate is an opening in the roof of the mouth. The cleft may involve only part of the palate or may run the entire length of the palate. It affects one in 2,500 babies and is more common in females.

A baby born with cleft lip with or without cleft palate will need surgery, dental work, and possibly speech therapy. These children are also at greater risk for ear infections and should be closely monitored by their physicians. Surgery can occur within the first few months for those with cleft lips, and within a year for those with a cleft palate. The more immediate problem is feeding. A specially designed prosthesis, or replacement device, may be fitted over the palate. A special nipple for babies with cleft lip is available for use when bottle-feeding.

Educational Implications
Aside from the above-described conditions, the child with cleft lip is usually physically and intellectually normal. If speech therapy is needed, teachers can support therapeutic activities in the school curriculum.

Speech therapy should not be isolated in the school environment. The child should be given opportunities to discuss feelings, hospital experiences, and other concerns, if appropriate. Teachers should encourage theme-related hospital/doctor play in the dramatic play or block-building activity centers, giving the child an avenue for self-expression and an opportunity for gaining mastery and control of feelings.

Diabetes

Definition

Diabetes is a chronic, complex metabolic disease, which results in the inability of the body to properly maintain and use carbohydrates, fats, and proteins. Most individuals with diabetes—95 percent of all cases—have a form known as non-insulin-dependent diabetes (NIDDM) or Type II diabetes. NIDDM occurs more often in people over the age of forty.

A less common form of diabetes, known as insulin-dependent diabetes (IDDM) or Type I diabetes, tends to occur in young adults and children. In cases of IDDM, the body produces little or no insulin of its own. People with IDDM must receive daily insulin injections.

Characteristics

Type I diabetes occurs when most of the insulin-producing cells in the pancreas have been destroyed. Usually the cause of this type of diabetes is not known. Sometimes the diabetes is the result of a viral infection or injury of the pancreas. It may also result from an immune system disorder.

Symptoms may develop suddenly or gradually over days to weeks. Symptoms vary widely from person to person. Common symptoms include:
* increased urination
* excessive thirst, dry mouth, and the drinking of a lot of fluids
* increased appetite or loss of appetite
* visible weight loss from loss of body fluids, muscle wasting, or loss of fat
* blurred vision, skin infections, vaginal infection, or tiredness
* abnormal feelings of prickling, burning, or itching of the skin, usually on the hands or feet.

Giving the body more insulin is the primary treatment for Type I diabetes. In addition, children with diabetes must learn how to control their blood sugar through diet and exercise. The goal is to be able to lead as normal a life as possible. If diabetes is not treated, serious complications can occur.

Educational Implications

It is important to determine whether a child diagnosed with diabetes is maintaining a special diet and regular meal and snack times and whether the child is receiving insulin.

Procedures for the maintenance of these important disease management techniques should be adhered to in the school. School personnel should know the steps to take if a child experiences an insulin reaction.

Adults should keep an ongoing record of any behavior or symptoms that occur at school. Indication of activities or situations that seem to precipitate the onset of a symptom should be shared with the child's family and physician. If a symptom occurs suddenly and dramatically, contact with the child's parents should be made immediately.

Regular meals and snacks are essential to disease management. If a meal is delayed at school, an appropriate snack should be provided. Normal activity should be encouraged, but time engaged in physical activity should be managed. It is important to maintain a balance between food intake, exercise, and medication.

Having a sugar source available at all times, such as when the children are playing outdoors or are on school excursions, is advised. If possible, provide a sugar source the child is accustomed to. The child's family and physician should always be consulted for guidance in the management of the child.

Epilepsy and Seizure Disorders

Definition

Epilepsy is a physical condition that occurs when there is a sudden, brief change in how the brain works. When brain cells are not working properly, a person's consciousness, movement, or actions may be altered for a short time. These physical changes are called epileptic seizures. Epilepsy is therefore sometimes called a seizure disorder. Epilepsy affects people of all races in all nations.

Some people can experience a seizure and not have epilepsy. For example, young children may experience a convulsion from a rapid onset fever. These febrile convulsions are one type of seizure. Other types of seizures not classified as epilepsy include those caused by an imbalance of body fluids or chemicals or by alcohol or drug withdrawal. A single seizure does not mean that the person has epilepsy.

Characteristics

Although the symptoms listed below are not necessarily indicators of epilepsy, it is wise to communicate immediately with a member of the child's family if a student experiences one or more of them.

- "blackouts" or periods of confused memory
- episodes of staring or unexplained periods of unresponsiveness
- involuntary movement of arms and legs
- "fainting spells" with incontinence or followed by excessive fatigue
- perception of odd sounds, distorted perceptions, and episodic feelings of fear that cannot be explained.

Families should be advised to seek professional medical care for their young child should any of these symptoms occur.

Seizures can be generalized, meaning that all brain cells are involved. One type of generalized seizure consists of a convulsion with a complete loss of consciousness; another type looks like a brief period of fixed staring.

Seizures are partial when those brain cells not working properly are limited to one part of the brain. Such partial seizures may cause periods of "automatic behavior" and altered consciousness. This is typified by purposeful-looking behavior, such as buttoning or unbuttoning a shirt. Such behavior, however, is unconscious, may be repetitive, and is usually not recalled.

Educational Implications
Seizures may interfere with the child's ability to learn. If the student has the type of seizure characterized by a brief period of fixed staring, he or she may be missing parts of what the teacher is saying. It is important that the teacher observes and documents these episodes. Report the episodes promptly to the child's parents and the medical professionals treating the child.

Depending on the type of seizure and how often seizures occur, some children may need additional assistance to help them keep up with classmates. Assistance can include adaptations in classroom instruction, first aid instruction on seizure management for the student's teachers, and counseling. All such assistance should be included in educational planning for the individual.

It is important that teachers and school staff be informed about the child's condition, any possible effects of medication, and what to do in case a seizure occurs at school. Most parents find that an open conversation with the school administrators and teachers at the beginning of the school year is the best way to handle the situation. It is important to assess the child's medical history periodically during the school year. Even if a child has seizures that are largely controlled by medication, it is still best to notify the school staff about the condition.

School personnel and the family should work together to monitor the effectiveness of medication as well as any side effects. If a child's physical or intellectual skills seem to change, it is important to share these observations with the family and the child's medical doctor. There may also be associated hearing or perception problems caused by the brain changes. Written observations by both the family and school staff will be helpful in discussions with the child's doctor.

Some students may have additional conditions, such as learning disabilities, along with the seizure disorders. Students can benefit the most when both the family and school are working together. There are many materials available for families and teachers so that they can understand how to work most effectively as a team.

Children and youth with epilepsy must also deal with the psychological and social aspects of the condition. These include public misperceptions and fear of seizures, uncertain occurrence, loss of self-control during the seizure episode, and compliance with medications. To help children feel more confident about themselves and accept their epilepsy, the school can provide epilepsy education programs for staff and students, including information on seizure recognition and first aid.

What to Do When A Child Has a Seizure
- Remain calm.
- Once a seizure has started, let it run its course.
- Ease the child onto the floor or ground and loosen any restrictive clothing.
- Protect the child from striking the head or body against any hard or sharp object. Otherwise, do not interfere with the child's bodily movement.
- Turn the child's face to the side so that saliva can flow from the child's mouth.
- Do not insert anything into the child's mouth.
- Allow the child to rest or sleep following the seizure.
- Notify the school nurse, the school director, and the child's parents that a seizure has occurred.

If, following a seizure, the child appears groggy, confused, or weak, the child may need to rest at home.

Human Immunodeficiency Virus Infection and Acquired Immunodeficiency Syndrome

Definition

Acquired immunodeficiency syndrome (AIDS) is caused by the human immunodeficiency virus (HIV). By killing or impairing cells of the immune system, HIV progressively destroys the body's ability to fight infections and certain cancers. Individuals diagnosed with AIDS are susceptible to life-threatening diseases called opportunistic infections, which are caused by microbes that usually do not cause illness in healthy people.

Characteristics

Medical evidence indicates that AIDS is contagious only through the exchange of semen and blood. That is, it is sexually transmitted or transmitted through contaminated blood or nonsterile hypodermic needles. Because AIDS is a somewhat newly recognized disease, medical treatment and vaccines are at an early stage of research.

The majority of children with AIDS have been born with it. Other children have acquired AIDS from AIDS-contaminated blood transfusions. Children with increased risk for HIV/AIDS are those with hemophilia and certain types of anemia, which require repeated blood transfusions. Or, a child may have had surgery that required blood transfusions.

Children with AIDS have:
- extremely low resistance to all viruses, colds, and infections
- persistent fatigue and/or unexplained weight loss
- other symptoms that are presently considered as diagnostic markers of AIDS, such as developmental delays, kidney and heart problems, frequent staphylococcus salmonella infections, frequent diarrhea, thrush (white coating on the tongue) and/or enlarged lymph glands in the neck, armpits, and/or groin, and night sweats or fevers.

Because HIV infection often progresses quickly to AIDS in children, most of the close to three million children under the age of fifteen who have been infected since the start of the epidemic have developed AIDS, and most of these have died.

There is still no cure or effective vaccine for HIV. Children orphaned by AIDS are the largest and fastest growing group of children in difficult circumstances in those countries most affected by the epidemic. The socioeconomic fallout from the epidemic in hard-hit communities and countries affects even children who are neither infected with HIV nor orphaned by AIDS.

Educational Implications
All children have a right to education. Children with AIDS are victims of circumstances. They have the right to the same educational opportunities as other children. If a child with AIDS participates in a Step By Step Program, program administrators should get a written, signed statement of procedures to follow, including essential information from the child's physician. Program staff should follow the usual precautions taken for avoiding the spread of any germ or infectious condition when cleaning up or diapering a child with HIV:
- Use rubber gloves while changing diapers, cleaning up vomit, or attending to an open wound.
- Wash toys or rugs with disinfectant if a child has vomited or bled on them.
- Each day, wash with disinfectant all toys that are frequently mouthed.

Lead Poisoning
Definition
Lead poisoning occurs when lead, which is poisonous at certain high levels of concentration, is absorbed into the body, causing chemical changes in the blood. This exposure may affect many organs and can cause permanent developmental deficiencies.

Characteristics
Children experience more problems than adults do with lead poisoning because of their greater exposure, absorption, and sensitivity to lead. Though the effects of lead poisoning may not be noticeable during the early years, once a child who has been exposed to high levels of lead reaches school age and encounters more demands on his or capacity to learn and concentrate, the damage may become more obvious.

If a mother has been exposed to high levels of lead intake, a child's brain may be damaged prenatally, as well as after birth if the child is nursing. Because lead may interfere with the amount of calcium absorbed, the teeth, bones, and nervous system of the child may be affected. Lead often interferes with a child's metabolism. This may result in abnormal functioning in many body systems and in tissue development.

Additional physical symptoms include:
- anemia
- constipation and nausea
- headaches and fatigue
- pain in joints and muscles
- pallor
- loss of appetite
- seizure disorders.

Children who have been exposed to an excess of lead intake before or after birth may exhibit the following:
- delays or regression in overall development
- poor coordination and slow reaction time
- irritability
- aggressive behavior disorders and inappropriate social behaviors
- speech and language learning problems
- problems in focusing attention
- difficulties in processing of information
- learning disabilities
- decreased intellectual ability or the inability to reach intellectual potential.

Neural Tube Defects: Spina Bifida and Myelomeningocele

Definition

Spina bifida means cleft spine, which is an incomplete closure in the spinal column. In general, the three types of spina bifida (from mild to severe) are:

Occulta—There is an opening in one or more of the vertebrae (bones) of the spinal column without apparent damage to the spinal cord.

Meningocele—The meninges, or protective covering around the spinal cord, have pushed out through the opening in the vertebrae in a sac called the "meningocele." However, the spinal cord remains intact. This form can be repaired with little or no damage to the nerve pathways.

Myelomeningocele—This is the most severe form of spina bifida, in which a portion of the spinal cord itself protrudes through the back. In some cases, sacs are covered with skin; in others, tissue and nerves are exposed. Generally, people use "spina bifida" and "myelomeningocele" interchangeably.

Educational Implications

Although spina bifida is relatively common, until recently most children born with a myelomeningocele died shortly after birth. Now that surgery to drain spinal fluid and protect children against hydrocephalus can be performed in the first 48 hours of life, children with myelomeningocele are much more likely to live. Quite often, however, they must have a series of operations throughout their childhood. School programs should be flexible in accommodating their special needs.

Many children with myelomeningocele need training to learn to manage their bowel and bladder functions. Some require catheterization, or the insertion of a tube to permit passage of urine. Clean, intermittent catheterization is necessary to help the child benefit from and have access to special education and related services; many children learn to catheterize themselves at a very early age. A successful bladder management program can be incorporated into the regular school day.

In some cases, children with spina bifida who also have a history of hydrocephalus experience learning problems. They may have difficulty with paying attention, expressing or understanding language, and grasping reading and math. Early intervention with children who experience learning problems can help considerably to prepare them for school.

Including the child with spina bifida in a school attended by nondisabled young people sometimes requires changes in school equipment or the curriculum, although the day-to-day school pattern should be as "normal" as possible. In adapting the school setting for the child with spina bifida, structural changes—such as adding elevators or ramps—can be made or the schedule or location of a classroom can be changed—for example, by providing a classroom on the ground floor of the school building.

Children with myelomeningocele need to learn mobility skills, and often require the aid of crutches, braces, or wheelchairs. It is important that all members of the school team and the parents understand the child's physical capabilities and limitations. Physical disabilities like spina bifida can have profound effects on a child's emotional and social development. To promote children's personal growth, families and teachers should encourage them, within the limits of safety and health, to be independent and to participate in activities with their nondisabled classmates.

Nutritional Deficits

Definition
A nutritional deficiency is caused by the absence of an essential nutrient, such as iron, in the body.

Characteristics
A child with a nutritional deficiency may have any of the following physical characteristics:
- A pale complexion or skin that appears dull or rough.
- A body build or structure that deviates from the norm, such as a bulging, bloated stomach; a rib cage that protrudes; legs that are badly bowed.

237

- Poor posture, poor muscle tone, and/or poor motor coordination.
- Poor or no appetite.
- An increasing loss of energy or lethargic reactions.
- Frequent illness and infection.
- Frequent constipation or diarrhea and nausea.
- Upper-respiratory infections, wheezing, stuffiness of the nose, sneezing, and eyes that look red or infected.

Behavioral characteristics may include:
- Refusal to eat, being a selective eater, or having a depressed appetite.
- A short attention span.
- Hyperactive or hypoactive activity levels.
- Lack of motivation and a poor self-concept.
- Sluggish and withdrawn behavior, being sleepy or irritable.
- Poor visual and motor coordination.
- Frequent absence from school.

Educational Implications
The causes of a child's symptoms of nutritional deficit should be investigated. Medical records should be sought and contact with the child's family and physician should be established and focused on this matter.

The child will require nutritional snacks, such as cheese, fruit, and vegetables. Trying different methods of food preparation may increase the child's appetite. Eating in the social setting of school may have positive benefits. Serve the child small amounts of each type of food. Encourage the child to taste everything, but do not force or bribe the child to eat. Maintain a relaxed and happy meal time.

Maintain an ongoing dialogue with the parents. Obtain nutritional information in the parents' native language and share this with them.

Encourage the child to participate in noncompetitive games and physical activities that do not demand a great amount of physical stamina. Encourage the child to extend the amount of time involved in school activities, including mealtime, by emphasizing pleasant conversation, using music or counting games if appropriate, and discussing color, texture, and other aspects of mealtime activities.

Prenatal Exposure to Alcohol

Definition
Fetal alcohol syndrome (FAS) is a group of abnormalities directly related to alcohol ingestion during pregnancy. Alcohol can injure a developing fetus throughout pregnancy; however, the most severe cases of FAS result from consumption of alcohol, particularly during the first trimester when the brain and the heart are formed. There is at present no established amount of alcohol that a pregnant woman can consume without risk to her unborn baby.

Characteristics

Children with FAS are usually diagnosed by their physical characteristics, which include: prenatal and postnatal growth deficiency, delay of gross and fine motor development, and congenital malformations, some of which result in a characteristic facial appearance. FAS is one of the most common known causes of mental retardation. Children with FAS may exhibit behavior problems, such as hyperactivity. Children with FAS may also be susceptible to mental health problems.

Physical abnormalities associated with this syndrome include: a small head, eyes, and mouth, as well as droopy eyelids; a wide space between the nose and upper lip; a thin upper lip and occasionally cleft lip with or without cleft palate; hearing loss; myopia; strabismus; dental malocclusions; and congenital heart disease.

Educational Implications

Many children with FAS have cognitive limitations and behavior problems that require appropriate adjustments in educational programming. Intellectual impairment may range from average intelligence to profound retardation. Learning disabilities in children with FAS are often associated with short-term-memory difficulties.

Behavioral characteristics include hyperactivity, irritability, and poor attention to tasks and learning situations. Children with FAS often have poor eye-hand coordination, resulting in difficulties with tasks requiring fine motor skill. They may have weak hand grasp.

Children with FAS may also have impairments of speech and language acquisition. They may have voice and fluency problems or deficits in syntactic, semantic, and pragmatic aspects of language. They may have oral-motor and articulation problems. Some children have specific problems associated with cleft palate and hearing loss. These conditions may directly affect all aspects of language learning, including listening to spoken language and understanding the meaning of what is said. As the child grows older these early deficits may carry over into difficulties with reading, writing, and spelling.

The following educational strategies have proven to be helpful to children with FAS:
- Provide routine and structure to the school day. Explain ahead of time what will happen, when it will happen, and what is expected. If there is to be a change in schedule, the child with FAS will benefit from advance warning.
- Use the technique of over-teaching. In addition to direct instruction, teachers will find that use of repetition is helpful to children with FAS in comprehending new skills and concepts. Use the same language when explaining rules or ideas is also helpful.
- Break tasks into their composite steps.
- Provide extra time to complete tasks.
- Use visual and activity-based learning tasks, backed up with spoken information.

- Use creative, flexible strategies.
- Teach the child how to ask for help.
- Provide direct instruction in the recognition of emotions and the use of appropriate social skills, with many opportunities for practice in functional settings with concrete experiences.

The developmental prognosis for children with FAS will be different for each individual. Some children will be mildly affected, some severely. Some of the difficulties reflect damage to the central nervous system and will persist. Others represent delays in development that will diminish or be resolved with early intervention and treatment. The potential for retraining is related to the severity of alcohol's effects and is reflected in the child's birth weight and the degree of facial dysmorphology, or disfigurement.

Treatment for children and their families should include:
- early intervention, including appropriate therapies for the child (e.g., psychological counseling, speech and language therapy, and occupational therapy) and for the parents (e.g., setting behavioral limits and managing their child with FAS in the home and community)
- full discussion of the diagnosis of FAS with the child's parents
- encouraging the child's parents to talk to knowledgeable individuals about the impact of the diagnosis
- stressing the need for sobriety for both parents
- assessment of the child's medical needs to prevent complications
- assessment of neurological and behavioral needs
- an educational environment that provides consistency
- limited distractions
- a focus on the child's developmental potential.

Prenatal Exposure to Illicit Drugs and Tobacco

Exposure to Cocaine

Cocaine can cause vasoconstriction that is associated with increased uterine contractions and decreased blood flow across the placenta. This in turn is related to abruptio placenta, a condition where pre-term delivery, spontaneous abortions, and stillbirths can occur.

Infants born to cocaine-using mothers may be premature and have lowered birth weight and length at birth and smaller head circumference. They are often irritable and tremulous, interacting poorly and having difficulty with state regulation. These neurobehavioral problems are most likely associated with central nervous system immaturity rather than with brain damage. By two years of age, there is catch-up growth and few decrements in developmental scores. There is no evidence that children are born addicted to cocaine.

Exposure to Heroin

The most serious effect of heroin to a newborn is neonatal abstinence syndrome or withdrawal, which includes sweating, gastro-intestinal upsets, high-pitched crying, and excessive yawning. Heroin use can also contribute to low birth weight.

Growth deficiencies may be present until one year. Short attention span, frequent temper tantrums, and difficulty with social adjustment are often observed in young children who have been exposed prenatally, but these symptoms decrease as the child develops.

Exposure to Tobacco

Smoking increases the chances of having an ectopic pregnancy, miscarriage, stillbirth, pre-term baby, low birth-weight baby, or a baby with sudden infant death syndrome.

Sensory Integrative Dysfunction

Definition

Sensory motor integration is the ability to:

- take in information through the senses, including the sense of touch, movement, smell, taste, vision, and hearing;
- put these sense perceptions together with prior information, memories, and knowledge stored in the brain; and
- make meaningful physical responses based on constructive use of perceptual input.

Sensory motor integration occurs in the central nervous system and is generally thought to take place in the mid-brain and brain-stem levels in complex interactions of those portions of the brain. These areas are responsible for such things as coordination, attention, arousal levels, autonomic functioning, emotions, memory, and higher level cognitive functions.

In contrast, sensory integrative dysfunction is a disorder in which sensory input is not integrated or organized appropriately in the brain and may produce varying degrees of problems in development, information processing, and behavior—problems that adversely affect an individual's ability to learn.

Characteristics

Sensory integration focuses primarily on three senses: the tactile, vestibular, and proprioceptive senses. The neural interconnections of these senses start forming before birth and continue to develop as a young child matures and interacts with the environment. The three senses are not only interconnected but are also connected with other systems in the brain. Although these three sensory systems are less familiar than vision and hearing, they are critical to our basic survival. They allow us to experience, interpret, and respond to different stimuli.

The Tactile Sense—includes the nerves under the skin's surface that send information to the brain. This information includes light touch, pain, temperature, and pressure. These

241

nerves play an important role in perceiving the environment as well as providing protective reactions for survival.

Dysfunction in the tactile system can be seen in an individual's withdrawing when being touched, refusing to eat certain textured foods, and/or refusing to wear certain types of textured clothing. A child may demonstrate touch sensitivity by complaining about having a hair cut or face washing. A child may avoid activities, such as using glue, playing in mud, or using finger paint; these activities would dirty the hands. Touch avoidance can also be observed when a child manipulates objects with only the fingertips rather than the whole hand. A dysfunctional tactile system may lead to a misperception of touch and/or pain and may lead to self-imposed isolation, general irritability, distractibility, and hyperactivity.

The Vestibular Sense—refers to the structures within the inner ear, the semicircular canals that detect movement and changes in the position of the head. The vestibular system tells you when your head is upright or tilted or even when your eyes are closed.

Dysfunction within this system may manifest itself in two different ways. Some children may be hypersensitive to vestibular stimulation and have fearful reactions to ordinary movement or play equipment such as swings, slides, ramps, or inclines. They may also have difficulty learning to climb or descend stairs or hills; and they may be apprehensive walking or crawling on uneven or unstable surfaces. As a result, they seem fearful in space. In general, these children appear clumsy.

On the other extreme, a child may actively seek very intense sensory experiences such as excessive body whirling, jumping, and/or spinning. This type of child demonstrates signs of a hypoactive vestibular system; that is, they are trying continuously to stimulate their dysfunctional vestibular system.

The Proprioceptive Sense—common signs of proprioceptive dysfunction are clumsiness, a tendency to fall, a lack of awareness of body position in space, odd body posturing, minimal crawling when young, difficulty manipulating small objects (buttons, snaps), eating in a sloppy manner, and resistance to new motor movement activities.

Another dimension of proprioception is praxis or motor planning. This is the ability to plan and execute different motor tasks. In order for this system to work properly, it must rely on obtaining accurate information from the sensory systems and then organizing and interpreting this information efficiently and effectively. It also allows us to manipulate objects using fine motor movements, such as writing with a pencil, using a spoon to drink soup, and buttoning one's shirt.

Educational Implications
In general, dysfunction within these three systems manifests itself in many ways. Children may be over- or under-responsive to sensory input. Their levels of activity may

be either unusually high or unusually low, or a child may be in constant motion or fatigue easily. In addition, some children may fluctuate between these extremes. Gross and/or fine motor coordination problems are also common when these three systems are dysfunctional and may result in speech and/or language delays and in academic under-achievement. Behaviorally, the child may become impulsive, easily distractible, and show a general lack of anticipation of routine events. Some children may also have difficulty adjusting to new situations and may react with frustration, aggression, or withdrawal.

Occupational therapists and/or physical therapists perform evaluation and treatment of basic sensory integrative processes. The therapist's general goals are:
- to provide the child with sensory information that helps the child better organize his or her central nervous system
- to assist the child in inhibiting and/or modulating unproductive sensory information
- to assist the child in producing organized responses to sensory stimuli.

REFERENCES

Abraham, M.R., Morris, L.M., and Wald, P.J. (1993). *Inclusive early childhood education.* San Antonio, TX: Communication Skill Builders.

Bagnato, S. J., and Neisworth, J. T. (1991). *Assessment for early intervention: Best practices for professionals.* New York, NY: Guilford.

Bailey, D. B., and Wolery, M. (1992). *Teaching infants and preschoolers with disabilities* (2nd ed.). Columbus, OH: Merrill.

Bailey, P., Cryer, D., Harms, T., Osborn, S., & Kniest, S. (1996). *Active learning for children with disabilities.* Menlo Park, CA: Addison Wesley Publishing Company.

Bayley, N. (1968). *Bayley infant scales of development.* New York: Psychological Corporation.

Beaty, J.J. (1994). *Observing development of the young child.* Englewood Cliffs, NJ: Merrill.

Beckman, P.J., Frank N., and Newcomb, S. (1996). Qualities and skills for communicating with families. In P.J. Beckman (Ed.), *Strategies for working with families of young children.* Baltimore, MD: Brookes Publishing.

Benjamin, S. (1989). An ideascape for education: What futurists recommend. *Educational Leadership, 47(1),* 8.

Berger, J. and Cunningham, C.C. (1981). *Developmental Psychology,* 17.

Bredekamp, S., (Ed.). (1987). *Developmentally appropriate practice in early childhood programs serving children from birth through age 8.* Washington, DC: National Association for the Education of Young Children.

Bredekamp, S., and Rosegrant, T. (Eds.). (1992). *Reaching potentials: Appropriate curriculum and assessment for young children, Vol. 1.* Washington, DC: National Association for the Education of Young Children.

Bruner, J. S. (1966). *Toward a theory of instruction.* New York: W. W. Norton.

Cohen, P.C. (1964). *The impact of the handicapped child in the family.* New Outlook for the Blind, 58.

Cook, R. E., Tessier, A., and Armbruster, V. B. (1987). *Adapting early childhood curricula for children with special needs.* Columbus, OH: Merrill.

Cook, R.E., Tessier, A., and Klein, M.D. (1996). *Adapting early childhood curricula for children in inclusive settings*, (4th ed.). Columbus, OH: Merrill.

Copple, C.E., Dehisi, R., and Sigel, E. (1982). Cognitive development. In B. Spodek (Ed.), *Handbook of research in early childhood education* (pp. 3-26). New York: The Free Press.

Coughlin, P. A., Hansen, K. A., Heller, D., Kaufmann, R. K., Stolberg, J. R., and Walsh, K. B. (1997). *Creating child-centered classrooms: 3 – 5 year olds*. Washington, DC: Children's Resources International, Inc.

Dunlop, K., (1977). Mainstreaming: Valuing diversity in children. *Young Children*, 33, no. 5. Washington, DC: NAEYC.

Dunst, C. J., Trivette, C. M., and Deal, A. (1988). *Enabling and empowering families: Principles and guidelines for practice*. Cambridge, MA: Brookline.

Erickson, M.F., and Pianta, R.C. (1989). New lunchbox, old feelings: What kids bring to school. *Early Education and Development*, 1, (1), 40.

Essa, E. (1992). *Introduction to early childhood education*. Albany, NY: Delmar.

Fairfax County Public Schools Developmental Language Instruction Curriculum, (1991). County School Board of Fairfax County, VA.

Fallen, N.H. and Umansky, W. (1985). *Young children with special needs*. New York: Macmillan

Fraiberg, S. (1972). Separation crisis in two blind children. *Psychoanalytic Study of the Child*, 26.

Fromberg, D.P. (1987). Play. In C. Seefeldt (Ed), *The early childhood curriculum: A review of current reserach* (pp.35-74). New York: Teacher's College Press.

Garwood, S. G. (Ed.). (1985). *Developmental toys*. Topics in Early Childhood Special Education, 5.

Gesell, A. (1940). *The first five years of life*. New York: Harper and Row.

Glasser, W. (1969). *Schools without failure*. New York: Harper and Row.

Goodman, K. (1986). *What's the whole in whole language?* Portsmouth, NH: Heinemann.

Goodwin, W. R., and Driscoll, L. A. (1980). *Handbook for measurement and evaluation in early childhood education*. San Francisco: Jossey-Bass.

Greenspan, S., and Meisels, S. (June/July 1994). Toward a new vision for the developmental assessment of infants and young children. *Zero to Three, 14(6),* 1-8.

Hanson, M. J. and Lynch, E. W. (1989). *Early intervention: Implementing child and family services for infants and toddlers who are at-risk or disabled.* Austin, TX: PRO-ED, Inc.

Hills, T. W. Reaching potentials through appropriate assessment. In Bredekamp, S. and Rosegrant, T. (1992). *Reaching potentials: Appropriate curriculum and assessment for young children, Vol. 1.* Washington, DC: National Association for the Education of Young Children.

Hohmann, M., Banet, B., and Weikart, D.P. (1979). *Young children in action.* Ypsilanti, MI: High/Scope.

Imamura, S. (1965). *Mother and the blind child.* Research Series, American Foundation for the Blind, No. 14.

Jenkins, J.R., Speltz, M.L., and Odom, S.L. (1985). Integrating normal and handcapped preschoolers: effects on child development and social interaction. *Exceptional Children,* 52.

Johnson, D.W., and Johnson, R.T. (1980). Integrating handicapped students into the mainstream. *Exceptional Children,* 47, no. 2, 10: 90-98.

Jones, E., and Reynolds, G. (1992). *The play's the thing: Teacher's roles in children's play.* New York: Teachers College Press.

Katz, L. G., and Chard, S. C. (1989). *Engaging children's minds: The project approach.* Norwood, NJ: Ablex Publishing Corporation.

Klinnert, M.D., Emde, R.N., Butterfield, P., and Campos, J.J. (1986). Social Referencing: The infant's use of emotional signals from a friendly adult with mother present. *Developmental Psychology,* 22(4), 427-432.

Kostelnik, M.J., (1997). Guiding emotional development. In E. Szanton, (Ed.), *Creating child-centered programs for infants and toddlers* (Chapter IV). Washington, DC: Children's Resources International, Inc.

Kostelnik, M.J., (1997). Guiding Social Development. In E. Szanton, (Ed.), *Creating Child-Centered Programs for Infants and Toddlers* (Chapter V). Washington, DC: Children's Resources International, Inc.

Kostelink, M. J., and Stein, L. C., Whiren, A. P., and Soderman, A. K. (1993*). Guiding children's social development,* (2nd ed.). Albany, NY: Delmar Publishers, Inc.

Lerner, J. (1988). *Learning disabilities: Theories, diagnosis, and teaching strategies.* Boston, MA: Houghton Mifflin.

Lieberman, A.F. (1993). *The emotional life of the toddler.* New York: Free Press.

Linder, T. W. (1993). *Transdisciplinary play-based intervention: Guidelines for developing a meaningful curriculum for young children.* Baltimore, MD: Paul H. Brookes.

Malofeev, N.N. (1998). Special education in Russia: Historical aspects. *Journal of Learning Disabilities, 31.*

Mandell, C. J., and Gold, V. (1984). *Teaching handicapped students.* St. Paul, MN: West Publishing Co.

McAfee, O., and Leong, D. (1994). *Assessment and guiding young children's development and learning.* Boston: Allyn and Bacon.

McLean, M., and Hanline, M. F. (1990). Poviding early intervention services in integrated environments: challenges and opportunities in the future. *Topics in early childhood special Education, 10.*

Meisels, S. J., and Provence, S. (1989). *Screening and assessment: Guidelines for identifying young disabled and developmentally vulnerable children and their families.* Washington, DC: National Center for Clinical Infant Programs.

Mindel, E.D. and Vernon, M. (1971). *They grow in silence: The deaf child and his family.* Silver Spring, MD: National Association for the Deaf.

National Association for the Education of Young Children (NAEYC). (1997, May). The benefits of an inclusive education: Making it work [9 paragraphs]. *Early years are learning years* [On-line series]. Available: pubaff@naeyc.org.

Neisworth, J. T. (1993). Assessment. In *DEC recommended practices: Indicators of quality in programs for infants and young children with special needs and their families.* Reston, VA: The Council For Exceptional Children.

Neuman, S.B. (1998). How can we enable all children to achieve? In S.B. Newman and K.A. Roskos (eds.), *Children achieving: Best practices in early literacy.* Newark, DE: International Reading Association.

O'Brien, J., and O'Brien, C. L. (1996). Inclusion as a force for school Renewal. In S. Stainback and W. Stainback (Eds.), *Inclusion: A guide for educators* (pp. 29 – 45). Baltimore, MD: Paul H. Brookes.

Owens, R. (1988). *Language development.* Columbus, OH: Charles E. Merrill.

Piaget, J. (1950). *The psychology of intelligence.* London: Routledge and Kegan Paul.

Piaget, J. and Inhelder, B. (1969). *The psychology of the child.* New York: Basic Books.

Rapin, I. (1979). *Effects of early blindness and deafness on cognition.* In R. Katzman (Ed.), Congenital and acquired cognitive disorders. New York: Raven Press.

Smith, C.R. (1983). *Learning disabilities: The interaction of learner task and setting.* Boston: Little, Brown.

Snell, M. E., and Vogtle, L. K. (1996). Interpersonal relationships of school-aged children and adolescents with mental retardation. In R. L. Schalock (Ed.), *Quality of life: Its application to persons with disabilities, 2,* 43-61. Washington, DC: American Association on Mental Retardation.

Stainback, S., & Stainback, W. (1996). *Inclusion: A guide for educators.* Baltimore. MD: Paul H. Brookes Publishing Co.

Staub, D., and Peck, C. A. (1995). What are the outcomes for non-disabled students? *Educational Leadership, 52 (4),* 36 - 40.

Staub, E. (1978). *Positive social behavior and morality: Social and personal influences, Vol. 1.* New York: Academic Press.

Sommers, V.S. (1944). *The influence of parental attitudes and social environment on the personality development of the adolescent blind.* New York: American Foundation for the Blind.

Tait, P. (1972). The effect of circumstantial rejection on infant behavior. *New Outlook for the Blind,* 66.

Tait, P. (1972). Play and the intellectual development of blind children. *New Outlook for the Blind,* 66.

U.S. Department of Health and Human Services (1997). *Headstart: Social services training guide.* (DHHS Publication). Washington, DC: U.S. Government Printing Office.

Vaughn, S., Bos, C., and Lund, K. (1986). But they can do it in my room: Strategies for promoting generalization. *Teaching Exceptional Children,* Spring, 176 – 180.

Vygotsky, L. (1967). Play and its role in the mental development of children. *Soviet Psychology,* 12, 62-67.

Vygotsky, L. S. (1978). *Mind in society: The development of higher psychological processes* (M. Cole, V. John-Steiner, S. Scribner, and E. Souberman, Eds. And Trans). Cambridge, MA: Harvard University Press.

Wolery, M., Strain, P. S., and Bailey, Jr., D. B. (1992). Reaching potentials of children with special needs. In S. Bredekamp and T. Rosegrant (Eds.), *Reaching potentials: Appropriate curriculum and assessment for young children, Vol. 1.* (pp. 91 - 111). Washington, DC: National Association for the Education of Young Children.

Wolery, M., and Wilbers, J. S. (Eds.). (1994). *Including children with special needs in early childhood programs.* Washington, DC: National Association for the Education of Young Children.

Wood, C. (1997). *Yardsticks: Children in the classroom ages 4-14; a resource for parents and teachers.* Greenfield, MA: Northeast Foundation for Children.

Wood, D. J., Bruner, J. S., and Ross, G. (1976). The role of tutoring in problem solving. *Journal of Child Psychiatry, 17,* 89 – 100.

PUBLICATIONS BY
CHILDREN'S RESOURCES INTERNATIONAL

Creating Child-Centered Classrooms: 3–5 Year Olds — curriculum and methods for teachers of children ages three to five

Creating Child-Centered Classrooms: 6–7 Year Olds — curriculum and methods for teachers of children ages six and seven

Creating Child-Centered Classrooms: 8-10 Year Olds — curriculum and methods for teachers of children ages eight to ten

Creating Child-Centered Materials for Math and Science — a book that assists teachers in designing and making their own classroom materials for active exploration in math and science

Education and the Culture of Democracy: Early Childhood Practice — a book explaining the link between democracy and early childhood teaching

Early Childhood Faculty Seminar: Individualized Teaching — a university-level course designed for use by early childhood education faculty

Early Childhood Faculty Seminar: Learning Through Play — a university-level course outline designed for use by early childhood education faculty

Early Childhood Faculty Seminar: School and Family Partnerships — a university-level course outline designed for use by early childhood education faculty

Early Childhood Faculty Seminar: Child-Centered Curriculum — a university-level course designed for use by early childhood education faculty

Early Childhood Faculty Seminar: The Study of Children Through Observation and Recording — a university-level course outline designed for use by early childhood education faculty

CHILDREN'S RESOURCES INTERNATIONAL
5039 Connecticut Ave, NW, Suite 1
Washington, DC 20008

(202) 363-9002 phone
(202) 363-9550 fax
email: criinc@aol.com